THE CORRUPTION OF CAPITALISM
RICHARD DUNCAN

ABOUT CLSA BOOKS

CLSA Books is a series of financial publications written by independent experts commissioned by CLSA Asia-Pacific Markets. As one of Asia's most independent brokers, CLSA recognises the value of going straight to the source. Being able to tap into unfiltered primary research is essential to making better-informed investment decisions.

CLSA's first effort to bridge the information gap resulted in CLSA U's executive education courses for institutional investors, led by independent experts. CLSA Books takes investment research even further, with even greater depth and breadth available to a wider audience. With independent research and an emphasis on outside sources, CLSA helps institutional investors draw their own conclusions.

A Financial Series by CLSA Asia-Pacific Markets
www.clsa.com

The
Corruption
of
Capitalism

A strategy to rebalance the global economy and restore sustainable growth

by

Richard Duncan

BOOKS
Hong Kong Tokyo Singapore New York London

CLSA BOOKS
CLSA Asia-Pacific Markets
18/F, One Pacific Place
88 Queensway, Hong Kong

Printed December 2009

The text of this book is set in Goudy, with display set in Optima.

Cover design by Jennifer Luk and Simon Harris.

Printed in Hong Kong
ISBN: 978-988-98942-4-5

Contents

Acknowledgements

Since beginning my career in Hong Kong in 1986, I have watched CLSA grow and thrive while its British competitors withered away during the 1990s and its American rivals had to be rescued by taxpayers' money in 2008. The CLSA Investors' Forum has long been the undisputed investment event of the year in Asia, being both enormously informative and a great deal of fun. I am therefore delighted that CLSA Books chose to publish this edition of *The Corruption of Capitalism*. I would like to thank CLSA Chairman and CEO Jonathan Slone, as well as Grace Hung for overseeing the project and Simon Harris for organizing the book's publication. Finally, thanks to Liz Keenan and Jeremy Halden for their editorial improvements to the text.

Richard Duncan
December 2009

.

Introduction

Abandoned principles

There should be no confusion as to the origins of the global economic crisis that began in 2008. This crisis was set in motion in the 1960s, when policymakers in the United States abandoned the core principles of economic orthodoxy: balanced government budgets and sound money backed by gold.

Large budget deficits and the possibility of financing them with paper money fundamentally changed the way the economy functioned and brought about a worldwide transformation that, over time, has deindustrialized the United States and left it heavily in debt. Paper money revolutionized all economic relationships by making credit abundant instead of scarce. In a complete break with the past, the government was no longer constrained in its ability to spend, and international trade was no longer required to balance. Economists, however, remained oblivious to this corruption of capitalism, and economic theory was left entirely unrevised.

Most damagingly, economists and policymakers continued to believe that "free trade" would continue to produce the same benefits under a paper-money regime as it had under the gold standard. They altogether failed to notice as free trade evolved into something entirely different: debt-financed trade. Moreover, they failed to grasp that debt-financed trade did not bring about the same permanent expansion of well-being as free trade, but instead permitted the development of extraordinary, debt-financed global imbalances that have thrown the world into a new depression now they have begun to come unwound.

The economic crisis confronting the United States—and, therefore, the world—is not cyclical. It is structural. The US economy is simply no longer viable as it is currently structured. The hard truth is that the United States produces very little that the rest of the world cannot buy much more cheaply from developing countries, where wage rates are 95% lower. The forces of globalization are hollowing out US industry and leaving the country incapable of producing as much as it consumes. These trends will only accelerate in the years ahead, so long as current policies continue and current misconceptions about the benefits of debt-financed trade under a paper-money regime persist.

A multi-trillion-dollar policy response in the United States and around the world has halted the downward spiral in economic output and asset prices—at least for the moment. It has also demonstrated that we really are all Keynesians now. Keynesian stimulus is not enough, however. Government spending is propping up the economy without correcting—or even targeting—the structural flaws that caused the crisis.

Keynes was right to advocate government spending to stimulate the economy during a depression. However, as his advice was not put into practice during his lifetime, he left us no exit strategy—no theory of how to eventually wean the economy off government life support. Therefore, it is now necessary to take Keynesian analysis a step further. Stimulus is not sufficient; a structural overhaul is required.

Japan's 20-year Great Recession offers insights into how this might be done. The expansion of government debt in Japan to more than 200% of GDP has demonstrated just how great a government's capacity to borrow actually is. It is not enough for the government to borrow just enough to support 1-2% GDP growth year after year. Japan's experience shows that the government of a large industrialized country has enough debt capacity to borrow on a large enough scale not merely to support the economy with a steady drip of stimulus but to completely restructure the economy so as to restore its viability. Japan did not do that, but the United States could and must.

It will require only a few more years of double-digit unemployment before a grassroots protectionist backlash sets in and Americans vote for high trade barriers. Protectionism would deal a great blow to global prosperity, but it is inevitable unless the United States completely reformulates its economic policy. Fortunately, a five- to 10-year window of opportunity exists for the US government to get to grips with the nature of this crisis and implement the radically different policies needed to permanently resolve it.

The US economy must be fundamentally restructured if the country is to avoid moving toward terminal decline. New advanced industries must be developed to enable the country to produce products the rest of the world needs and can't buy anywhere else at any price. This will require the government to invest in 21st-Century industries on a scale great enough to give the United States an unassailable lead in the technologies of the future.

It is tragic that a series of terrible policy mistakes has led to this situation where the United States must now rely on the government to restructure the economy. However, America's economic degeneration began long ago, when Presidents Johnson and Nixon broke the link between dollars and gold. Regrettably, only the US government has sufficient financial and organizational capacity to carry out the economic overhaul necessary to restore the nation to the path of sustainable prosperity. The private sector in the United States did not win World War II. The government took the reins of the economy during that war and steered it to victory. This national emergency will also require a government-directed solution.

The Corruption of Capitalism explains the nature of the present crisis and the reforms—budgetary, monetary, regulatory and political—needed to permanently resolve it. The book is divided into three parts. Part 1 describes the state of the global economy and the multi-trillion-dollar policy response keeping it afloat. Part 2 gives an account of the policy mistakes from the 1960s onward that have resulted in this New Depression. Part 3 outlines what must be done to restructure the US economy so as to restore global economic equilibrium and growth, as well as the domestic reforms required in the United States to make that possible.

Great crises create great opportunities. The United States has the resources to reverse its economic decline by reengineering its industrial base. Ample funding is available. The real impediments are a lack of understanding of what must be done and the opposition of vested interests who stand to lose from restructuring and reform. American democracy has not faced greater challenges than these since 1945.

PART 1: The present

The world in crisis

A worldwide economic depression began in 2008. This New Depression was cased by the same factors as the Great Depression and followed exactly the same pattern. Thus far, however, the New Depression has been milder than the Great Depression because the policy response this time has been completely different.

Figure 1

THEN AND NOW

The Great Depression	The New Depression
Gold standard breaks down (1914)	Bretton Woods breaks down (1971)
Credit boom: Roaring Twenties	Credit boom: Global economic bubble
Boom leads to bust when the credit can't be repaid	Boom leads to bust when the credit can't be repaid
Banking collapse	Banking collapse
International trade collapses	International trade collapses

Source: Author

Both depressions were caused because governments began creating money. The Great Depression originated with the collapse of the gold standard in 1914, whereas the New Depression had its origins in the 1971 breakdown of the Bretton Woods system. In the earlier period, the gold standard collapsed because the European nations created more credit to finance World War I than could be supported by their gold reserves. Similarly, the Bretton Woods system broke down because the United States created more credit to finance the Vietnam War abroad and social-welfare spending at home than could be underwritten by American gold reserves.

In both instances, a great economic boom was brought about by an explosion of credit creation; and in both instances the boom turned to bust when that credit could not be repaid. At that point, a systemic crisis brought down the international banking system. Immediately thereafter, international trade collapsed.

During the 1930s, the forces of creative destruction, largely unimpeded by government intervention, ravaged the global economy as the excesses produced by the credit boom bankrupted a civilization unable to repay its debts. This time, governments have intervened and, in effect, taken over the management of the economy to prevent market forces from correcting the imbalances brought about by the paper-money-induced credit bubble. The commanding heights of global finance have been nationalized or bailed out, either openly or furtively, while the broader economy is sustained by government life support.

Thus far, these measures have greatly mitigated the pain of the New Depression. However, the policies introduced to date have not resolved the causes of this crisis or even targeted them. Moreover, government resources, while vast, are finite. Government spending will not be able to carry the economy forever. Policymakers must aim to do more than simply perpetuate the existing global economic disequilibrium. So far, there is no indication they understand the origins of the crisis, much less how to permanently end it. Part 1 describes the current state of the global economy and the extent of its dependence on government intervention.

Chapter 1
The policy response to the New Depression

A money-financed tax cut is essentially equivalent to Milton Friedman's famous "helicopter drop" of money.

Ben Bernanke[1]

When American policymakers abandoned the core principles of economic orthodoxy—balanced budgets and sound money—in the 1960s and early 1970s, capitalism began to evolve into something different: debtism. Until then, the creation of wealth had depended on the manufacture and exchange of tangible goods within a framework constrained by a limited supply of capital. By the late 1990s, however, a new economic paradigm had evolved in which the creation of wealth derived primarily from the invention and manipulation of debt, which seemingly faced no constraints. The emergence of debtism transformed the US economy and brought about a period of unprecedented global prosperity. It was inherently unsustainable, however, and in 2008 debtism collapsed.

---

[1] Fed Governor Ben S. Bernanke, "Deflation: Making Sure 'It' Doesn't Happen Here" (remarks before the National Economists Club, Washington, DC, 21 November 2002).

Debtism has now been replaced by a different economic paradigm: statism. Rather than standing by while the economy replayed the 1930s, the US government has mobilized on a war footing to prevent the annihilation of the financial sector and to support aggregate demand. Dole has replaced debt as the new driver of global growth. Statism is dangerous, however. It is a threat to democracy. For how can the citizenry control the state when the state controls the livelihood of the citizens? Moreover, statism is ultimately no more sustainable than debtism, since in reality it is only a variation thereof, where the state is the debtor and where prosperity still depends on the expansion of debt.

Was there an alternative to the statist policy response to the New Depression? No. Given the transformation of public expectations in this age of paper money, there wasn't. Americans have come to expect, and demand, to be bailed out by the government. A multi-trillion-dollar government intervention in response to the economic collapse could never have been more than one or two election cycles away.

That does not mean statism cannot be rolled back, however. Grave policy mistakes have corrupted the capitalist system and led to a crisis that has left the economy on government life support. US government debt will almost certainly increase by at least $10 trillion over the next ten years. As that debt will be required to prevent an economic collapse, it is politically inevitable. What is not yet fixed, however, is how that money will be spent. If it is spent foolishly or stolen by special interest groups, the American era will come to a swift end. However, if that money is spent wisely, miracles could be created and the American Century could prove to have been only the first of many.

Misunderstood lessons from the Great Depression

Milton Friedman, Ben Bernanke and many other prominent economists laid most of the blame for the Great Depression on the failure of the US Federal Reserve to prevent a contraction of the money supply when a large number of banks began to fail in 1930[2]. That theory—the "Just Keep the Balloon Inflated" theory—was wrong, and it has contributed significantly to creating the new crisis. The Great

---

[2] 1) Milton Friedman and Anna Jacobson Schwartz, *A Monetary History of The United States, 1967-1960* (Princeton University Press, 1963); 2) Ben S. Bernanke, *Essays on The Great Depression* (Princeton University Press, 2000); 3) Barry Eichengreen, *Golden Fetters: The gold standard and the Great Depression 1919-1939* (Oxford University Press, 1995).

Depression was not caused because the Fed did not pump a lot of new credit into the economy when the credit created earlier by the private sector could not be repaid. It was caused because too much credit had already been created in the first place during World War I and the Roaring Twenties. Excessive credit created a boom, and the boom created the bust. The first law of macroeconomic cycles is: If you don't prevent the boom, you can't prevent the bust. The second law is: The bigger the boom, the bigger the bust. China, take note!

By teaching the Just Keep the Balloon Inflated theory, its proponents created a widespread belief that there could never again be an economic calamity like the Great Depression. By persuading the public that policymakers had learned from the past and would not make the same mistakes again, they contributed to the reckless risk-taking that ended in the systemic financial-sector meltdown that began in 2008.

As chairman of the US Federal Reserve, Ben Bernanke is now in charge of the monetary response to the New Depression. He is finding it much harder to keep the balloon inflated than he had anticipated. Washington has been forced to nationalize much of the US financial sector and to guarantee the debt of a good part of the rest to prevent the credit bubble from deflating. Even so, preventing credit from contracting has proven insufficient to forestall economic disaster. The government was forced to increase its spending by 24% in 2009 to support aggregate demand. Despite all this, US unemployment is moving into double digits and international trade has plunged dramatically.

These measures have kept the New Depression from becoming as severe as the Great Depression. But the crisis is far from over: the economy is on government life support, the commanding heights of global finance have been nationalized, and the macroeconomic imbalances that brought about this crisis have not yet even begun to be addressed. Other than during the two world wars, the government's control over the economy has never been greater. Indeed it is no longer accurate to describe the US as having a capitalist economy.

While the ultimate cost of this crisis is still unknown, some of its lessons are perfectly clear. Prudent government regulation of and control over credit creation are required to prevent a destabilizing economic boom and bust. This crisis occurred because US lawmakers, regulators and monetary officials shamefully failed to carry out their duties in this respect. It is not enough to respond to bubbles after they pop or to Just Keep the Balloon Inflated. Credit bubbles must be prevented from forming by controlling money and credit creation. Any policy response that does not restore sound money and prevent runaway credit growth will be inadequate to permanently resolve this crisis.

9

Thus far the government has only attempted to patch up the holes in the balloon. That is far from enough.

What it takes

The credit-inflated bubble whose decades-long expansion had become the driver of global economic growth imploded in 2008 when too much of the credit extended could not be repaid. The US government was forced to respond on two fronts to prevent a breakdown of the global economy. First, it was required to stop the destruction of the financial system. To do this, Washington had to assume responsibility for repaying the debts of a large part of the financial industry. Second, to prevent a devastating plunge in US economic output, the government had to spend enough to offset the collapse in private-sector demand.

The ultimate cost in monetary terms of the government's policy response will not be known for years. Thus far, however, the cost of preventing the disappearance of the financial system has been much more than the government has spent on directly supporting aggregate demand. It is likely to remain much higher. In fact, the costs of maintaining the current financial system could prove to be so costly that the system may be impossible to save at all.

Saving the financial industry

> The government is prepared to do what it takes to maintain the stability of our financial system.
>
> US Treasury Secretary Henry Paulson[3]

Had the Federal National Mortgage Association (Fannie Mae), the Federal Home Loan Mortgage Corporation (Freddie Mac), AIG, Citigroup, or any of a hundred other "too-big-to-fail" financial institutions failed, in the absence of large-scale government intervention, its collapse would have bankrupted most of the other financial institutions in the world and destroyed the bulk of the world's savings. The global economy would have come to a standstill. Without government intervention, the worst horrors of the Great

---

[3] Treasury Secretary Henry Paulson, interview on *Fox News Sunday*, 16 March 2008.

Depression would have returned. This is so because each of these institutions is connected to the rest as the result of billions of dollars of conventional loans and trillions of dollars of derivatives contracts. It was the catastrophic consequences inherent in these counterparty risks that forced the government to nationalize much of the sector's losses.

The US government has acted very aggressively to prevent the financial sector's destruction. The Treasury Department and the Federal Reserve have played the most visible roles in the bailout, but many other government agencies have also been involved. As the principal rescue vehicle, the Troubled Asset Relief Program (TARP) has attracted the most public attention, but it represents only a portion of the money committed by the government to stave off systemic collapse.

The Office of the Special Inspector General for the Troubled Asset Relief Program (SIGTARP) was established in late 2008 to monitor how the money allocated to the TARP program is spent. Its quarterly reports to Congress provide a comprehensive overview of government efforts to support the financial system. For instance, SIGTARP's July 2009 report states:

> By itself, the Troubled Asset Relief Program ("TARP") is a huge program at $700 billion. As discussed in SIGTARP's April Quarterly Report, the total financial exposure of TARP and TARP-related programs may reach approximately $3 trillion. Although large in its own right, TARP is only a part of the combined efforts of the Federal Government to address the financial crisis. Approximately 50 initiatives or programs have been created by various Federal agencies since 2007 to provide potential support totaling more than $23.7 trillion.[4]

Figure 2

INCREMENTAL FINANCIAL-SYSTEM SUPPORT SINCE 2007, BY FEDERAL AGENCY

($ trillion)	Current balance	Maximum balance as of 30 June 2009	Total potential support related to crisis
Federal Reserve	1.4	3.1	6.8
FDIC	0.3	0.3	2.3
Treasury—TARP (incl. Federal Reserve, FDIC components)	0.6	0.6	3.0
Treasury—Non-TARP	0.3	0.3	4.4
Others—FHFA, NCUA, GNMA, FHA, VA	0.3	0.3	7.2
Total	3.0	4.7	23.7

Note: Amounts may include overlapping agency liabilities, "implied" guarantees and unfunded initiatives.
Total potential support does not account for collateral pledged. Other agencies include: Federal Housing Finance Agency, National Credit Union Administration, Government National Mortgage Association, Federal Housing Administration, and US Dept of Veterans Affairs.
Source: SIGTARP *Quarterly Report to Congress*, 21 July 2009, p. 138

---

[4] Office of the Special Inspector General for the Troubled Asset Relief Program (SIGTARP), *Quarterly Report to Congress*, 21 July 2009, p. 137.

The Department of the Treasury, the Federal Reserve and the Federal Deposit Insurance Corporation (FDIC) have played the leading role in carrying out government policy. Coordination between these three bodies has been effective in achieving maximum impact on the financial system for minimum overt commitment of taxpayers' money. The Treasury Department requires Congressional approval to spend money. Obtaining that approval for the $700 billion TARP was an arduous experience that Treasury officials would prefer not to have to live through again. By contrast, the Fed can create as much paper money as it pleases without asking anyone's permission. It is also relatively unrestricted in what it does with the paper money it creates. However, it is constrained by its concerns over how the markets will respond to its actions. If it creates too much money, it could spook investors and cause market-determined interest rates to rise or the dollar to fall—perhaps very sharply. The Fed is also constrained by its fear that lawmakers will rewrite the laws in order to bring it under Congressional control.

The FDIC has been very useful as a guarantor not only of deposits, its traditional role, but also now of bank-issued debt as well. Although the FDIC cannot spend taxpayers' money like the Treasury, or create money from thin air like the Fed, it can still guarantee hundreds of billions of dollars of bank-issued debt so long as it does not lose more money in this exercise than it earns by charging the financial sector fees for its services. Whether or not the FDIC actually will lose money will not be known for some time; should the worst occur and losses outstrip fee revenues, then that situation can be dealt with when it arises. The coordination of Treasury, Fed and FDIC action has been worked out on the run, and there has been considerable overlap in their efforts.

The government's rescue of the financial system comprises five broad categories of measures: nationalization, money creation, debt acquisition, debt guarantees, and regulatory forbearance.

Nationalization

Technically, the government has not fully nationalized any of the troubled financial institutions. Fannie Mae and Freddie Mac were put into "conservatorship" at the price of $291 billion so far. AIG has become 79.9% government-owned, following three rounds of bailouts involving government commitments in excess of $180 billion. Taxpayers have a 34% stake in Citigroup, for which the government paid $45 billion and guaranteed the losses on most of a $301 billion portfolio of questionable assets. The government has also paid $45 billion to date for roughly a 6% stake in Bank of America. Finally, it has invested approximately $168 billion more to take smaller equity stakes in 647 or so other banks.

Money creation

While the Treasury had to struggle with Congress to obtain the $700 billion to fund TARP, the Federal Reserve found it considerably easier to get cash. It simply created it. Between the beginning of 2008 and July 2009, the "Reserve Bank Credit" of the Federal Reserve increased by $1.12 trillion, to a total of $2.0 trillion.[5] In other words, over 19 months, the Fed created money and grew its balance sheet by 125%. The Fed used some of that money to buy debt securities outright (see Figure 3) and most of the rest to lend to financial institutions. The Term Auction Facility allows banks to borrow from the Fed by putting up collateral. It was designed to give banks an alternative to borrowing at the Fed's discount window, which had come to be seen as a sign of weakness. Term Auction Credit lending peaked at $493 billion in March 2009, with $237 billion still outstanding in July 2009. The amount of Fed credit outstanding to AIG at that date was $43 billion. The Fed also extended an additional $30 billion to other institutions through its Term Asset-Backed Securities Loan Facility.

The $1.12 trillion created by the Fed is 60% more than the total funds allocated to TARP and the equivalent of approximately 8% of US GDP. Nevertheless, it represents only a part of the amount the Fed has really committed to the rescue of the financial sector. According to SIGTARP:

> The Federal Reserve's $2 trillion balance sheet, however, does not reflect the true potential amount of support the Federal Reserve has provided to those programs, which is estimated to be at least $6.8 trillion. This is because many of the programs involve guarantees that, although not listed on the balance sheet, expose the Federal Reserve to significant losses if the assets they are backing deteriorate in value.[6]

Central banks are meant to be able to regulate the economy by tweaking interest rates in one direction or the other. When a huge credit bubble collapses, however, a "liquidity trap" emerges in which interest rates fall toward zero. That occurs because too much capacity is built during the boom. When the boom busts, there are no longer any viable new projects in which to invest. Therefore the demand for loans (from viable borrowers) collapses, and interest rates, the cost of renting money, plunge.

When this crisis began to unfold, the Fed responded by cutting the federal funds rate. As that rate moved toward zero, confronting the Fed with a liquidity

---

[5] Federal Reserve Statistical Release H.4.1, "Factors Affecting Reserve Balances of Depository Institutions", 3 January 2008 and 30 July 2009. Amounts are averages for the weeks ending 2 January 2008 and 29 July 2009.

[6] Office of the Special Inspector General for the Troubled Asset Relief Program (SIGTARP), *Quarterly Report to Congress*, 21 July 2009, p. 137.

trap, the central bank began its program of "quantitative easing", otherwise known as "helicopter money".

Figure 3

FACTORS AFFECTING RESERVE BALANCES OF DEPOSITORY INSTITUTIONS

($ million)	Averages of daily figures for the weeks ended:	
	2 Jan 08	29 Jul 09
Reserve Bank Credit	**891,743**	**2,010,048**
Securities held outright	740,611	1,343,891
US Treasury	740,611	695,318
Bills	227,841	18,423
Notes and bonds, nominal	470,984	627,146
Notes and bonds, inflation-indexed	36,911	44,438
Inflation compensation	4,876	5,311
Federal agency debt securities	0	104,066
Mortgage-backed securities	1	544,507
Repurchase agreements	39,750	0
Term auction credit	40,000	237,629
Other loans	5,787	108,531
Primary credit	5,770	33,803
Secondary credit	0	105
Seasonal credit	16	88
Primary dealer and other broker-dealer credit	1	0
Asset-Backed Commercial Paper Money- Market Mutual Fund Liquidity Facility	1	1,073
Credit extended to AIG, net	1	43,054
Term Asset-Backed Securities Loan Facility	1	30,408
Other credit extensions	1	0
Net portfolio holdings of Commercial Paper Funding Facility		94,414
Net portfolio holdings of LLCs funded through the Money Market Investor Funding Facility	1	26,029
Net portfolio holdings of Maiden Lane LLC	1	
Net portfolio holdings of Maiden Lane II LLC	1	15,672
Net portfolio holdings of Maiden Lane III LLC	1	19,166
Float	(1,017)	(1,778)
Central-bank liquidity swaps	1	87,738
Other Federal Reserve assets	66,612	78,756
Gold stock	**11,041**	**11,041**
Special drawing rights certificate account	**2,200**	**2,200**
Treasury currency outstanding	**38,821**	**42,487**
Total factors supplying reserve funds	**943,805**	**2,065,776**

¹ Not a category in 2008. Source: Federal Reserve Statistical Release, 3 January 2008 and 30 July 2009

Quantitative easing means the creation of more paper money. Interest rates are determined by both the demand for money and the supply of money. The Fed is now creating more money, effectively to replace the money/debt destroyed in the economic crash, in order to prevent the money supply from contracting. But by doing so, it is simply perpetuating the imbalances that triggered the crash in the first place. Society had more debt than it could afford to support. Creating more debt to replace the old, destroyed debt won't change that. The Fed is in charge of US monetary affairs. The emergence of a liquidity trap is its fault and the resort to quantitative easing is testimony to its failure.

Debt acquisition

A third method the government has employed to save the financial sector is to buy debt securities outright from that sector. For example, the Fed announced in March 2009 that it would buy up to $1.25 trillion of agency mortgage-backed securities and up to $200 billion in agency debt. "Moreover, to help improve conditions in private credit markets, the Committee decided to purchase up to $300 billion of longer-term Treasury securities over the next six months."[7] By the end of July 2009, the Fed had acquired $545 billion in mortgage-backed securities and $104 billion in federal agency debt securities. It had also bought more than half of the $300 billion in targeted longer-term Treasury securities. In addition, the Fed had accumulated a $94 billion portfolio of commercial paper.

The Department of the Treasury has also been involved in debt purchases from the financial sector. It bought $141 billion worth of government-sponsored enterprises' (GSEs) mortgage-backed securities in the open market as part of its takeover of Fannie Mae and Freddie Mac. That acquisition preceded and, therefore, was not part of the $700 billion the Treasury was permitted to spend through TARP.

Together, the Fed and Treasury had bought well over $1 trillion in debt securities by the end of July 2009. That amount exceeds 2% of all outstanding dollar-denominated credit-market debt. This intervention served a number of purposes. It provided a buyer at times when the market was dominated by panicked sellers and therefore prevented prices from becoming oversold and unnecessarily depressed. The purchases also pushed up the price of the debt and thereby held down its yield. Lower yields supported mortgage rates at a time when the property market needed all the help it could get. Lower yields on Treasury bonds also reduced the cost to the government of financing its rapidly expanding debt.

Debt guarantees

The fourth set of measures to save the financial system involve the US government's guaranteeing both new and previously issued debt. The FDIC established a Debt Guarantee Program that guarantees the newly issued senior unsecured debt (securities that have priority over other debt for repayment in the event of default) of banks and other depository institutions. Its goal is to increase the availability and reduce the cost of funding for participating banks in order to help "get the credit flowing again". The maximum potential size of

---

[7] Board of Governors of the Federal Reserve System, Federal Open Market Committee press release, 18 March 2009.

this program is $785 billion. Of that amount, $346 billion has been used so far.

In a completely different kind of program, the Treasury, Fed and FDIC joined together to guarantee a select set of troubled assets on the books of Citigroup. The government has entered an agreement with Citigroup in which $301 billion of the bank's assets will be "ring-fenced". Citigroup must absorb the first $29 billion of losses on those assets. After that, the government will split the remaining losses with Citigroup 90:10. Of the 90% of losses that will be borne by the government, the first $5 billion will be absorbed by the Treasury with TARP funds, the next $10 billion by the FDIC, and the remaining losses covered by the Federal Reserve with a non-recourse loan. This loss-sharing agreement was announced in November 2008, at a time when extreme weakness in Citigroup's share price called the bank's viability into question. Committing taxpayer money to guarantee Citigroup's losses helped restore confidence in its future.

In January 2009, the government and the Bank of America announced a similar arrangement in which $118 billion of Bank of America's assets would be ring-fenced and the losses on those assets shared between the bank and the government. Four months later, however, Bank of America announced it was no longer seeking such assistance.

Forbearance

Finally, the government adopted forbearance as a policy tool. This was not the moment, so the thinking went, to stand on principle in every case, especially where a little flexibility could help the survival of the country's banking sector. For instance, in April 2009, the Financial Accounting Standards Board announced that it would relax fair-value (i.e. "mark-to-market") accounting rules that had required banks to value all assets at the current market price. The new guidelines gave banks greater flexibility in the way they valued distressed assets.

The government also acted with remarkable speed in approving the conversion of Goldman Sachs and Morgan Stanley into bank holding companies in September 2009, the month the investment banking industry disappeared. This move gave those highly leveraged institutions better access to funding.

The government's Home Affordable Modification Program provided support to both home owners and their creditors by using TARP funding to "modify" mortgages so as to ease payments, thus reducing foreclosures and the financial-sector's losses on delinquent mortgages.

In combination, these five broad areas of government intervention succeeded in preventing the collapse of the financial sector, at least as of October 2009.

The cost of the measures adopted so far seems certain ultimately to be reckoned in the trillions. Yet they have not solved, or even addressed, the problems that *caused* the systemic crisis. Therefore they should only be viewed as stopgap measures. The cost of truly cleaning up the financial industry could ultimately reach tens of trillions should the $700 trillion unregulated derivatives market prove to be just one more financial-sector Ponzi scheme.

Supporting aggregate demand

The entire US economy is on government life support, not only the financial sector. The Congressional Budget Office (CBO) has projected that the government will spend $3.7 trillion in 2009—$700 billion, or 24%, more than the year before. Government outlays will jump to 26% of GDP, from 21% in 2008. The last time government expenditure exceeded that proportion of GDP was during World War II. Had the government not increased its spending, the downward spiral in the economy would have been far worse than it has been to date.

There are a number of ways to assess what the government has spent to stimulate the economy. None of them are straightforward. Two economic stimulus packages have been implemented since the crisis began. The Economic Stimulus Act of 2008, passed in February of that year, provided approximately $150 billion in stimulus to the economy through tax reductions and rebates. One year later, the American Recovery and Reinvestment Act of 2009 (ARRA) was passed. It will provide $787 billion in stimulus, spread between 2009 and 2011. Figure 4 shows how that money will be spent.

Figure 4

AMERICAN RECOVERY AND REINVESTMENT ACT OF 2009

Category	Amount ($ billion)
Tax relief	288
State and local fiscal relief	144
Infrastructure and science	111
Protecting the vulnerable	81
Healthcare	59
Education and training	53
Energy	43
Other	8
Total	**787**

Source: Recovery.gov (http://www.recovery.gov/?=node/88)

The government outlays projected by the CBO provide a shocking view of the increase in government spending in 2009. However, these projections include estimates of government spending to save the financial sector as well as all other types of expenditure. Moreover, the estimates are complicated by the necessity of incorporating numerous assumptions—for instance, that the net present value of the government's future losses will be $133 billion on TARP and $291 billion on Fannie May and Freddie Mac, though its actual expenditure and losses to date both differ from those amounts.[8]

Figure 5

US FEDERAL GOVERNMENT OUTLAYS

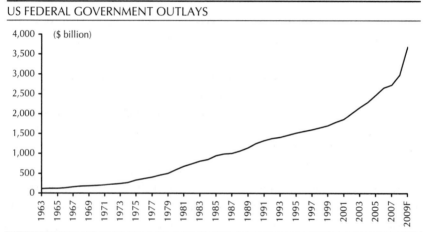

Source: CBO, *The Budget and Economic Outlook: An Update*, August 2009

The CBO's budget deficit projections yield a different and even more harrowing insight into the stimulus provided to the economy by the government. The CBO forecasts that the 2009 budget deficit will be $1.6 trillion, three-and-a-half times higher than the largest deficit on record and the equivalent of 11% of US GDP. Again, these levels have not been exceeded since World War II. In fact, after 1946, the highest previous budget deficit was 6% of GDP, in 1983—roughly half the shortfall projected for 2009.

---

[8] Congressional Budget Office: 1) *The Budget and Economic Outlook: Fiscal Years 2009 to 2019, Testimony, Statement of Robert A. Sunshine Acting Director before the Committee on the Budget United States Senate*, 8 January 2009; 2) *A Preliminary Analysis of the President's Budget and an Update of CBO's Budget and Economic Outlook*, March 2009.

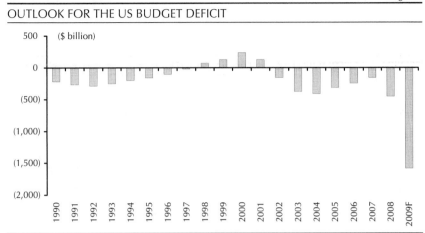

Source: CBO, *The Budget and Economic Outlook: An Update*, August 2009

However, the increase in the deficit does not accurately reflect the impact of government spending on the economy either. Not only does this projection share the same shortcomings as the outlay projections on the expenditure side, it also incorporates the collapse in government tax receipts on the revenue side. In 2009, federal government revenues are projected to fall to 15% of GDP due to the collapse in the economy and the evaporation of capital-gains taxes on property and stocks. The last time government revenues were so low as a percentage of GDP was in 1950. Lower tax payments do represent a kind of stimulus of the "automatic-stabilizer" variety, but they are far less effective in creating jobs than outright government spending.

The bottom line is that it is very difficult to precisely quantify how much direct stimulus the government has so far provided to the economy. The $150 billion from the 2008 stimulus package is straightforward. It has certainly helped support the economy. As for 2009, the best way to estimate the total may be to subtract roughly $425 billion in financial-sector support from the $700 billion increase in outlays, yielding $275 billion of real stimulus spending, an amount equivalent to 2% of US GDP. In addition to that, it would not be inaccurate to point out that bailing out the financial sector also provided some direct stimulus to the economy, as the large bonus payments received by the employees of Merrill Lynch and other troubled firms trickled down to the rest of the public.

Much more government spending will be required over the years ahead.

America's old economic-growth model of debt-fuelled private consumption will not be resuscitated. The new growth driver is government deficit spending.

Figure 7

FEDERAL GOVERNMENT REVENUES AND OUTLAYS

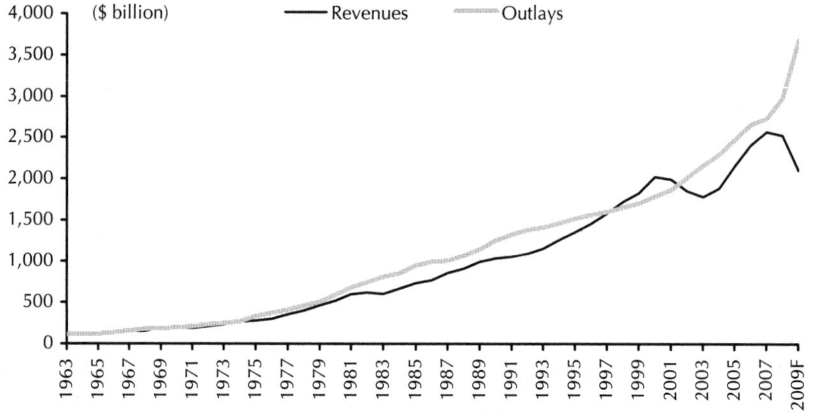

Source: CBO, *The Budget and Economic Outlook: An Update*, August 2009

Helicopter money

As described above, the government's policy response to the New Depression has been first, to stop the disintegration of the financial sector by using taxpayers' money and newly created money to buy the industry's equity and debt, and by promising to inject more of both in the future as required; and second, to radically increase public spending to offset the collapse in private-sector spending so as to prevent a downward spiral in the economy. Had the government not taken these steps, the New Depression would have been the New Great Depression.

A great deal can be learned about the government's response to this crisis, as well as the mistaken policies that necessitated it, by analyzing a speech delivered by Ben Bernanke on 21 November 2002. At that time, Bernanke was a Governor of the Federal Reserve. The speech, to the National Economists Club, was titled "Deflation: Making Sure 'It' Doesn't Happen Here". In light of subsequent events, Bernanke's comments expose his misunderstanding of the state of the US economy, and, in particular, the forces driving it. This is important because the policies he advocated in that speech are the ones that have been employed in this crisis. Those policies were conceived as a solution to an economic situation Bernanke did not understand. Consequently, they will not cure the imbalances that caused the New Depression. In the short run, their effect will be palliative at best. Over the long run, unless combined with new policies to restructure the US economy, they will only exacerbate past mistakes and permanently undermine American prosperity.

Bernanke gave this speech soon after the collapse of the NASDAQ bubble, when deflation threatened the US for the first time since the 1930s. His ideas about how to prevent deflation are important if we are to understand his ideas about curing it. He began by stating, "I believe that the chance of significant deflation in the United States in the foreseeable future is extremely small..." He went on: "A particularly important protective factor in the current environment is the strength of our financial system: Despite the adverse shocks of the past year, our banking system remains healthy and well-regulated, and firm and household balance sheets are for the most part in good shape."[9]

At the end of 2002, the US banking sector was not healthy, and it was certainly not well regulated. Within five years of those remarks it began to collapse, pulling the global economy down with it. Nor were household balance sheets in "good shape". American households had never been more indebted. As for corporate balance sheets, who can say what condition they were in, given the long series of accounting scandals involving Enron, WorldCom, Fannie Mae, Freddie Mac, and many others? To take just the most recent example: in August 2009, General Electric agreed to pay a $50 million fine to settle accounting-fraud charges by US regulators related to the use of improper accounting methods in 2002 and 2003. "GE bent the accounting rules beyond the breaking point," the *Financial Times* quoted Robert Khuzami, director of the SEC's enforcement division, as saying.[10] In light of present knowledge, it is difficult not to conclude that Bernanke in 2002 greatly overestimated the health of the US economy.

The Fed governor went on to discuss the causes of deflation and its relationship to aggregate demand:

> The sources of deflation are not a mystery. Deflation is in almost all cases a side effect of a collapse of aggregate demand—a drop in spending so severe that producers must cut prices on an ongoing basis in order to find buyers. Likewise, the economic effects of a deflationary episode, for the most part, are similar to those of any other

---

[9] Fed Governor Ben S. Bernanke, "Deflation: Making Sure 'It' Doesn't Happen Here" (remarks before the National Economists Club, Washington, DC, 21 November 2002).
[10] *Ibid.*

sharp decline in aggregate spending—namely, recession, rising unemployment, and financial stress.[11]

Next, Bernanke suggested it would be far better to prevent deflation rather than to be forced to cure it once it had taken hold, as it had in Japan:

> The basic prescription for preventing deflation is therefore straightforward, at least in principle: Use monetary and fiscal policy as needed to support aggregate spending, in a manner as nearly consistent as possible with full utilization of economic resources and low and stable inflation.[12]

According to Bernanke, then, deflation is caused by a collapse in aggregate demand and can be prevented by using monetary and fiscal policy "to support aggregate spending". But he does not address the question of why aggregate demand would collapse in the first place. Nor does he explain why the economy cannot be righted by market forces but instead must rely on government intervention to hold off deflation.

These questions are too important to overlook. Deflation took hold in the US in the 1930s and in Japan in the 1990s because policymakers in those countries failed to prevent credit bubbles from forming there in the 1920s and the 1980s. Credit bubbles cause aggregate demand for goods and services to expand far beyond the point that can be sustained by the underlying income of society. That is why aggregated demand collapses when the credit bubble pops. Therefore, it must be understood that deflation is the consequence of misguided government policies that allow the formation of credit bubbles. Bad policies were responsible for the NASDAQ bubble. Its collapse produced the deflationary pressures Bernanke was discussing in 2002. Bad policies are also responsible for the deflationary threat now confronting the US following the rise and fall of the housing-credit bubble.

Bernanke ended by describing what the Fed could do to cure deflation in the "unlikely" event that prevention did not work and the overnight federal funds rate fell to zero: The following excerpts convey most of his recommendation on the subject:

> We conclude that, under a paper-money system, a determined government can always generate higher spending and hence positive inflation....

> Of course, the U.S. government is not going to print money and distribute it willy-nilly (although as we will see later, there are practical policies that approximate this behavior). Normally, money is injected into the economy through asset purchases by the Federal Reserve. To stimulate aggregate spending when short-term interest rates have reached zero, the Fed must expand the scale of its asset purchases or, possibly, expand the menu of assets that it buys....

---

[11] *Ibid.*
[12] *Ibid.*

Yet another option would be for the Fed to use its existing authority to operate in the markets for agency debt (for example, mortgage-backed securities issued by Ginnie Mae, the Government National Mortgage Association)....

Historical experience tends to support the proposition that a sufficiently determined Fed can peg or cap Treasury bond prices and yields at other than the shortest maturities....

If lowering yields on longer-dated Treasury securities proved insufficient to restart spending, however, the Fed might next consider attempting to influence directly the yields on privately issued securities. Unlike some central banks, and barring changes to current law, the Fed is relatively restricted in its ability to buy private securities directly. However, the Fed does have broad powers to lend to the private sector indirectly via banks, through the discount window. Therefore a second policy option, complementary to operating in the markets for Treasury and agency debt, would be for the Fed to offer fixed-term loans to banks at low or zero interest, with a wide range of private assets (including, among others, corporate bonds, commercial paper, bank loans, and mortgages) deemed eligible as collateral....

Each of the policy options I have discussed so far involves the Fed's acting on its own. In practice, the effectiveness of anti-deflation policy could be significantly enhanced by cooperation between the monetary and fiscal authorities. A broad-based tax cut, for example, accommodated by a program of open-market purchases to alleviate any tendency for interest rates to increase, would almost certainly be an effective stimulant to consumption and hence to prices.[13]

While most of those measures were not required in 2002-03, they have been put into effect in 2008-09. Their purpose is to prevent a contraction of aggregate demand after a credit bubble has burst. This policy is inherently flawed because it fails to recognize that the bubble (and the aggregate demand it created) could not be kept inflated indefinitely by the private sector because the private sector did not have sufficient income to sustain it. It is no cure to use aggressive fiscal and monetary policy to inflate a new credit bubble to replace the one that just burst. The second bubble will be no more sustainable than the first.

The policies employed to prevent deflation and support aggregate demand after the NASDAQ bubble burst were only a mild version of those laid out in Bernanke's 2002 speech. Aggressive fiscal and monetary measures were implemented that pumped up aggregate demand by fuelling the US property bubble. That approach worked in the short run: the US experienced no significant deflation at the time. Over the long run, however, those policies made matters very much worse. If private-sector income was insufficient to support the NASDAQ credit bubble in 2001, how could anyone have supposed that it would be sufficient to support the much larger housing credit bubble a few years later?

---

[13] *Ibid.*

Yes, as Bernanke pointed out, "Indeed, under a fiat (that is, paper) money system, a government (in practice, the central bank in cooperation with other agencies) should always be able to generate increased nominal spending and inflation, even when the short-term nominal interest rate is at zero". That is certainly true in the short run, but what is the exit strategy? Given the scale of government intervention required to prevent complete economic collapse during this round, at this rate, a continuation of the fiat-money bubble-blowing strategy will soon end in nothing less than total collectivization of society.

The policy response to the New Depression has not cured the causes of the economic breakdown, it has merely nationalized the cost of attempting to perpetuate them. Once the bubble began to collapse, there was no realistic alternative to nationalization. Nationalization has kept the patient alive, but a radically different policy will be required if the patient is actually to be cured.

Chapter 2
Condition critical: the state of the US economy

Our economy is badly weakened, a consequence of greed and irresponsibility on the part of some, but also our collective failure to make hard choices and prepare the nation for a new age.

President Barack Obama[1]

The bankruptcy of the private sector in 2008 has left the US economy on government life support. The patient is alive, but cannot sustain itself. Its survival, at least in its previous capitalist state, is far from assured. A long convalescence may restore the economy to health. However, complete recovery is not possible without physical rehabilitation to reestablish self-sufficiency and intense psychological therapy to cure persisting delusions of monetary omnipotence and societal psychosis related to trade. A number of malignancies will also have to be removed. This chapter examines the critical condition of the American economy.

---

[1] President Barack Obama, inaugural address, 20 January 2009.

Government life support

The CBO expects the US budget deficit to be $1.6 trillion in 2009, $1.4 trillion in 2010, $921 billion in 2011 and $590 billion in 2012.[2] These are shocking numbers. They are also far too optimistic for two reasons. First, reckless credit growth has distorted the US economy and left it with excess industrial capacity, overinflated asset prices and unsustainable spending patterns that will leave the private sector crippled for years. Second, the CBO projections greatly understate the financial-sector losses that the government will have to absorb in the future.

The United States' old economic model of debt-fuelled consumption has imploded. Government deficit spending is now the country's sole driver of growth. Government outlays are projected to expand by $700 billion, or 24%, to a total of $3.7 trillion during 2009. Even so, US GDP is expected to contract by 1% to $14.2 trillion. If the government had not massively increased its spending, the economy would have collapsed. Moreover, Washington will have to continue propping up the economy for the foreseeable future. Like it or not, statism is the new economic paradigm.

The outlook for the private sector

GDP is made up of private consumption, private investment, net trade and government spending and investment. Figure 8 presents a breakdown of US GDP in 2008.

Spending on personal consumption accounted for 70.5% of GDP in 2008; private investment 14.0%; and government spending 20.2%. Net exports deducted 4.7% from GDP. This breakdown is somewhat misleading, however, in the sense that it underestimates the true impact of government spending on the economy. Federal spending totaled $2.98 trillion in 2008, nearly three times the sum shown in Figure 8. The reason for the discrepancy is that in the GDP breakdown, the government spending line represents only direct purchases of goods and services. It does not include unemployment benefits, Social Security and Medicare spending, assistance to state and local governments, or emergency assistance to the financial sector. In other words, federal government outlays make a significant contribution to other sectors of the economy, particularly personal consumption spending and state and local

---

[2] CBO, *The Budget and Economic Outlook: An Update*, August 2009.

government. Figure 8 thus overstates those sectors' contribution to GDP and understates that of the federal government.

Figure 8

COMPONENTS OF US GDP (NOMINAL)

	Amount ($ billion)		% of total	
	2007	2008	2007	2008
Gross domestic product (nominal)	13,808	14,265	100.0	100.0
Personal consumption expenditure	9,710	10,058	70.3	70.5
Gross private domestic investment	2,130	1,994	15.4	14.0
Net exports of goods and services	(708)	(669)	(5.1)	(4.7)
Exports	1,662	1,859	8.4	13.0
Imports	2,370	2,529	17.2	17.7
Government	2,675	2,882	19.4	20.2
Federal	979	1,072	7.1	7.5
State and local	1,696	1,810	12.3	12.7

Source: Bureau of Economic Analysis

Personal consumption expenditure

Between 2002 and 2007, American households increased their borrowing by an average of $1 *trillion* each year. That incredible increase in debt drove personal consumption expenditure to its current level of $10 trillion a year, and was chiefly responsible for pushing GDP to its current size of $14 trillion.

Figure 9

ANNUAL INCREASE IN HOUSEHOLD-SECTOR DEBT

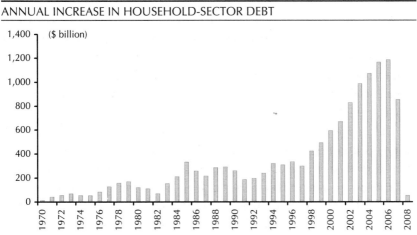

Source: US Federal Reserve Flow of Funds

There was never any possibility that the household sector could repay that much debt. When American households began defaulting en masse on debt repayments in 2007, the finance industry's originate–securitise–sell-to-sucker scam unraveled and households were cut off from further credit. In 2008, household-sector borrowing increased by only $54 billion. The inability of households to borrow more threw the world into the worst economic crisis in 80 years.

For large numbers of Americans, debt had become the main source of "income". Cut off from new credit, they had no alternative but to spend less. Retail sales plunged.

Figure 10

US RETAIL SALES

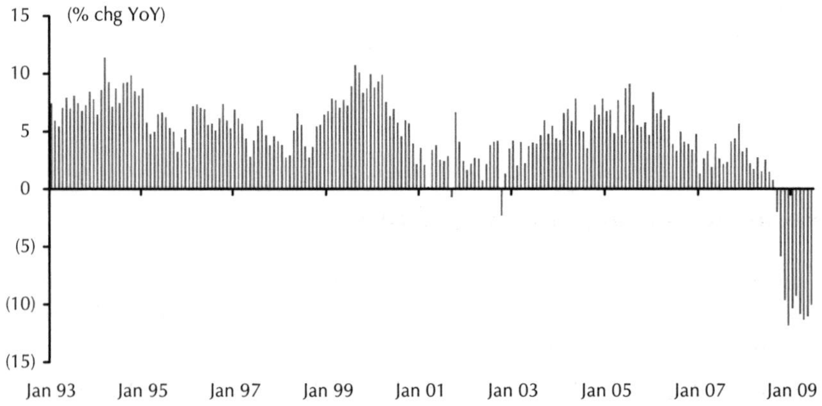

Source: Federal Reserve Bank of St. Louis

When the NASDAQ bubble collapsed in 2000-01, retail sales barely wavered. Compared to the same month of the previous year, they dipped by 0.7% one month and by 2.3% a few months later. And that was it. The stock market might have crashed but the credit was still flowing. House prices were rising fast, thanks mostly to the Fed, and there was plenty of home equity to extract and spend.

This time around, the story is completely different. Retail sales fell by 2% year on year in September 2008, and by 5.8% in October. Over the next eight months, retail sales were down by an average of 10.5% each month. This was— and remains—a disaster. There had not been a downturn remotely like it since the Great Depression. Since then the worst time for retailers was a couple of months where retail sales were down 5% or so, but that did not last long.

There is no reason to expect that household borrowing will increase again in the foreseeable future. Keep in mind, households did not pay down their debt in 2008. They were merely denied access to more credit because they couldn't repay the debt they had already incurred. Simply put, the US household sector as a whole is no longer creditworthy. It does not earn enough to service the interest on its debt. And to make matters worse, unemployment is rising rapidly.

Figure 11

US UNEMPLOYMENT RATE

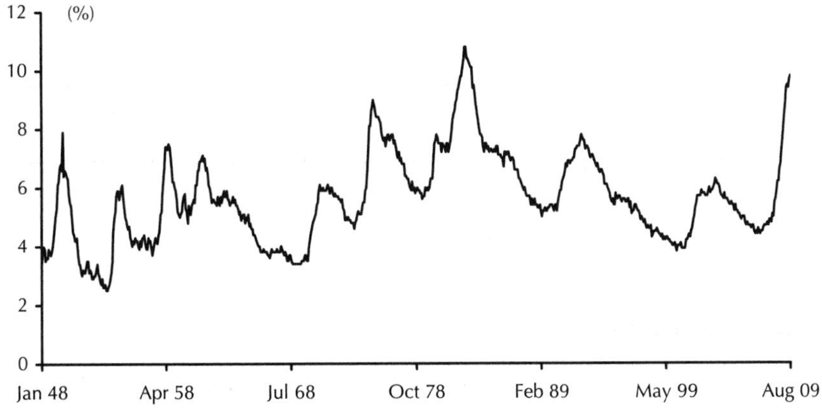

Source: US Department of Labor

Furthermore, households now have fewer assets to offer as collateral for additional loans. An individual's home is generally his or her most valuable asset and the most widely accepted form of collateral. Property prices in the US have fallen by an average of 30% in the past three years, however. Household net worth has already slumped 21% from its peak in the second quarter of 2007. Moreover, years of equity extraction, now combined with record home foreclosures, mean the amount of equity the average homeowner actually still has in the home has fallen to a record low of 43%. Therefore the average American, already heavily indebted, has less and less to borrow against.

It is a distinctly gloomy picture. US households are heavily indebted, cut off from additional access to credit, and facing the worst job market in at least a generation. Anyone hoping for a spontaneous revival of private-sector spending should think again. Personal consumption expenditure is being supported by government transfer payments. That support will have to remain in place for years to prevent a very severe economic outcome.

Figure 12

OWNERS' EQUITY AS % OF HOUSEHOLD REAL ESTATE

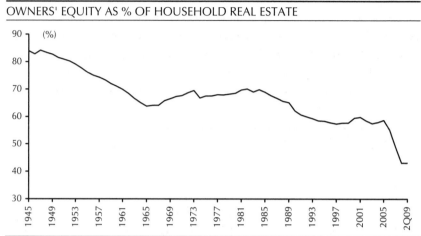

Source: Federal Reserve Flow of Funds

Private investment

The prospects for private investment are also very poor. With sales so depressed, there is little reason for industry to produce more goods. It is therefore not surprising that US industrial production has fallen by a larger percentage than at any time since World War II. In absolute terms, it is no greater than it was 10 years ago.

Figure 13

INDUSTRIAL PRODUCTION

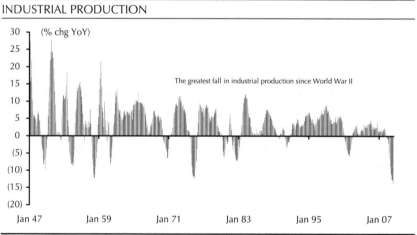

Source: Federal Reserve Bank of St. Louis

Capacity utilization has also plummeted to its lowest level since the data series began in 1967. In all probability, it is at its lowest level since the 1930s. With so much excess capacity, new investment will be restricted for many years. Weak investment will also mean higher unemployment.

Figure 14

US CAPACITY UTILIZATION

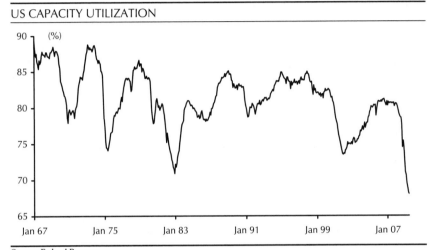

Source: Federal Reserve

Trade

Net trade subtracted 5% from GDP in 2008. That is not unusual: trade has reduced US economic output every year since 1975. At least that is how the impact of net trade is depicted in the official GDP breakdown (as shown in Figure 8). The reality is rather different. As explained in later chapters, the huge trade deficit necessitated enormous flows of capital into the US. These pushed up asset prices, pushed down interest rates, fuelled economic growth and eventually created an economic bubble. Therefore the large trade deficit actually produced much more economic growth than would have occurred if net trade had been balanced. Nevertheless, in official treatments of GDP, trade deficits act as a large drag on economic output.

Those in charge of US trade policy have long believed the expansion of international trade would make everyone better off. Even though a very large trade deficit developed as trade expanded, US policymakers apparently convinced themselves that this trade deficit would one day correct itself. The high rates of economic growth in countries like China, India, Brazil and Russia gave rise to the belief in policy circles that as those countries grew richer, they would import much more from the US. In the years just before the global credit bubble popped, the theory arose that the global economy had "decoupled", meaning that various parts of the world could grow independently of each other. This further bolstered the hope that the rest of the world would eventually buy more from the US than the US bought from the rest of the world.

Figure 15

US GOODS IMPORTS VERSUS EXPORTS, 1960-2009

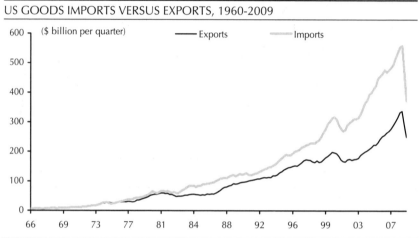

Source: Bureau of Economic Analysis

That was a fantasy. Growth in US exports is tied to growth in US imports: the more the US buys from the rest of the world, the more the rest of the world buys from the US. Unfortunately, export growth is consistently smaller than import growth. In other words, the ratio between them is less than 1. Since the beginning of 2000, it has averaged 0.58. So, for example, if the United States were to import $100 billion more this year than last, it would be able to export $58 billion more, but it would have to borrow $42 billion from abroad to finance the difference between what it imports and what it exports. As long as it lasted, this arrangement benefited America's trading partners, US exporters, and the financiers who arrange the credit. However, not only were the very large US trade deficits inherently unsustainable, they were also responsible for the global imbalances that are now coming unwound.

It is not surprising that the rest of the world would buy more from the US when the US buys more from the rest of the world. The large trade surpluses enjoyed by America's trading partners mean they have much more money available to buy American-made products. But it is also not surprising that the rest of the world buys less from the US than it sells to the US. Many of the countries the US trades with have much lower wage rates than the US does. That means they can make most manufactured goods at a much lower cost than the US can. Given two differently priced products of similar quality, everyone will buy the cheaper one. Therefore, Americans buy products made with low-cost labor, and so do the people living in countries where labor costs are low. Average wage rates in China, for example, are roughly 95% lower than average wages in the US. The US trade deficit with China was $268 billion in 2008 largely for that reason.

Decoupling was a myth. During the recession that followed the bursting of the NASDAQ bubble in 2000, imports into the US fell by 15% from peak to trough. US exports fell even more, by 17% from peak to trough. Furthermore, imports rebounded well before exports did. By the time US exports recovered to their previous peak level, in the second quarter of 2004, imports into the US were already 15% above their previous peak. Obviously, when the US imports less from the rest of the world, the rest of the world has less income with which to import products from the US. When the economic crisis began in the US at the end of 2008, economic growth rates and trade between nations did not decouple. Instead, the global economy crashed as one highly interdependent unit. The World Bank has forecast that world trade volumes will plunge by 10% in 2009. Between the third quarter of 2008 and the first quarter of 2009 (the most recent quarter for which figures are available), imports into the US had fallen by 33%, while US exports had dropped by 26%.

Even after this drop, the value of imports into the US was still 18% higher than it was at the peak of the NASDAQ bubble. This suggests there is still considerable potential for further falls. Also, the value of imports remains 50% higher than that of exports. Finally, and most importantly when considering the outlook for the US economy, if the 2001 experience is any guide, exports will ultimately fall more than imports and remained depressed for some time after imports begin to rebound. Depressed exports are likely to remain a drag on the US economy for at least several more years. They will also depress employment and new investment within the United States.

It is time US policymakers woke up to the fact that the US trade deficit is not going to go away by itself. At no time in the foreseeable future will the rest of the world have the money or the desire to buy enough of the products America now makes to close the trade gap. The US simply does not produce enough things the rest of the world wants at a price it can afford. The only possibility of correcting the trade deficit without resorting to protectionism is for the US to develop revolutionary new industries in which it will have an unassailable technological lead. This idea is described in Chapter 11.

To summaries: If the federal government had not come to the rescue of the private sector, the outlook for the US economy would be harrowing. Personal consumption expenditure would shrink because households, already mired in debt and unable to get more credit, would have no choice but to spend less. Private investment, faced with the lowest capacity-utilization rate in living memory, would drop dramatically. Net trade would continue to deduct from GDP, with no realistic hope that exports would ever rise faster than imports. A downward spiral in economic activity would take hold as a reduction in spending in each of the above categories negatively impacted all of the other categories, compounding the crisis by necessitating a further round of spending cuts across the board. In other words, if the federal government had not stepped in and supplied the aggregate demand now lacking everywhere else in the economy, then the United States would have fallen into an economic depression very much like that of the 1930s, a depression from which it would not quickly emerge.

The outlook for the public sector

Chapter 1 described how Washington intervened with a $700 billion increase in spending in 2009 to support aggregate demand following the breakdown of the private sector. This section will focus on what the government will have to do to prop up the US economy over the next three years.

The $1.6 trillion budget deficit expected for 2009 is the result of decreased tax revenues as well as increased government spending. Tax revenues decline when the economy is weak without providing any stimulus to the economy. In 2008 and 2009, tax revenues were further reduced by tax cuts of $157 billion and $288 billion, respectively. Tax cuts do stimulate the economy, but only to the extent that people spend the money they would otherwise have paid as taxes.

Government spending has a much more direct impact on the economy. Government outlays increased by roughly $700 billion in 2009. However, of that amount, approximately $425 billion was related to the injection of government money into the collapsing financial sector. That spending aided the economy indirectly, of course, since it prevented the systemic annihilation of the financial sector. But it did not directly increase aggregate demand.

34

Figure 16

US BUDGET BALANCE

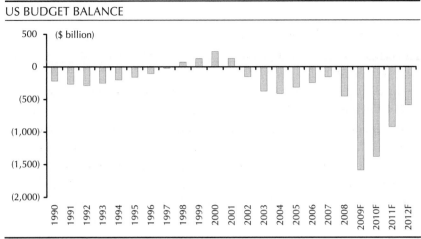

Source: CBO, *The Budget and Economic Outlook: An Update*, August 2009

Stripping out the financial-sector rescue money from the estimates of government spending in 2009 yields a more accurate picture of the true support the government provided to economic output. The charts below incorporate the CBO assumptions that $425 billion was spent on financial sector bailouts in 2009 and that $106 billion will be spent in 2010. These amounts reflect the CBO's estimates of the net present value of the costs the government will incur as a result of TARP and the rescue of Fannie Mae and Freddie Mac.

Figure 17

INCREASE IN FEDERAL OUTLAYS

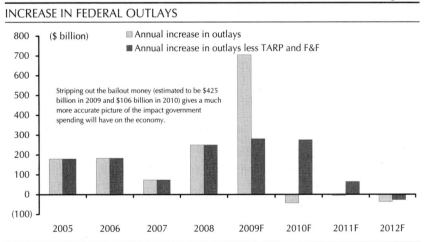

Source: CBO (historic), author (forecasts)

If the bailout costs are stripped out, the increase in spending that directly boosted the economy in 2009 was approximately $280 billion. A quarter of a trillion dollars and then some is still a great deal of money. However, it provided much less economic stimulus than would be suggested at first glance by a $1.6 trillion budget deficit.

In 2010, non-bailout-related federal spending is projected to increase by $275 billion over 2009. That increase is unlikely to be sufficient to prevent the economy from contacting again in 2010. Current CBO projections show federal spending (not related to bailouts) increasing by only $64 billion in 2011 and actually decreasing by $28 billion in 2012. If those projections turn out to be accurate, then US GDP will probably continue to contract in both those years as well. It should be noted, however, that federal government outlays have not decreased from one year to the next since 1965 (and even then the reduction was only marginal), so they are unlikely to decline again any time soon.

Figure 18

MORE REALISTIC ESTIMATE OF ANNUAL INCREASE IN FEDERAL OUTLAYS

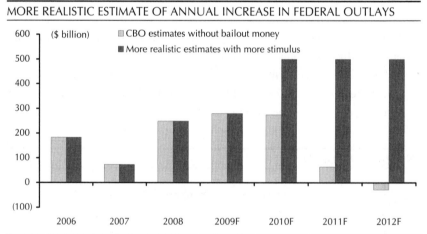

Source: CBO (historic), author (forecasts)

A more likely scenario is that several more government stimulus packages will be required to pull the economy out of recession and keep it from sliding into recession again. The debt-fuelled consumption model of economic growth will not be revived in 2010, or even by 2012. America's new economic paradigm is one driven by government deficit spending. It will take much more government stimulus than current official projections incorporate to keep the US economy afloat over the next five years. In 2010, roughly $225 billion in additional stimulus should be expected (on top of that currently incorporated into the CBO projections). More than that—

perhaps $500 billion a year—will be required in 2011 and 2012, since most of the 2009 stimulus package will have been spent by the end of 2010.

These more realistic projections for government outlays would take the budget deficit up to $1.6 trillion in 2010, $1.4 trillion 2011 and $1.1 trillion in 2012. Even then, these estimates do not include the trillions of dollars the government is also likely to lose as a result of its vast contingent liabilities in the financial and housing industries.

The government's contingent liabilities

The financial sector

The financial sector represents a $700 trillion contingent liability for the government. Its losses are highly likely to increase the US budget deficit by several trillion dollars more over the next 10 years. Crazed financial-sector deregulation is responsible for this disaster. That $700 trillion is the size of the largely unregulated over-the-counter derivatives market—the market that puts the "too" in "too big to fail". Although the government has only partially nationalized the financial sector, it has implicitly guaranteed the solvency of all the industry's major players. Their web of counterparty exposure has entangled the government and restricted its policy options. Policymakers are convinced that the only alternative to a taxpayer-funded bailout of every large bank in need would be the complete systemic collapse of the financial sector. Their concern is well-founded.

The severe financial stress at AIG and Citigroup sheds considerable light on the government's predicament. AIG's losses in derivatives threatened its solvency. According to the insurance giant's 2008 annual report, "AIG was providing protection to banks and other clients around the world through its credit default swap business." As it turned out, it was taxpayers who were providing the protection. AIG lost $99 billion in 2008. Thus far, the government has pumped in more than $180 billion in loans and equity in exchange for a 79.9% equity stake and the right to lose potentially hundreds of billions of dollars more on any future AIG losses. At the end of 2008, AIG's on-balance-sheet liabilities amounted to $808 billion. In addition, the notional amount of AIG Financial Products Corp's interest rate, credit default and currency swaps and swaptions derivatives portfolio was $1.5 trillion, down from $2.1 trillion at the end of 2007. Had the government not come to the rescue, AIG would have collapsed, with catastrophic consequences for counterparties in its derivatives trades.

As for Citigroup, the government has injected $45 billion of capital (more than the former industry giant's entire market capitalization at the time of its second bailout in January 2009) and guaranteed most of a $300 billion "ring-fenced" pool of questionable debt in exchange for a 34% stake in the corporation. Citi's on-balance-sheet liabilities totaled $1.8 trillion at the end of 2008, while the notional amount of its derivatives portfolio was $33 trillion—more than twice the size of US GDP. The bankruptcy of Citi would have been an extinction-level event that stretched considerably beyond the financial industry.

AIG and Citigroup are just two of many high rollers in the derivatives market that the government views as too big to fail. There is a long list of others.

Derivatives and the threat they pose to the global economy are the subject of Chapter 9. Here it will suffice to note that the derivatives industry has grown so big so fast, and its workings are so opaque, that the losses potentially concealed in the $700 trillion notional amount of derivatives contracts now in existence could greatly exceed even the US government's ability to redeem them. For instance, a 1% loss ratio would amount to a $7 trillion loss, 5% to $35 trillion and 10% to $70 trillion. To overlook the threat posed by these "financial instruments of mass destruction" is to ignore the 800-pound gorilla in the room. Preventing derivatives from destroying the financial sector remains one of the government's greatest challenges. The cost of doing so will be much higher than is currently understood.

The housing industry

As "conservator" for Fannie Mae and Freddie Mac, the government is exposed to future losses on nearly half of the entire US mortgage market. At the end of 2008, outstanding residential mortgage debt totaled $11.9 trillion. Fannie Mae owned or guaranteed 26% of that amount; Freddie Mac an additional 19%. Thus Fannie and Freddie's combined exposure to the mortgage market was $5.3 trillion.

Fannie Mae's Form 10-Q filing for the first quarter of 2009 states:

> Following a decline of approximately 10% in 2008, we expect that home prices will decline another 7% to 12% on a notional basis in 2009. We also continue to expect that we will experience a peak-to-trough home price decline of 20% to 30%.

And in the following paragraph:

> ...our 20% to 30% peak-to-trough home price decline estimate compares with an approximately 33% to 46% peak-to-trough decline using the S&P/Case-Schiller index method.3

---

[3] Federal National Mortgage Association, Form 10-Q, Quarterly Report to the US Securities and Exchange Commission, p. 15.

In light of the extraordinary collapse in the housing market, the eventual cost to the government related to Fannie Mae and Freddie Mac could significantly exceed the $373 billion estimate the CBO has incorporated in its projections for the government budget between 2009 and 2019. The Making Home Affordable Program announced by President Obama in March 2009 suggests that Fannie and Freddie will take on an even greater role in government attempts to support homeowners at risk of losing their homes. This program further increases the government's contingent liabilities related to the housing market.

Finally, Fannie and Freddie are both important participants in the derivatives markets. The notional amount of derivatives on Fannie's 2008 consolidated balance sheet is shown as $1.2 trillion; that on Freddie's totaled $1.3 trillion. These amounts too represent contingent liabilities for the government.

Government debt: Is it sustainable?

What will happen to government debt over the next decade? Two scenarios are considered in Figure 19.

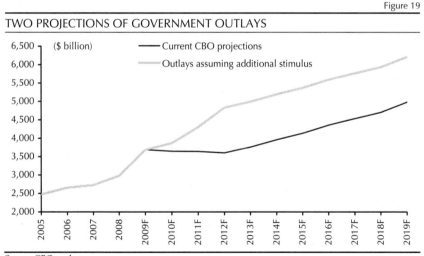

Figure 19

TWO PROJECTIONS OF GOVERNMENT OUTLAYS

Source: CBO, author

The first uses the CBO's current projections for government spending. The second assumes that additional government stimulus will be required on top of the CBO's estimates—$225 billion more in 2010, and $500 billion more in each of 2011 and 2012.

Both scenarios ignore the possibility of additional losses flowing from the government's contingent liabilities.

Figure 20

PROJECTIONS OF PUBLICLY HELD FEDERAL DEBT AS % OF GDP

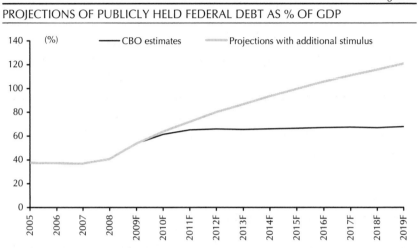

Source: CBO, author

The different assumptions about government outlays yield very different estimates of how much debt the government will be in by 2019 (see Figure 20). If the CBO's projections are correct, government debt held by the public (that is, by all entities outside the federal government) will increase from $5.8 trillion in 2008 to $9.8 trillion in 2011 and to $14.3 trillion by 2019, at which point it will be the equivalent of 68% of GDP. If the projections assuming additional stimulus are correct, government debt held by the public will be much higher by 2019—120% of GDP.

The CBO's projections are based on the wishful-thinking view that the government's intervention in the economy is a one-off event and that everything will return to normal as soon as US policymakers can "get the credit flowing again". These projections are likely to prove far too optimistic. The second scenario is the more probable. If it pans out, government debt held by the public in 2019 will be higher than at the end of World War II, when it peaked at 115% of GDP.

Figure 21

PUBLICLY HELD FEDERAL DEBT AS % OF GDP, 1900-2019

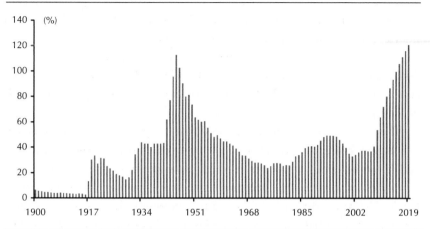

Note: Projections assume additional stimulus. Source: CBO

The US government will not be able to avoid incurring a much higher level of debt to keep the economy afloat in its present post-bubble dysfunctional state. Financing that debt, however, will be much easier than most would expect. To understand why, consider what has taken place in Japan over the past two decades.

Figure 22

JAPAN'S GOVERNMENT DEBT AS % OF GDP

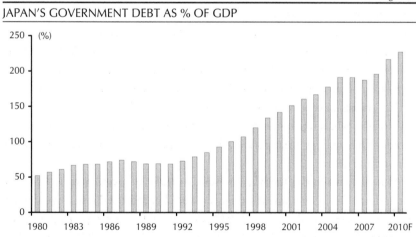

Source: IMF World Economic Outlook database, April 2009

When the great Japanese bubble economy popped in 1990, Japan's ratio of government debt to GDP was approximately 69%. The Japanese government has been forced to run very large budget deficits every year since then to

41

prevent a downward spiral in the economy. The ratio of government debt to GDP is now more than 200%. Although this aggressive deficit spending did not succeed in pulling the economy permanently out of recession, it did save Japan from a 1930s-style depression, or at least it has so far.

Japan's experience foreshadows what the US can expect over the next decade. Both economies were transformed by credit bubbles that left the private sector crippled when they burst. In both cases, the government then stepped in to provide life support.

The lesson to be learned from Japan is that it is possible for the government of a large industrialized economy to finance an enormous increase in its debt—and it can be done without resorting to paper-money creation. The Bank of Japan did not monetize the government's debt by printing money and buying bonds. The private sector has financed the increase in Japan's debt by buying government securities, and it has even been willing to do so at concessionary interest rates. The yield on the 10-year Japanese government bond is only 1.4%.

This was possible in Japan, and will be possible in the US, because in a post-bubble economy there is a tremendous amount of money that will be destroyed unless it is invested in the safe haven of government debt. During the bubble years, a great deal of profit is made. Up until the boom ends, that growing pool of money is invested in speculative ventures of one kind or another. However, when the bubble pops, the owners of that money quickly realize that if their funds remain in speculative investments they will be wiped out. Therefore, most of that pool of money becomes available to finance the increase in the government's debt. This is fortunate, because if the central bank had to print money to finance the debt, hyperinflation would result and culminate in depression no matter what the government did to stimulate the economy.

US policymakers will be shocked to learn how much money the government will have to spend to stave off economic collapse over the coming decade. They will be equally shocked to see just how easy it turns out to be to finance that debt.

However, while the funding available to the US government is vast, it is not infinite. The government's finances were headed for disaster even before the private sector collapsed in 2008. The CBO's long-term projections show the ratio of government debt to GDP climbing to 300% by 2082 as a result of out-of-control spending on Medicaid, Medicare and Social Security. A policy change is essential if Washington is to avoid fiscal ruin.

Figure 23

PUBLICLY HELD FEDERAL DEBT AS % OF GDP

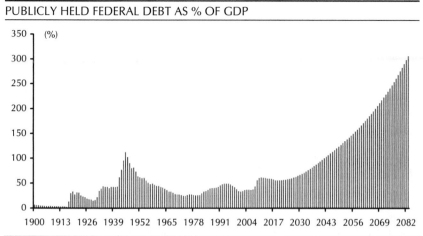

Source: CBO, *The Long-Term Budget Outlook*, June 2009

Conclusion

The government hopes its policy response to the economic crisis is a one-off effort that has nearly succeeded and that soon everything will go back to normal once it gets the credit flowing again. That hope is misguided. The government's intervention to support the economy is not a one-off event. The policy mistakes that caused the crisis have not been corrected. Everything will not go back to normal.

Over the past 40 years, those errors have seen the economy degenerate to the point where the United States is no longer capable of producing as much as it consumes, while much of the rest of the world has expanded its industrial capacity to the point where it is incapable of consuming as much as it produces. This is an unprecedented crisis of worldwide economic imbalances. Now only trillions of dollars of government deficit spending can keep the global economy afloat.

Chapter 3
The global economy:
A crisis of imbalances

For some two hundred years both economic theorists and practical men did not doubt that there is a peculiar advantage to a country in a favourable balance of trade, and grave danger in an unfavourable balance, particularly if it results in an efflux of the precious metals. But for the past one hundred years there has been a remarkable divergence of opinion.

John Maynard Keynes[1]

The global economy is in crisis because of trade imbalances that developed in the years following the breakdown of the Bretton Woods international monetary system. The United States is largely to blame. It created the Bretton Woods system but failed to abide by its rules, thus causing its collapse. Since then, the US has taken advantage of its position as issuer of the world's reserve currency by incurring enormous trade deficits and financing them with dollar-denominated debt.

The United States accounts for 23% of global GDP. Its trade deficits, which far exceed those of any other nation, have long been the driver of global

---

[1] John Maynard Keynes, *The General Theory of Employment, Interest and Money* (Cambridge University Press, 1936), p. 333.

economic growth. Between 1996 and 2008, US imports tripled as two debt-fuelled economic bubbles inflated American purchasing power. When the second bubble popped, however, imports fell by a third and the global economy was plunged into a crisis of excess capacity and insufficient demand.

This chapter considers the outlook for the rest of the global economy by focusing first on five surplus countries: China, Japan, Germany, Korea and India. These five economies together account for a further 25% of global GDP. That the abrupt drop off of US imports has thrown all five into crisis demonstrates the extent to which the world depends on the United States for growth. Decoupling was a myth: global economic growth is a function of US demand.

Next, oil's contribution to global economic disequilibrium is considered—along with the possibility that its price is being manipulated. Finally, the chapter looks at the role paper-money creation played in bringing about the crisis in the global economy—as well as ways in which it could be used to help resolve it.

The chances that the Fed will create a third bubble that magically restores private-sector purchasing power in the United States are very slim. Consequently, there is no reason to expect US imports to return to their previous peak within the foreseeable future. The world has changed. All previous assumptions related to economic growth rates must be scrapped. The global economy has gone ex-growth. There can be no assurance that globalization will survive the New Depression.

The Unbalanced

Every country with a large trade imbalance is ultimately destabilized by it, regardless of whether the imbalance is a deficit or a surplus. Deficit countries go into debt and eventually cannot repay that debt. Since every country's balance of payments must balance, the larger a country's current-account deficit becomes, the more foreign money comes into the country to finance it. That money exacerbates the economic overheating that was responsible for the deficit. Eventually, the exogenous money is misallocated and much of it is lost. Then the credit stops flowing and consumers stop buying. That was the case in the United States, Spain, the UK, Australia and Italy, the five countries with the largest current-account deficits in 2007, the last full year of the global credit bubble.

The fate of the surplus countries depends on what they do with their surplus earnings. If the money stays in the country, it blows the domestic economy into a bubble. That's what happened to Japan in the 1980s and to many other countries—most notably China—since then. The alternative is for the surplus country to lend or invest the money abroad. That prevents the domestic economy from blowing into a bubble; however, it puts the money sent abroad at risk of being lost if the borrowers default. Very large losses provoke systemic banking crises. That is the danger now confronting Germany.

Figure 24

GLOBAL IMBALANCES

Country	Current-account balance 2007		2003 to 2007 ($ billion)	
	Amount ($ billion)	% of GDP	Current-account balance, cumulative	Change in FX reserves from end 2002
United States	(731)	(5.3)	(3,397)	(20)
Spain	(145)	(10.1)	(425)	(29)
UK	(81)	(2.9)	(299)	5
Australia	(57)	(6.3)	(206)	1
Italy	(51)	(2.4)	(165)	(5)
Russia	76	5.9	350	416
Saudi Arabia	96	25.1	366	10
Japan	211	4.8	855	417
Germany	250	7.5	747	(15)
China	372	11.0	900	1,192

Source: IMF World Economic Outlook database, April 2009

The United States has the world's largest trade deficit. In 2007, the US current-account deficit was $731 billion, five times larger than that of Spain, the country with the second largest deficit, and nine times that of the UK, the country next in line. All the countries with trade deficits share the United States' problems, which are explored throughout this book. This chapter, therefore, focuses on those with trade surpluses, beginning with China, the country with the largest trade surplus.

The rise and fall of the Chinese economy

China and the United States

Since the beginning of the Industrial Revolution, every economic boom has been followed by an economic bust. The bigger the boom, the bigger the bust. Over the past 20 years, China has experienced the greatest economic boom in history. Consequently, the prospects for China's economy are terrible.

China's economic model is based on export-led growth. That model is now even more bankrupt than the American model of debt-fuelled consumption, since Chinese exports are dependent on US consumption. The rise of China's economy over the past 20 years has changed the world. Its fall over the next 20 years may have equally profound consequences. Every boom busts. China's boom will be no exception.

Figure 25

CHINA'S TRADE SURPLUS WITH THE UNITED STATES AS % OF CHINA'S GDP

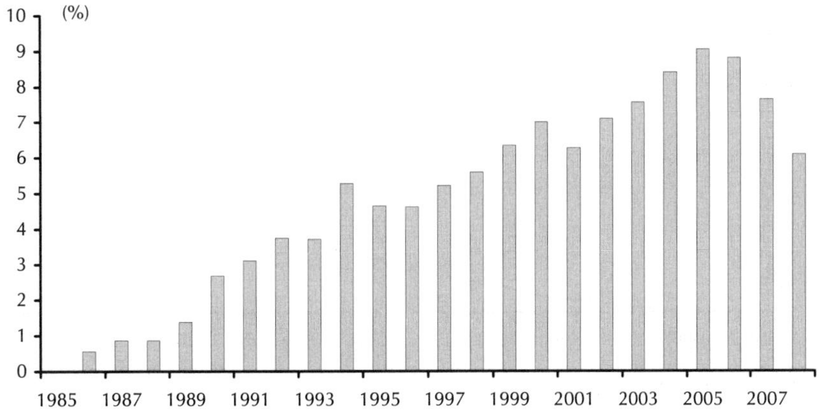

Source: US Census Bureau

In 1990, China's economy was only twice the size of Belgium's. In 2008, it was the third largest in the world. That economic transformation was due entirely to China's trade surplus with the US, which soared from $10 billion in 1990 to $268 billion, or the equivalent of 6% of China's GDP, in 2008. Its surplus peaked at 9% of GDP in 2005.

One way of gauging the importance of that trade surplus with the US is simply to subtract it from China's GDP. Doing so shows that without that surplus, China's economic output would have been 6% lower than it actually was in 2008. That approach would radically understate the importance of that surplus to China, however. In reality, a large multiplier should be applied to that figure, since there are three other, less direct ways in which the trade surplus with the US drives Chinese growth. First, tens of millions of Chinese workers are employed in factories producing goods for sale to the United States. The wages they earn and spend boost consumption in China, and therefore appear in China's GDP accounts under the heading of personal consumption expenditure rather than exports.

47

Moreover, there is a multiplier on this consumption figure as well. When those workers buy from merchants, that boosts the merchants' purchasing power, too. Therefore, the wages earned by Chinese factory workers making products for the US market make a significant contribution to personal consumption throughout the Chinese economy.

Figure 26

CHINA'S TRADE SURPLUS WITH THE UNITED STATES

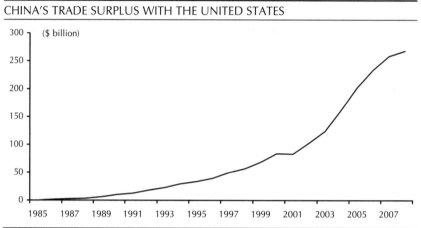

Source: US Census Bureau

Second, much of the gross fixed capital formation (i.e. investment) in China has gone into the construction of factories that make goods for export to the US. This includes investment not only from domestic Chinese investors but also from abroad (i.e. direct foreign investment). During 2008, $148 billion of direct foreign investment entered China. A significant amount of that would have been directly or indirectly related to investments aimed at producing goods to sell to the United States. Therefore, much of the gross fixed capital formation in China's GDP accounts is tied to US demand for Chinese exports.

A further route by which China's trade surplus with the US drives China's economy is the banking system. When Chinese exporters bring back their earnings from selling goods in the United States, that money goes into the Chinese banking system and leads to rapid growth in deposits. This in turn leads to rapid growth of loans, since to pay interest on those deposits, Chinese banks need to earn interest on loans. Chinese bank loans have expanded at an extraordinary pace for 20 years, and rapid loan growth has been a major driver of the country's economic growth. Such rapid loan growth would not have been possible without China's large trade surplus with the US.

So even though China's $268 billion trade surplus with the US directly accounted for an already astounding 6% of China's GDP in 2008, it had an even larger impact through its indirect effects on personal consumption expenditure, gross fixed capital formation and credit expansion. It would not be unreasonable to estimate that as much as 40% of China's economy must be attributed to its dependence on exporting to the United States.

Seen in this light, it should be clear why the breakdown of the American economic model of debt-fuelled consumption has thrown China into a terrible crisis of its own. Whereas the United States' problem is that it cannot make as much as it consumes, China's problem is even worse. China can't consume as much as it makes. Chinese factory workers do not earn enough to buy the products they make. If China can't export those products, there is no domestic market for them. Then production must stop, and the workers lose their jobs.

That is the situation China confronts now. Chinese exports began to collapse in November 2008. During the first eight months of 2009, they were 22% lower than during the same period one year earlier. In February 2009, a director of the Office of the Central Rural Work Leading Group told a news conference that 20 million Chinese factory workers had lost their jobs and been forced to return jobless to the countryside. The employment situation is not likely to have improved since then.

China's extraordinary policy response

High unemployment often leads to social unrest. The Chinese government takes the threat of such unrest very seriously. Accordingly, its response to the country's economic crisis has been exceptionally aggressive. In November 2008, the government announced a $590 billion stimulus package (equivalent to 13.4% of 2008 GDP) that will focus on infrastructure spending. In addition, during the nine months between September 2008 and June 2009, bank lending expanded by 27%, the equivalent of $1.2 trillion or 27% of Chinese GDP. Through this combination of fiscal spending and state-directed lending, China has provided more stimulus to the global economy than any other nation, not only relative to the size of its economy but in absolute terms as well.

China's ratio of government debt to GDP is very low—only 20%. That is now the nation's greatest strength, because it gives the government the ability to support the economy through deficit spending. The banking sector, however, is likely to prove to be a source of great vulnerability. Excessive loan growth causes systemic banking-sector crises. With few exceptions, every country where loans have expanded by 10% or more a year for 10 years in succession has suffered a severe banking crisis when loan growth eventually slowed down. Loan growth drives economic growth. So long as lending expands at a double-digit rate, nonperforming loans appear low for two reasons. First, the rapid loan growth supports rapid economic growth. Second, it is very easy for debtors to borrow more money this year and use it to pay the interest on the money they borrowed last year. Eventually, the economy becomes warped by too much credit and misallocated investment. At that point the credit cannot be repaid, loan growth slows or lending contracts, and the economy goes into crisis.

Loan growth in China has averaged 18% a year for the past 20 years. Consequently, the Chinese banking sector was vulnerable even before the global economic crisis caused a breakdown of Beijing's export-led growth strategy. The eye-popping 27% surge in lending between September 2008 and June 2009 greatly increases the likelihood that China's banking sector will suffer a systemic crisis. A real possibility exists that a significant portion of the new lending (and much of the old lending, too, for that matter) will not be repaid. In that case, the government will have to make good the banking sector's losses to ensure that Chinese depositors do not lose their savings.

This huge increase in bank lending gave China's economy tremendous support that was badly needed when exports plunged. However, the stimulus provided by that credit jolt will soon wear off—and exports have not recovered. Before long, the government will have to decide whether to force the banks to expand credit by another 27% over the next six months, and again over the following six months—and again in the six months after that. If it does, China's economy will continue to grow by 10% a year; but the losses accumulating in the banking sector will rapidly climb toward 100% of China's GDP, because credit growth on that scale has never been and never will be viable. On the other hand, if the government begins to rein in credit growth, the economy will not meet its 8% annual growth target. In fact, large fiscal deficits will be required if China is to achieve any economic growth at all.

Japan was able to avoid a depression following the collapse of its bubble economy in 1990 thanks to government deficit spending that pushed the ratio of government debt to GDP from 69% to more than 200% today. China looks set to join the United States on the same course Japan has followed. It would not be surprising to see Chinese government debt blow through 100% of GDP before too many more years have passed—even if the banking sector does not collapse. China's export-led growth model is broken. Government deficit spending is now the country's sole driver of growth. Ironically, China and the United States now share the same economic paradigm. It is unfortunate it is debt-funded government spending rather than capitalism.

Post-bubble China should be able to finance a very large expansion of government debt, just as post-bubble Japan did. That is because when large economic bubbles burst and no viable investment opportunities remain in the rest of the economy, the profits earned during the bubble years seek the safe haven of government bonds.

In any case, the years of 10% annual GDP growth in China are over. Economic growth of 2-4% would be a very respectable outcome in the post-bubble world. Whether the Chinese government can live with this new reality is an important question. The price of much higher rates of credit-induced growth now could be complete economic collapse in a few years. Either way, it would be a serious mistake to continue to extrapolate China's rapid economic growth rates of the past decade into the future. The China boom is over. That has important implications for the rest of the world.

China and the rest of the world

Before the global crisis, China was hailed as the second engine of global economic growth alongside the United States. That assessment was correct. However, it was misleading unless it was also understood that China's engine was not just running in tandem with the US but was powered by it. As China's exports and trade surplus with the US expanded, China's imports from the rest of the world soared—to $1.13 trillion in 2008, nearly eight times their 1998 level.

Figure 27

IMPORTS INTO CHINA

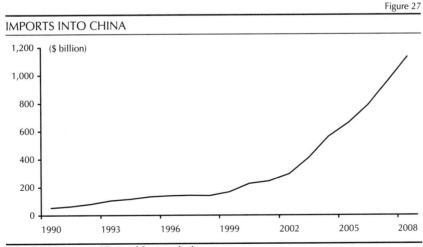

Source: IMF International Financial Statistics database

Skyrocketing Chinese imports have been a great boon to the global economy. The country's Asian neighbors, European exporters and commodity-producing nations from Saudi Arabia to Brazil have all benefited from surging Chinese demand.

Any hope that the Chinese economy had "decoupled" from the United States' economy was completely dispelled, however, when the US bubble burst in 2008. When US goods imports fell 33% between the third quarter of 2008 and the first quarter of 2009, Chinese imports did not continue to shoot skyward on the back of strong domestic demand. Instead, they slumped by 25%. That is because China's imports are a function of its exports. When the US bubble burst, it was not only China's exports to the US that plummeted. Its exports to most other countries fell too, because China's other trading partners depend on their trade surpluses with the US to buy things from China and from each other. When their exports to the US fell, they had far less money to spend on Chinese products, and their imports from China fell accordingly.

Consequently, the Chinese engine of global growth failed right in sync with the American one. The extraordinarily aggressive policy response by the Chinese government has provided enormous support to the Chinese economy. But that support cannot be sustained indefinitely. The economy is already losing altitude fast, and a crash landing cannot be ruled out. China's trading partners are more likely to be hit by debris from the wreckage than by a new surge in Chinese purchasing orders. Yet although China's economy is in crisis, most of the world continues to view it as an engine of global growth. Aligning those misconceptions with reality will be a painful process for all those countries that have benefited from the great China boom.

A glance at Figure 28 shows that China has had a surplus on both its current account and its financial account for many years. (The current account relates primarily to trade in goods and services; the financial account to capital flows.) These surpluses have together produced a very large overall balance each year that has rapidly augmented China's foreign-exchange reserves. (The overall balance comprises the current account, the capital account and the financial account plus net errors and omissions; a positive overall balance accumulates as foreign-exchange reserves.) History shows that countries with rapidly expanding foreign-exchange reserves experience impressive economic booms followed by equally impressive economic busts. That was the case with Japan in the 1980s and all the Asian Crisis countries in the 1990s. It seems inevitable that China's economic boom will end the same way and for the same reasons.

Figure 28

CHINA'S BALANCE OF PAYMENTS

($ billion)	2002	2003	2004	2005	2006	2007	2008
Current account, n.i.e.	35,422	45,875	68,659	160,818	253,268	371,833	426,107
Goods: exports f.o.b.	325,651	438,270	593,393	762,484	969,682	1,220,000	1,434,600
Goods: imports f.o.b.	(281,484)	(393,618)	(534,410)	(628,295)	(751,936)	(904,618)	(1,073,920)
Trade balance	44,167	44,652	58,982	134,189	217,746	315,381	360,682
Services: credit	39,745	46,734	62,434	74,404	91,999	122,206	147,112
Services: debit	(46,528)	(55,306)	(72,133)	(83,796)	(100,833)	(130,111)	(158,924)
Balance on goods & services	37,383	36,079	49,284	124,798	208,912	307,477	348,870
Income: credit	8,344	16,095	20,544	38,959	54,642	83,030	91,615
Income: debit	(23,290)	(23,933)	(24,067)	(28,324)	(39,485)	(57,342)	(60,177)
Balance on goods, serv. & inc.	22,438	28,241	45,761	135,433	224,069	333,165	380,308
Net current transfers	12,984	17,634	22,898	25,386	29,199	38,668	45,799
Capital account, n.i.e.	(50)	(48)	(69)	4,102	4,020	3,099	3,051
Financial account, n.i.e.	32,341	52,774	110,729	58,862	2,642	70,410	15,913
Net errors and omissions	7,504	17,985	26,834	(16,441)	(13,075)	16,349	(26,080)
Overall balance	75,217	116,586	206,153	207,342	246,855	461,691	418,993
Total reserves minus gold	291,128	408,151	614,500	821,514	1,068,490	1,530,280	1,949,273

Source: IMF International Financial Statistics database

Japan: Still deflating 20 years on

Japan's economy, the world's second largest, has been on government life support since the great Japanese bubble popped in 1990. The government's budget went into deficit in 1993. Since then the deficit has averaged 5.4% of GDP a year.

Figure 29

JAPAN'S GDP

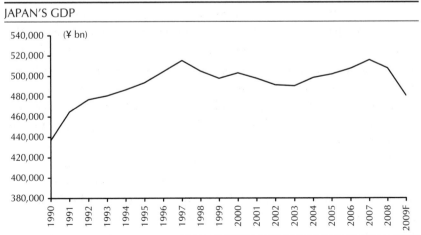

Source: IMF World Economic Outlook database

As a result, Japanese government debt now exceeds 200% of GDP, by far the highest ratio of any industrialized country. Despite nearly two decades of massive government spending, the Japanese economy is the same size now as it was in 1993 if not adjusted for deflation.

The country did benefit from the 2003-08 global economic boom. Exports doubled between early 2002 and mid-2008. But the global crash has hit Japan hard. Exports have shrunk by well over 40%, to levels not seen since 1995.

Figure 30

JAPAN'S EXPORTS

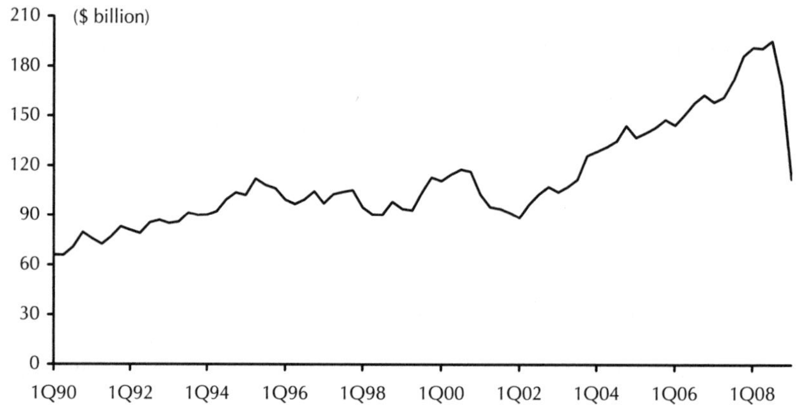

Source: IMF International Financial Statistics database

Japan faces a series of severe challenges. Like China, it depends on export-led growth in a world where private-sector demand has just collapsed. But while China's population is growing, Japan's is shrinking. Fewer people mean less consumption. Japanese wages are very high compared to those in most other countries. High wages reduce the nation's industrial competitiveness (although they do support domestic consumption). This has become an increasing problem over the past decade as China's fast-growing industrial output has begun to eat into Japanese export markets. Finally, credit growth has been very anemic for years. In post-bubble Japan, deflating asset prices have slowed the demand for loans.

The Japanese government has responded to the crisis with aggressive fiscal stimulus. The budget deficit is projected to exceed 9% of GDP in both 2009 and 2010. Nevertheless, Japan's GDP is expected to contract by 6% in 2009 and to expand by only 0.5% in 2010—by which time the ratio of government debt to GDP will exceed 225%.

Aggressive government spending has kept Japan out of a 1930s-style depression for nearly two decades, but it has not restored the economy to sustainable growth. It is unclear how much longer the Japanese economy can continue to be propped up by government deficit spending before the debt burden becomes insupportable. As of now, however, government debt is Japan's only growth driver. The likelihood that Japan might become a driver of global economic growth in the foreseeable future is therefore nil.

Figure 31

JAPAN'S BALANCE OF PAYMENTS

($US billion)	2002	2003	2004	2005	2006	2007	2008
Current account, n.i.e.	**112**	**136**	**172**	**166**	**171**	**210**	**157**
Goods: exports f.o.b.	396	449	539	568	616	678	746
Goods: imports f.o.b.	(302)	(343)	(407)	(474)	(535)	(573)	(708)
Trade balance	**94**	**106**	**132**	**94**	**81**	**105**	**38**
Services: credit	66	78	98	110	117	129	149
Services: debit	(108)	(112)	(136)	(134)	(136)	(150)	(170)
Balance on goods & services	**52**	**72**	**94**	**70**	**63**	**84**	**17**
Income: credit	91	95	113	141	166	199	212
Income: debit	(26)	(24)	(28)	(38)	(48)	(61)	(60)
Balance on goods, serv. & inc.	**117**	**144**	**180**	**173**	**181**	**222**	**170**
Net current transfers	(5)	(8)	(8)	(8)	(11)	(12)	(13)
Capital account, n.i.e.	**(3)**	**(4)**	**(5)**	**(5)**	**(5)**	**(4)**	**(5)**
Capital account, n.i.e.: credit	1	0	0	1	1	1	1
Capital account: debit	(4)	(4)	(5)	(6)	(6)	(5)	(6)
Financial account, n.i.e.	**(63)**	**72**	**23**	**(123)**	**(102)**	**(187)**	**(173)**
Net errors and omissions	**0**	**(17)**	**(29)**	**(16)**	**(31)**	**17**	**52**
Overall balance	**46**	**187**	**161**	**22**	**32**	**37**	**31**
Total reserves minus gold	461	663	834	834	880	953	1,009

Source: IMF International Financial Statistics database

Japan has the world's second-largest foreign-exchange reserves after China. However, those reserves have grown much more slowly than China's in recent years. As Figure 31 shows, Japan has consistently run large current-account surpluses, but also quite large financial-account deficits since 2005. Exporting capital by investing in and lending to other countries helped offset the capital entering Japan through its current-account surplus, leaving the nation with a smaller overall balance of payments and a less rapid buildup of foreign-exchange reserves. This suggests that policymakers learned from the mistakes made in the 1970s and 1980s, when large inflows of foreign money (as reflected in the buildup in reserves) inflated Japan's economy into a great bubble. Recall the grounds around the Imperial Palace in Tokyo were then said to be worth more than California. On the other hand, the capital Japan exported would have contributed to economic overheating and therefore the possibility of default in the countries receiving the capital, increasing the risk that a significant amount of that money could be lost. The repatriation of those Japanese investments explains the strength of the yen since the crisis began, despite the poor prospects for the Japanese economy.

Germany: Surplus and deficit

Germany is another interesting case. In 2007 it had the fourth-largest economy in the world and the second-largest current-account surplus. Between 2002, when the recession caused by the NASDAQ crash bottomed out, and 2007, the last full year of the US property bubble, Germany's exports rose by 120% and its current-account surplus by 540%. However, the economy did not record particularly impressive GDP growth (averaging 1.2% a year) and unemployment remained quite high, averaging 9.4% a year and remaining at 8.4% in 2007.

Figure 32

GERMAN GOODS EXPORTS

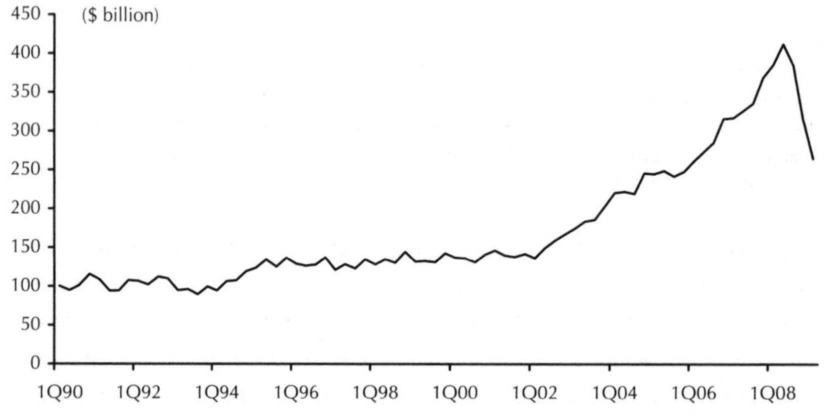

Source: IMF International Financial Statistics database

Normally, when a country's current account expands sharply, the domestic economy overheats as the money brought in from abroad by the current-account surplus goes into the banking sector and causes rapid credit growth and asset-price inflation. That did not occur in Germany because instead of allowing that foreign capital to stay in the country, the Germans exported it.

This can be seen in the very large financial-account deficits in Figure 33. Capital outflows also explain why Germany's foreign-exchange reserves remained flat despite such a large annual current-account surplus.

Figure 33

GERMANY'S BALANCE OF PAYMENTS

($US billion)	2002	2003	2004	2005	2006	2007	2008
Current account, n.i.e.	41	47	128	143	190	263	244
Goods: exports f.o.b.	612	747	908	983	1,136	1,350	1,498
Goods: imports f.o.b.	(486)	(603)	(722)	(790)	(938)	(1,079)	(1,232)
Trade balance	126	145	186	193	198	271	266
Services: Credit	103	124	146	164	191	223	247
Services: debit	(145)	(173)	(196)	(209)	(223)	(258)	(285)
Balance on goods & services	84	96	137	148	166	236	228
Income: credit	98	119	170	200	253	328	361
Income: debit	(115)	(136)	(145)	(169)	(195)	(258)	(296)
Balance on goods, serv. & inc.	67	79	162	179	224	306	292
Net current transfers	(26)	(32)	(34)	(36)	(34)	(43)	(49)
Capital account, n.i.e.	(0.225)	0.353	0.521	(1.816)	(0.336)	0.114	(0.002)
Capital account, n.i.e.: credit	2	3	3	4	4	5	5
Capital account: debit	(2)	(3)	(3)	(6)	(4)	(5)	(5)
Financial account, n.i.e.	(41)	(72)	(153)	(164)	(223)	(325)	(299)
Net errors and omissions	(2)	24	23	21	29	63	58
Overall balance	(2)	(1)	(2)	(3)	(4)	1	3
Total reserves minus gold	51	51	49	45	42	44	43

Source: IMF International Financial Statistics database

By investing so much capital overseas, Germany avoided developing a domestic economic bubble like the one Japan had in the 1980s or the one China has today. But it also helped inflate economic bubbles in other countries, for instance in Eastern Europe, Ireland, Iceland and, of course, the United States. Now that the bubbles have burst in the countries with large trade deficits, Germany is likely to take large losses on its investments in those countries. Those losses are at the heart of the considerable problems facing German banks.

Even though Germany avoided a large domestic bubble, it is still very vulnerable to the collapse in international private-sector demand. Its exports have fallen 36% from their second-quarter 2008 peak and the number of unemployed workers has risen by nearly half a million, to 3.4 million. The IMF forecasts that the German budget deficit, insignificant in 2008, will rise to 4.7% of GDP in 2009 and to 6.1% of GDP in 2010. Despite the government's fiscal stimulus, the economy looks set to contract by 5.6% in 2009 and a further 1.0% in 2010, by which time the unemployment rate is projected to rise to 10.8% (from 7.3% at the end of 2008).

Germany will not be an engine of growth for the global economy. As in Japan, the population has begun to shrink. Having peaked at 82.4 million in 2005, it is now about 82.3 million—more or less where it was in 2002. Global excess capacity will deter new investment. Finally, the government sector is unlikely to provide much additional growth. The government will be reluctant to expand fiscal stimulus further. Moreover, Germany has not forgotten that "quantitative easing" was the cause of hyperinflation in Germany during the 1920s. As a result, it can be counted on to discourage the European Central Bank from aggressive experiments with paper-money creation.

Korea: Double surplus

Having long pursued a strategy of export-led growth, Korea is no less vulnerable to the collapse in global private-sector demand than any of the countries discussed above. However, its situation presents some interesting variations on the theme.

Figure 34

KOREAN EXPORTS AND IMPORTS

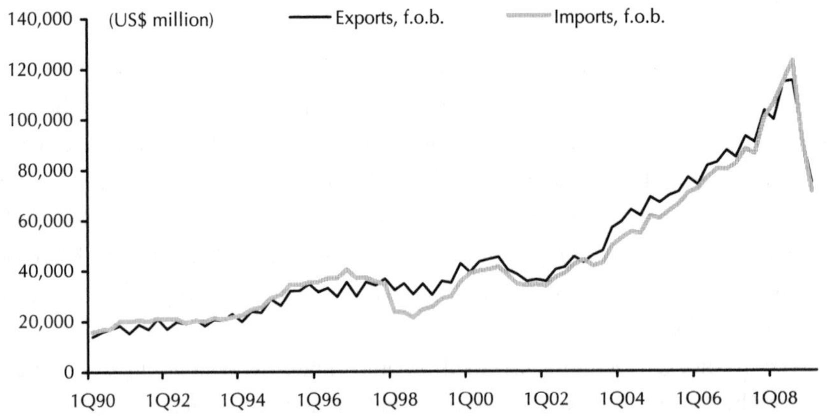

Source: IMF International Financial Statistics database

Between the post-NASDAQ-bubble trough and the property-bubble peak, Korean exports more than tripled. Although Korea did a better job than most export-oriented economies in insuring that its imports kept pace with its exports, the country still racked up a cumulative current-account surplus of $67 billion during the five years from 2003 to 2007. Rather than offsetting that amount by

58

investing outside the country as Germany did, Korea imported an additional $62 billion through a financial-account surplus as its banks and corporations borrowed cheaper funds from abroad. The surplus on both the current account and the financial account resulted in a great deal of exogenous money entering and stimulating the Korean economy, as can be seen in the US$141 billion increase in Korea's foreign-exchange reserves during that period.

Figure 35

KOREA'S BALANCE OF PAYMENTS

($ million)	2002	2003	2004	2005	2006	2007	2008
Current account, n.i.e.	5,394	11,950	28,174	14,981	5,385	5,954	(6,350)
Goods: exports f.o.b.	163,414	197,289	257,710	288,971	331,842	378,982	433,472
Goods: imports f.o.b.	(148,637)	(175,337)	(220,141)	(256,288)	(303,937)	(349,573)	(427,421)
Trade balance	14,777	21,952	37,569	32,683	27,905	29,409	6,051
Services: credit	28,388	32,957	41,882	45,129	49,891	63,034	75,990
Services: debit	(36,585)	(40,381)	(49,928)	(58,788)	(68,851)	(83,609)	(92,723)
Balance on goods & services	6,580	14,528	29,523	19,025	8,945	8,835	(10,683)
Income: credit	6,900	7,176	9,410	10,432	14,547	19,327	22,726
Income: debit	(6,467)	(6,850)	(8,328)	(11,994)	(14,014)	(18,558)	(17,620)
Balance on goods, serv. & inc.	7,012	14,854	30,606	17,462	9,478	9,603	(5,576)
Current transfers, n.i.e.: credit	7,314	7,859	9,151	10,004	9,588	10,934	13,636
Current transfers: debit	(8,932)	(10,764)	(11,583)	(12,486)	(13,680)	(14,583)	(14,410)
Net current transfers	(1,618)	(2,905)	(2,432)	(2,482)	(4,093)	(3,649)	(773)
Capital account, n.i.e.	(1,087)	(1,398)	(1,753)	(2,340)	(3,126)	(2,390)	(39)
Capital account, n.i.e.: credit	47	59	72	147	290	522	1,688
Capital account: debit	(1,133)	(1,457)	(1,825)	(2,487)	(3,416)	(2,912)	(1,727)
Financial account, n.i.e.	7,338	15,308	9,359	7,104	21,098	8,622	(50,894)
Net errors and omissions	124	(68)	2,895	119	(1,267)	2,922	835
Overall balance	11,769	25,791	38,675	19,864	22,090	15,109	(56,447)
Total reserves minus gold	121,345	155,284	198,997	210,317	238,882	262,150	201,144

Source: IMF International Financial Statistics database

Low-cost foreign borrowing boosted Korea Inc.'s profit margins. However, when the global crisis erupted it created a liquidity crisis in Korea. The foreign capital ran for the exits. In 2008, Korea registered a $51 billion financial-account deficit and its foreign-exchange reserves plunged by $61 billion. As the money left Korea, it was converted out of the won and into US dollars, causing the won to lose 26% of its value relative to the greenback. A large swap arrangement between the Bank of Korea and the Fed was set up to prevent matters from deteriorating further.

As it turned out, the sharp depreciation of the currency has greatly improved Korea's competitiveness in international markets. Of course, that improvement comes at the expense of trading rivals that did not devalue. Exports accounted for 42% of Korea's GDP in 2007; in 2008, following the drop in the value of the currency, they made up 53% of GDP. This level of dependence on trade leaves Korea very exposed to the global crisis. The country will be left with excess industrial capacity that will deter new investment. Unemployment will rise and damage consumption. The government is expected to run a budget deficit of 3.2% of GDP in 2009 and 4.7% in 2010. However, additional government spending will not be enough to offset the drop in exports. The IMF expects Korea's economy to contract by 4% in 2009, then grow by 1.5% in 2010. Even after its currency devaluation, Korea will still be in no position to drive global growth.

India: Deficit and surplus

India has followed a course of economic development very different from the other countries discussed in this chapter. Rather than running large trade surpluses, it has consistently experienced large trade deficits. In fact, since 1980 it has had a trade deficit every year and a current-account deficit every year, with the exceptions of 2001 to 2004 inclusive. In spite of this, India now has the world's fifth-largest foreign-exchange reserves (US$255 billion), a fact that is all the more remarkable given that as recently as the early 1990s, the country needed IMF support to cope with a balance-of-payments crisis.

Figure 36

INDIA'S BALANCE OF PAYMENTS							
($US million)	2000	2001	2002	2003	2004	2005	2006
Current account, n.i.e.	(4,601)	1,410	7,060	8,773	780	(7,835)	(9,415)
Goods: exports f.o.b.	43,247	44,793	51,141	60,893	77,939	102,176	123,617
Goods: imports f.o.b.	(53,887)	(51,212)	(54,702)	(68,081)	(95,539)	(134,702)	(166,695)
Trade balance	(10,640)	(6,419)	(3,561)	(7,188)	(17,600)	(32,526)	(43,078)
Services: credit	16,684	17,337	19,478	23,902	38,281	55,831	75,354
Services: debit	(19,187)	(20,099)	(21,039)	(24,878)	(35,641)	(47,989)	(63,537)
Balance on goods & services	(13,143)	(9,181)	(5,122)	(8,164)	(14,960)	(24,684)	(31,261)
Income: credit	2,521	3,524	3,188	3,491	4,690	5,082	7,795
Income: debit	(7,414)	(7,666)	(7,097)	(8,386)	(8,742)	(11,475)	(12,059)
Balance on goods, serv. & inc.	(18,036)	(13,323)	(9,031)	(13,059)	(19,012)	(31,078)	(35,525)
Net current transfers	13,434	14,733	16,091	21,831	19,793	23,242	26,109
Financial account, n.i.e.	9,623	7,995	11,985	16,421	22,229	21,622	37,776
Overall balance	6,069	8,690	18,854	25,665	23,646	14,555	23,737
Foreign-exchange reserves minus gold	37,902	45,871	67,666	98,938	126,593	131,924	170,738

Source: IMF International Financial Statistics database

The buildup in India's foreign-exchange reserves is the result of massive inflows of foreign capital, far exceeding the sums needed to finance the current-account deficit. Those inflows (made up of remittances by non-resident Indians, portfolio investment, direct investment, and borrowing from abroad by banks and corporations) have brought down domestic interest rates and fuelled credit growth, giving rise to an economic boom. Interest rates, which held steady at 16.5% throughout the 1980s, fell to 10.9% in 2004. As credit grew more affordable, loans to the private sector increased by 240% between 2002 and 2008, while the ratio of credit to GDP expanded from 33% to 51%.

The large capital inflows eventually led to economic overheating. That leaves India vulnerable on a number of fronts. First, it is at risk if demand for its exports contracts. Although exports have not been the principal driver of India's growth, they nonetheless tripled between 2002 and 2008.

Figure 37

INDIA'S EXPORTS

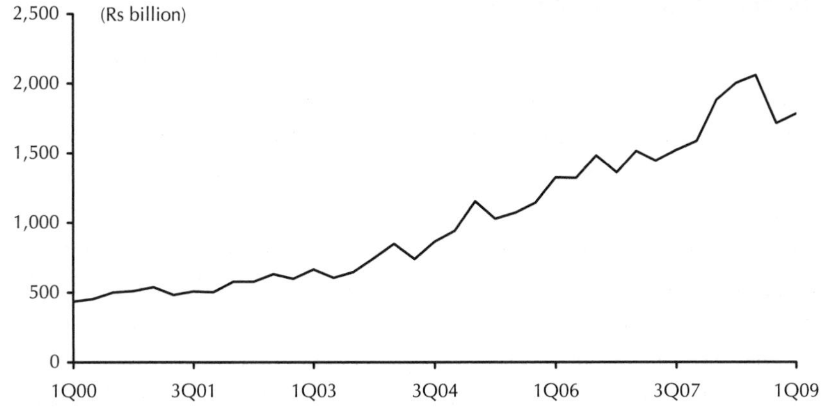

Source: IMF International Financial Statistics database

India's economy is also particularly vulnerable to the risk of foreign-capital outflow. Inflows drove the economic boom by pushing down interest rates and funding rapid credit growth. A prolonged reversal of those flows would push interest rates back up and limit credit expansion. Significantly less credit growth would cause the Indian economy to deflate and cause widespread distress in the financial sector.

When the global crisis began, India—like most other countries—did experience capital flight. Its foreign-exchange reserves contracted by 13% during the second half of 2008, and the rupee depreciated by 23% between the end of 2007 and April 2009. Exports fell 17% from the third to the fourth quarter of 2008. The government responded with fiscal stimulus. The IMF now expects India's budget deficit to be 9.8% of GDP in 2009 and 8.4% of GDP in 2010.

The economy is expected to keep growing in 2009 and 2010, however—by 4.5% and 5.6% respectively—supported by a weaker currency and government stimulus. The growing importance of India's services sector should also help insulate the economy from global shocks. Moreover, the central bank's still-large stockpile of foreign reserves will provide a buffer against the risk of further capital outflows. However, the global environment is now much less supportive to India, and growth will be harder to come by. In any case, the global impact of economic growth in India will be minimal at best. At $1.2 trillion, India's GDP is only one-tenth as large as that of the United States.

Oil and global imbalances

High oil prices have greatly exacerbated global trade imbalances in recent years. In 2007, thanks to oil exports, Saudi Arabia had the world's fourth-largest current-account surplus at $96 billion, followed by Russia with $76 billion.

A great deal of research was written claiming high oil prices were justified by the combination of rising demand and a shortage of supply. Events were to prove that analysis wrong on both counts. Global demand for oil is now expected to decline by 1.7 million barrels a day in 2009. This has left OPEC with excess capacity of 6 million barrels a day. OPEC oil inventories (on a days-to-cover basis) have not been this high since the 1990-91 recession. At that time oil cost less than $20 a barrel. Moreover, the global economy was clearly a great deal healthier then than it is now.

Therefore, the current oil price of $74 a barrel cannot be justified by economic fundamentals. Nor can the future price of oil (or its impact on the global economy) be estimated on the basis of fundamental supply and demand. Instead, it seems highly probable that oil prices have been and continue to be drastically inflated above fundamental value as a result of trading in the derivatives market. It is not clear whether derivatives are intentionally being used to manipulate prices higher or whether derivatives trading is simply driving prices higher because more and more speculators want to gamble on oil futures. The possibility of manipulation should be investigated. The trading of hundreds of trillions of dollars' worth of derivatives contracts through unregulated over-the-counter markets makes it impossible to see who is doing what. Clearly, many parties have a great deal to gain from $100-a-barrel oil. Oil at that price, for example, would make Russia a superpower, whereas oil at $10 a barrel would put Russia at risk of becoming a failed state. It could also make tens of billions of dollars' difference in the profits of banks trading in oil futures.

Figure 38

THE UPS AND DOWNS OF OIL: WEST TEXAS INTERMEDIATE

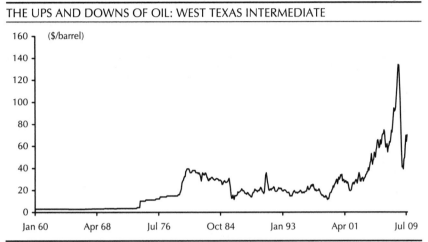

Source: Federal Reserve Bank of St. Louis

If everyone other than end users were banned from trading derivatives on oil (as was the case until numerous exceptions were granted), the price of oil would most likely fall back to $11 a barrel, where it traded in December 1998. This theory can easily be put to the test: ban speculators for six months and see what happens. Ten-dollar oil would do a great deal to restore global equilibrium.

Quantitative easing and the global savings glut

Quantitative easing is a euphemism for paper-money creation. The "quantity" being referred to is the quantity of paper money in existence. Quantitative easing is a very important part of the policy response to the New Depression. It plays a critical role in the Just Keep the Balloon Inflated approach to managing the crisis.

It is essential to understand, however, that quantitative easing is not new. In fact it was one of the two principal causes of the global economic bubble that led to the New Depression. The other was the US trade deficit. Mutually reinforcing, these two evils created the global imbalance that produced this crisis. The paper money created by countries with large trade surpluses funded the debt-fuelled excessive consumption in countries with large trade deficits. And the dollars brought back by exporters to the countries with surpluses were the assets central banks in those countries acquired in exchange for the paper money they created. The larger the US trade deficits became, the more paper money the surplus countries created to finance them.

The extraordinary scale on which global quantitative easing has occurred in recent years is best captured in the data showing total foreign-exchange reserves.

Figure 39

TOTAL WORLD RESERVES MINUS GOLD

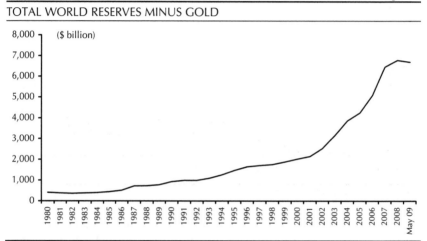

Source: IMF International Financial Statistics database.

Between 2000 and 2004, total reserves (not including gold) nearly doubled. In other words, during those four years international non-gold reserves increased by as much as in all previous centuries combined. Over the following four years they practically doubled again. Altogether, central banks created (from thin air) the equivalent of nearly $5 trillion over eight years. Never before during peacetime had paper-money creation (i.e. quantitative easing) on that scale taken place. The global disequilibrium it caused was also unprecedented.

When Fed Chairman Bernanke blamed the economic bubble in the United States on the global savings glut, it is curious that he did not explain that central banks were responsible for "printing" the "savings" behind the glut. The $5 trillion they had created since the turn of the century was enough to buy all the US government debt that existed before the crisis began. Little wonder that there was a glut of money.

Bernanke cannot have been so ill-informed that he didn't know the central banks of trade-surplus countries were creating the equivalent of trillions of dollars and using them to buy US dollars and then dollar-denominated assets. It must therefore be asked why he would not explain that this was the origin of the savings glut destabilizing the US economy. A global savings glut caused by a few hundred central bankers would be far easier to correct than one caused by hundreds of millions of individuals across the developing world. Clarification of this issue by Chairman Bernanke would be most welcome, particularly now that the Fed has joined the quantitative-easing club by printing a trillion dollars of its own.

Monitoring total foreign-exchange reserves is a very useful way to understand the state of the global economic bubble. As long as reserves expanded rapidly, the global economy boomed. When reserves stopped expanding and began to contract, the world went into economic shock. Which came first, the bubble or the reserves, is a chicken-and-egg kind of question. The reserves grew in line with (and financed) the US trade deficit. When the American private sector was incapable of bearing any more debt, consumption slowed, the current account corrected and total reserves stopped expanding.

At that point the government sector stepped in to supply the aggregate demand that had evaporated throughout the rest of the economy. The US government was joined by governments all around the world in providing debt-funded fiscal stimulus. The Fed and a number of other central banks (the Bank of England, the European Central Bank and the Swiss National Bank) that for the most part had not been large-scale paper-money printers in the past launched aggressive quantitative-easing programs to help underwrite growth by increasing the supply of "liquidity". The Bank of Japan also did its part and expanded its quantitative-easing activities by adding commercial paper and corporate debt to the list of assets it printed money to acquire (in addition to the dollars entering Japan through its trade surplus). There may have been a global saving glut, but that money was not so stupid as to stay in the toxic debt classes it had been speculating in before the bubble burst. So these central banks were compelled to create even more liquidity and provide credit to those parts of the credit market that the private sector would not touch.

The world's central bankers are doing everything in their power to get the credit flowing again, despite the glaring fact that the private sector is incapable of repaying the debt it has already incurred.

IMF: Global central bank?

The IMF took a giant step closer to becoming the global central bank on 28 August 2009, when it created from thin air the equivalent of $250 billion worth of new special drawing rights (SDRs). SDRs are an international reserve asset that can be exchanged for freely usable currencies. They could be described as IMF money. The new SDRs were allocated to IMF members in proportion to the size of their quotas. (Quotas, which are denominated in SDRs, determine member countries' voting power within the IMF.) The US, as the largest quota holder with a 17% share, received 17% of the newly created money, followed by Japan with 6.1%, and so on.

A second smaller allotment of SDRs worth $33 billion was created on 9 September and given to countries who became members of the IMF after 1981 and had therefore never received any SDR allotment. Together, these two allotments represent nearly a tenfold increase in the outstanding stock of SDRs. This increase in IMF assets will provide a nice boost to the world's total reserves (minus gold). The new IMF money was badly needed to help bail out global banks and other foolish investors, who had once again lent recklessly into the developing world and could suffer very large losses if their debtors cannot find the money to repay them. The contraction in world trade has created a balance-of-payments crisis throughout much of the developing world. Plunging export earnings mean many countries will be unable to repay their debt as it matures in the next few years. Normally, they do not have to repay this debt, merely roll it over. But every time there is a shock, global lenders run for the exits so fast they cannot all get out and a balance-of-payments crisis results. That was the case in Latin America in the early 1980s, in Mexico in 1995 and in much of Asia in 1997. Now developing countries everywhere are in trouble.

With its resources greatly expanded by the new money it has created, the IMF will once again be able to rescue the global banks from their reckless lending, as it did after all the previous shocks. Lucky bankers.

The IMF's ability to conjure up $283 billion at will does raise many interesting possibilities. If it can create $283 billion this year to bail out reckless investors, why can't it create $283 billion next year for some other (perhaps more socially useful) purpose? The next quota allotment could be earmarked for investment in sustainable energy, for example. A $283 billion investment in solar energy just might end the world's dependence on fossil fuels, and by bringing down energy costs could do more to alleviate poverty than all previous aid efforts combined. And another $283 billion the year after that? It could be used for education, to build infrastructure, for debt relief in developing countries, or for research to cure infectious diseases. The world is drowning in excess industrial capacity, which is putting strong downward pressure on prices. So long as there is no inflationary pressure, there is nothing to stop the IMF from creating much more paper money in the years ahead.

Something good could result from the New Depression after all. Central banks around the world are creating paper money to keep asset prices inflated, to support aggregate demand and to prevent the collapse of the global financial sector. If they allocated this conjured-up money wisely, they could work miracles.

Conclusion

The global economy has been distended by unprecedented trade imbalances that the deficit countries financed with debt and the surplus countries facilitated with paper-money creation. Global output and asset prices surged so long as the imbalances grew, but collapsed into crisis when private-sector borrowers in the deficit countries began defaulting on their debt. The world economy now depends on the expansion of government debt to perpetuate the imbalances so as to stave off global economic collapse. But government resources are finite. The clock is ticking. The global economy needs to be fundamentally reoriented to end the structural imbalances that created this crisis. If government resources run out before this occurs, the crisis will become very much worse.

Part 2: The past

What went wrong

Part 1 described the nature and extent of the global economic crisis, as well as the policies implemented to combat it. Part 2 looks back to consider the long series of policy mistakes that led us here.

Chapter 4 outlines the steps taken to restore stability following the onset of the Great Depression. By regulating banks, controlling credit, balancing the budget and establishing a strong international monetary system to promote balanced international trade, the United States government had, by the early 1950s, laid the foundations for strong and sustainable economic growth. These prerequisites for stability, however, were eroded away during the decades that followed.

Chapter 5 explains how excessive government spending forced the United States to break the link between the dollar and gold. Chapter 6 relates how floating exchange rates and unregulated cross-border capital flows created one debt crisis after another all around the world during the 1970s, 1980s and 1990s. Chapter 7 shows how the US economy was destabilized by the country's twin deficits, and Chapter 8 demonstrates how the United States itself, like so many smaller countries before it, was eventually overwhelmed by international credit flows.

Chapter 9 looks at the deregulation of the financial industry, the proliferation of derivatives and the threat that unregulated finance poses to the world. Finally, Chapter 10 explains why the New Depression is a structural economic crisis rather than merely another cyclical recession. Put bluntly, the US economy as it is now structured is simply not viable.

Chapter 4
Restoring stability after the Great Depression

Practices of the unscrupulous money changers stand indicted in the court of public opinion, rejected by the hearts and minds of men. True they have tried, but their efforts have been cast in the pattern of an outworn tradition. Faced by failure of credit they have proposed only the lending of more money. Stripped of the lure of profit by which to induce our people to follow their false leadership, they have resorted to exhortations, pleading tearfully for restored confidence. They know only the rules of a generation of self-seekers. They have no vision, and when there is no vision the people perish.

President Franklin D. Roosevelt[1]

The Great Depression was the worst economic calamity ever to befall the United States. It was caused by a credit boom that began with the breakdown of the gold standard during World War I and ended with the systemic collapse of the global financial sector a decade and a half later when that credit could not be repaid. At that point the international banking system broke down and

---

[1] President Franklin D. Roosevelt, first inaugural address, 4 March 1933.

international trade collapsed. The damage took decades to repair. During the 1930s, US lawmakers addressed the flaws in the domestic banking system with a series of measures that improved oversight and strengthened regulation. It took until the end of World War II, however, to reestablish a stable international monetary system within which global trade could once again begin to flourish.

In the years following the collapse of the 1914–30 credit bubble, the United States gradually regained control over credit creation and laid the foundations for sustainable prosperity. This chapter describes how that was accomplished.

What caused the Great Depression?

The origins of the Great Depression can be traced to 1914 and the start of World War I, when Great Britain, France, Germany and the other belligerents issued unprecedented amounts of government bonds to finance the war and instructed their central banks to print money to buy the debt. This triggered a global credit boom.

Before the war, the paper money in circulation was backed by—and freely convertible into—gold held by the central banks. However, once the central banks began to print large quantities of paper money to finance the war, their gold reserves were no longer sufficient to back it. The right of the public to convert paper money into gold had to be suspended. Thus the gold standard was among the first casualties of World War I.

The United States did not enter the war until 1917. Until then, it sold raw materials, equipment and weapons to both sides and, for the most part, demanded payment in gold. When it did enter the war, the United States supplied its allies with war materials on credit—with the understanding that it would be repaid in gold or in a currency fully backed by gold. The US central bank also began printing money to finance Washington's war bonds.

Between 1913 and 1919, central government expenditure rose from $715 million to $18.5 billion in the United States; from £192 million to £1.7 billion (it peaked at £2.7 billion in 1917) in Great Britain; from 5 billion francs to 40 billion francs in France; and from 3.5 billion marks to 55 billion marks in Germany—where it rose to 299 billion marks in 1921, ultimately ending in hyperinflation and the destruction of the currency.

Such massive government spending during the war destroyed the equilibrium between supply and demand for almost every manufactured good and commodity across the globe. Financing that spending destabilized global capital markets to an even greater extent. By the end of the war, paper money in circulation had doubled in the United States and Britain, tripled in France and quadrupled in vanquished Germany, which was also saddled with a $12 billion bill for war reparations. These were payable primarily to France and England, which in turn were very heavily indebted to the United States—now the world's greatest creditor nation. Moreover, US gold reserves had nearly doubled during the war.

The credit created during and immediately after the war fuelled the global economy but led to increasingly unsustainable economic distortions as the Roaring Twenties progressed. The United States lent money to other countries to enable them to buy American exports. Later, following the 1924 Dawes Plan agreement between Germany and its creditors, the United States also lent hundreds of millions of dollars to Germany. Those loans enabled Germany to pay war reparations to France and England, helping them repay part of their war loans from the United States. This merry-go-round of international credit created profitable opportunities for the bankers who arranged the credit and transferred the money, but it also created patterns of demand and supply that were unsustainable. When the global credit boom that began in 1914 gave way to bust at the end of the 1920s, a systemic financial-sector breakdown spread around the world and the credit merry-go-round stopped. Nations responded by devaluing their currencies, increasing tariff barriers or both. International trade collapsed and the Great Depression began.

Regaining control over credit, 1933–50

Between 1929 and 1933 in the United States, one bank in three collapsed, nominal GDP contracted by 45% and unemployment rose to 25%. Bank deposits were not guaranteed by the government. When a bank failed, its customers lost their money—$1.3 billion in total, according to the FDIC[2]. People queued for city blocks to withdraw their savings from the banks that were still open. The week Franklin Roosevelt was sworn in as President, in March 1933, a national "bank holiday" was declared to prevent all the rest of the banks from collapsing as well.

[2] FDIC Learning Bank, "The 1930s", http://www.fdic.gov/about/learn/learning/when/1930s.html.

Americans were in shock. Capitalism appeared to have collapsed just as Karl Marx had predicted it would. No one fully understood what had happened, but most people blamed the bankers. Congress launched investigations into banking and securities practices.

In March 1932, the US Senate Committee on Banking and Currency convened what came to be known as Pecora Committee Investigation, named for committee counsel Ferdinand Pecora. The committee was authorized:

> ...to make a thorough and complete investigation of the operation by any person, firm, co-partnership, company, association, corporation, or other entity of the business of banking, financing, and extending credit; and of the business of issuing, offering, or selling securities.[3]

For the next two years, counsel Pecora summonsed and interrogated the high and mighty of the US financial industry. Among the corporations investigated were National City Bank (which later became Citibank); J.P. Morgan & Co.; Chase National Bank; and Dillon, Read & Co. Those subpoenaed included Richard Whitney, president of the New York Stock Exchange, who was later jailed for embezzlement, and J.P. Morgan, Jr. himself.

The country was mesmerized by the hearings, which were widely covered in newspapers and on radio. Under close questioning, many of the country's most powerful bankers and financiers were revealed to be unscrupulous, foolish or both. Pecora uncovered widespread conflicts of interest and other unethical practices throughout the industry, particularly related to securities underwriting.

The Banking Committee compiled more than 12,000 printed pages and received 1,000 exhibits in evidence. Its report concluded:

> The cost of the investigation has been approximately $250,000. The expenditures, however, have been justified many fold by the incalculable benefits flowing to the American people from the hearings in the form of enlightenment as to practices which have cost them so dearly in the past and in the form of remedial measures designed to prevent such practices for all time in the future. The Federal Government has been or will be reimbursed many times over by the receipt of additional income taxes and penalties imposed on the basis of testimony developed at the hearings. To date (June 6, 1934) assessments for deficiencies and penalties have been levied by the Bureau of Internal Revenue in a sum exceeding $2,000,000 as a direct result of the revelations before the subcommittee.[4]

The outcome of the Pecora hearings was a wave of legislation designed to bring the financial industry under much tighter government control.

---

[3] US Senate Committee on Banking and Currency Report, submitted by committee member Fletcher, 6 June 1934.

[4] *Ibid.*

The Securities Act of 1933 (also known as the Truth in Securities Act) regulated the initial public offering of securities. Its purpose was to ensure that investors received adequate and truthful information regarding the securities sold. The following year, the Securities Exchange Act of 1934 regulated the trading of securities on the secondary market and established the Securities and Exchange Commission (SEC).

The Glass-Steagall Act (officially the Banking Act of 1933) included four measures that profoundly changed the American banking industry. First, it mandated the separation of commercial banking from investment banking and securities trading. Bankers were forced to choose which business they wished to conduct; they were not permitted to do both. For example, J.P. Morgan & Co. was forced to sell its investment banking business, which became Morgan Stanley, with new directors as well as owners. This ensured that deposits at commercial banks could not be used for speculative purposes by investment bankers.

Next, Glass-Steagall established the Federal Deposit Insurance Corporation (FDIC) to insure bank deposits against loss, initially up to a maximum of $2,500. This measure, opposed by the banking industry, was instrumental in restoring public confidence in the banking system. A third important measure introduced by Glass-Steagall imposed a ceiling on the interest rates banks could pay on deposits and banned the payment of interest on demand deposits. These are known as the Regulation Q restrictions. Finally, Glass-Steagall for the first time extended federal oversight to all commercial banks.

Two years later, the Banking Act of 1935 reorganized the structure of the central bank, concentrating power over the monetary system within the Board of Governors of the Federal Reserve System and the Federal Open Market Committee in Washington at the expense of the 12 Federal Reserve Banks. The Act made the Federal Reserve Board's power to alter the reserve requirements of banks permanent. When it was first granted, this power had been considered as only a temporary emergency measure. The Act also changed the status of the FDIC from temporary to permanent. Finally, it granted the Federal Reserve Board the power to set margin requirements for securities lending.

These New Deal laws together gave public officials much greater control over the banking and securities industries than ever before. Moreover, they created a structure and provided the tools that would ultimately enable the central bank to profoundly affect the economy by controlling the quantity and price of credit. It was not until the early 1950s, however, that the Fed was able to exercise that power. Throughout the Depression, excess capacity and weak product prices meant demand for credit was very limited. The business sector's reluctance to borrow and the banks' reluctance to lend both depressed interest rates and limited the Fed's control over the credit-creation process. Later, from World War II through the start of the Korean War, the Fed was again compelled to create money and buy government bonds, making it impossible for it to simultaneously control the money supply.

1951–69: Tight control and stability

Beginning in the early 1950s, however, circumstances became ideal to enable the Fed to control credit growth, and therefore economic growth, through small adjustments in the federal funds rate.

The financial industry was tightly regulated. Ceilings on the interest rates payable on deposits made it impossible for banks to compete with one another for funding—which, in turn, reduced their incentive to take risks. The economy was healthy and demand for loans was strong. Deposit growth could not keep pace.

The banks' portfolios were primarily made up of customer loans and US government bonds accumulated during the war. Banks were not yet permitted to issue debt to raise funds. To increase loans to customers, they had to raise funds by selling the government bonds in their portfolios. Those bonds were held at face value until they were sold.

The Fed could affect the price of the bonds, and therefore the profit banks would earn from selling them, by making small changes in interest rates. Higher rates would make the bonds less valuable and discourage the banks from selling them. In this way, the Fed could discourage an increase in lending. Conversely, lower interest rates would raise the price of the bonds, encouraging the banks to sell them and extend more credit to the public. Martin Mayer describes this mechanism with great clarity in his excellent book *The Fed*.[5]

Individuals and small- and medium-sized businesses had no alternative but to rely on local banks or thrifts for loans. Corporations had the choice of either borrowing from banks or raising funds by issuing bonds. However, since the size of the bond market was relatively small, businesses obtained the majority of their financing from commercial banks. There was very little possibility of obtaining credit from abroad. Outside the United States, capital was in short

---

[5] Martin Mayer, *The Fed: The inside story of how the world's most powerful financial institution drives the markets* (Detroit Free Press, 2001), pp. 167-169.

supply, and capital controls were still firmly in place throughout most of the world. The Eurodollar market did not yet exist.

Consequently, during the 1950s and most of the 1960s, the Fed had a very firm grip on the amount of credit that could be created and the price at which that credit would be made available. That power enabled the Fed to stimulate the economy by making credit more plentiful or slow the economy by making credit scarcer. However, there were limits on the amount of money and credit the Fed could create. When the Federal Reserve System was established in 1913, the Federal Reserve Act required the Federal Reserve Banks to maintain gold reserves equivalent to at least 40% of their Federal Reserve notes (US currency) outstanding and at least 35% of their deposits. In 1945, Congress had reduced both ratios to 25%; nonetheless, by maintaining the link between money and gold, these restrictions put a cap on the Fed's powers to create money and credit.

Balanced budgets

The Fed could not have achieved control over credit creation had the government not also reimposed budgetary discipline at the end of World War II. Between 1900 and 1930, the US government had run a budget surplus in 21 years out of 30. Of the nine years when it ran a deficit, three—1916 to 1918—coincided with the country's involvement in World War I. Economic orthodoxy demanded that the budget be balanced, and very few questioned that orthodoxy.

Figure 40

US BUDGET BALANCE AS A % OF GDP

Source: Bureau of Economic Analysis (GDP), White House Office of Management and Budget (budget)

The Depression created a budgetary crisis, however. In 1932, the last year of the Hoover presidency, the deficit rose to 4% of GDP when tax revenues collapsed. Between 1932 and 1940, the deficit averaged 3.6% of GDP a year. At that time, most Americans, including Hoover's successor, Franklin Roosevelt, believed it was the government's duty to maintain a balanced budget. During the 1932 election campaign, Roosevelt harshly criticized Hoover for the large shortfall in the federal budget that year. Two years later, with the budget still in deficit, President Roosevelt's first budget director, Lewis Douglas, resigned in protest. He later warned the President: "I hope, and hope most fervently, that you will evidence a real determination to bring the budget into actual balance, for upon this, I think, hangs not only your place in history but conceivably the immediate fate of western civilization."[6] Roosevelt was deeply concerned about the budget deficits. In mid-1937, with the economy showing signs of strength, he cut government spending and the budget went temporarily into surplus. However, the economy quickly deteriorated again and the deficits resumed.

When the United States entered World War II in late 1941, all thought of balancing the budget was put on hold until the war was won. In 1942, the budget deficit blew out to the equivalent of 14% of GDP. The next year it more than doubled, to 30% of GDP; and it remained above 20% of GDP in 1944 and 1945. In 1946, with the war won, the deficit improved substantially. By 1947 the budget had returned to surplus. Over the next decade, the budget remained in surplus more often than in deficit. The war had created a tremendous economic boom in the United States. Government spending had quickly eliminated the excess capacity that had weighed so heavily on the economy all through the 1930s. Strong postwar tax revenues and reduced military spending made it relatively easy to balance the budget.

More than that, however, US policymakers fundamentally believed that a balanced government budget was vital to a healthy economy. They understood that money didn't grow on trees: there was a limited amount of it. If the government borrowed to finance a budget deficit, it would push up interest rates and "crowd out" private-sector borrowers, who would then be forced to invest less. Ultimately, the economy would pay a price for the government's failure to balance its books. Therefore, policymakers were quick to bring the budget back into balance as soon as circumstances allowed.

---

[6] Arthur M. Schlesinger, Jr., *The Age of Roosevelt: The coming of the New Deal* (Houghton Mifflin Company Boston, 1959), p. 293.

Recreating a framework for international trade

Economic orthodoxy demanded balanced trade no less than balanced budgets. From the earliest days of the nation state, countries paid close attention to their balance of trade for one very practical reason: imports had to be paid for—and in gold. If a country imported more than it exported, its supply of gold—in other words, its money supply—would contract and its economy would suffer.

Gold had become money because centuries of experience had shown it to be the most reliable medium of exchange. Gold has an intrinsic value as jewelry and, as with other commodities, this value is determined by the market. Gold does not rot or rust. Unlike diamonds, it can be divided into parts without diminishing its value. It is light enough to carry and scarce enough to have considerable purchasing power even in small quantities. But most importantly, governments cannot create gold and thus reduce its value by making it less scarce. History had shown that gold could be trusted as a store of value, whereas money created by government fiat tended to lose its purchasing power over time—and sometimes become completely worthless.

By the 19th Century, the domestic and international commerce of most civilized nations was transacted in gold, and all financial instruments were understood to be ultimately convertible into gold. Thanks largely to the integrity of this gold standard, international trade expanded more rapidly than ever before.

Governments were right to be concerned about the balance of trade. Although the gold standard contained an inherent adjustment mechanism that made long-term trade imbalances unsustainable, the process of adjustment tended to be painful. For instance, in the mid-19th Century, if Great Britain had a large trade deficit with France, a portion of its gold would literally have been put on a ship and sent to France. Britain's money supply would thereupon have contracted, its economy would have gone into recession, unemployment would have risen and deflation would have occurred. In France, the opposite would have taken place: the money supply and credit would have expanded, the economy would have boomed, employment would have improved and prices would have risen. Before long, recessionary Britain would have stopped buying as many expensive French goods, prospering France would have bought more inexpensive British goods, and trade between them would have returned to balance.

Understanding this self-correcting process, in the late 18th Century economic theorists such as Adam Smith and David Ricardo showed that nations benefited from trade when they specialized in those industries where they possessed a natural advantage. Under their influence, faith in mercantilism—which held that international trade was a zero-sum game—gradually gave way to the logic of "free trade". Nevertheless, the benefits of free trade were not always distributed equally. Industrially less-developed countries—and during the 19th Century the United States was one—often preferred to protect their developing industries from foreign competition by raising protective tariffs. Regardless of a country's development status, however, its trade balance was always subject to the careful watchfulness of the government and its economic ministers. One way or the other, over time trade had to balance, either through an impartial automatic adjustment process or as the result of deliberate actions by governments.

The next best thing

World War I destroyed the gold standard. Attempts to restore it during the 1920s were unsuccessful. When the global financial sector broke down in the early 1930s, international trade collapsed. Then World War II eliminated any hope for a return to normalcy.

When the war ended, however, efforts to rebuild the world's financial architecture began again. In July 1944, representatives of 44 nations met at the United Nations Monetary and Financial Conference, in Bretton Woods, New Hampshire. Its aim was to establish a rule-based system to regulate international trade and monetary relations so as to promote balanced growth in international trade. The conference was a tremendous success. Never before had an international monetary system been created by an agreement among nations. The gold standard had simply emerged over the course of centuries because gold had proven to be the most reliable medium of exchange.

The Bretton Woods system was designed to replicate the best aspects of the gold standard. It was structured to prevent member countries from pursuing the kinds of unfair trade practices that had contributed to the Depression. In particular, it sought to prevent unilateral currency devaluations and trade tariffs.

Simply returning to the gold standard was not an option. By the end of the war, the victors held most of the world's gold. Gold was not distributed widely enough around the world to allow international trade to recommence. The United States had by far the largest gold holdings, followed by France. Moreover, the US had become the largest creditor nation in history.

To overcome this unequal distribution of gold, the Bretton Woods Agreement established a system of fixed exchange rates in which the US dollar served as the anchor currency. The United States pegged the dollar to gold at the fixed rate of $35 per ounce and agreed to buy or sell gold to or from the monetary authorities of other countries at that price in order to prevent any fluctuation in the dollar's value relative to gold. Other member countries undertook to maintain the value of their currency near an agreed par value, allowing fluctuation within only a narrow margin. In practice, most countries pegged their currency to the dollar and bought or sold dollars to prevent any significant change in their currency's established value They also had the right to exchange the dollars held by their monetary authorities for gold held as reserves by the United States via the "gold window" at the US Treasury.

The monetary authorities at the conference realized that no international trading system could survive for long if trade among nations did not balance. Trade had to be paid for. Imbalances could be financed on credit only over the short run at best. To ensure that trade did balance, the Bretton Woods system was designed to have the same automatic adjustment mechanism that the gold standard had. Trade deficits would cause monetary contraction and trade surpluses would cause monetary expansion, in both cases setting off macroeconomic forces that would restore balance. During the conference, the architects of the system created the International Monetary Fund (IMF) to help ease the adjustment process.

Maintaining equilibrium in global trade was clearly foremost in the minds of the creators of the Bretton Woods system and central to the IMF's mission. In the first six paragraphs of the IMF's Articles of Agreement, "balance of payments" or "balanced growth of international trade" is mentioned three times:

Article I. Purposes

The purposes of the International Monetary Fund are:

To promote international monetary cooperation through a permanent institution which provides the machinery for consultation and collaboration on international monetary problems.

To facilitate the expansion and balanced growth of international trade, and to contribute thereby to the promotion and maintenance of high levels of employment and real income and to the development of the productive resources of all members as primary objectives of economic policy.

To promote exchange stability, to maintain orderly exchange arrangements among members, and to avoid competitive exchange depreciation.

To assist in the establishment of a multilateral system of payments in respect of current transactions between members and in the elimination of foreign exchange restrictions which hamper the growth of world trade.

To give confidence to members by making the Fund's resources available to them under adequate safeguards, thus providing them with opportunity to correct maladjustments in their balance of payments without resorting to measures destructive of national or international prosperity.

In accordance with the above, to shorten the duration and lessen the degree of disequilibrium in the international balance of payments of members.

The Fund shall be guided in all its decisions by the purposes set forth in this Article.

The international monetary system created at Bretton Woods was a brilliant success. So long as the world's leading industrialized nations abided by its rules, it provided a structure in which international trade could (and did) flourish. It was only when the United States ceased to honor its obligations under this system from 1971 that the credit bubble that led to the New Depression began to form.

Conclusion

By the early 1950s, all the pieces had been put into place to eliminate the monetary and economic chaos that had begun with the breakdown of the gold standard in 1914. In the United States, banks were tightly regulated, the Fed had complete control over credit creation, dollars were backed by gold, and the government balanced its budgets. At the international level, the Bretton Woods system, modeled after the gold standard, provided a framework in which trade could again flourish as it had in the years before World War I.

These conditions created an economic environment closely resembling that in which capitalism had first emerged. They lasted for two decades. During the 1950s, the US economy expanded by 49%. During the 1960s, it expanded by 54%. These rates of growth have not been matched since.

By the early 1970s, the Bretton Woods system had collapsed, the dollar was no longer backed by gold and the US government had lost the will to balance its budgets. Before the end of that decade, the Fed had lost control over credit creation. The global credit bubble responsible for the New Depression formed during the 1980s and 1990s. It popped in 2008. The rest of Part 2 describes the policy mistakes that led to this disaster.

Chapter 5
Monetary LSD

Our commitment to maintain dollar convertibility into gold at $35 an ounce is firm and clear. We will not be a party to raising its price. The dollar will continue to be kept as good as or better than gold.

President Lyndon Johnson[1]

The credit bubble that caused the New Depression began on 15 August 1971, when President Nixon repudiated the United States' obligation to back its currency with gold. President Lyndon Johnson, advised by arrogant Keynesian economists who believed they could "fine tune" away the business cycle, had mismanaged the US economy during his five years in the White House by spending too much money at home and abroad. Loose fiscal and monetary policy caused the economy to overheat. The result was a spike in inflation beginning in 1966 and a balance-of-payments crisis by the end of the decade. The government's refusal to cut spending, raise interest rates and endure a recession or two during the 1960s undermined the Bretton Woods system and was directly responsible for its collapse in 1971. The international monetary system created at Bretton Woods required the key participants to live within their means. When the United States refused to do that, the system fell apart.

---

[1] Council of Economic Advisors, "President Johnson's Transmittal Letter", *1968 Economic Report of the President*, p. 16.

America: Living beyond its means

The 1960s was the only decade of the 20th Century when the US economy expanded every year without exception. Despite such strong growth, the government ran budget deficits during eight of those 10 years. The economists in charge of policymaking at the time called themselves Keynesians. John Maynard Keynes died in 1946, so he did not live long enough to see "Keynesianism". If he had, he would not have approved—not least because Keynesianism was ultimately responsible for undermining the international monetary system he had helped create in 1944. Keynes had argued that governments should borrow and spend during deep recessions and reduce expenditure and repay debt during economic expansions. By the 1960s, however, the Keynesian economists had read into *The General Theory of Employment, Interest and Money* (Keynes's masterpiece) that the business cycle could be done away with altogether.

A few lines from the 1969 Economic Report of the President—an annual review prepared by the President's Council of Economic Advisors—perfectly encapsulates both their misguided philosophy and their boastful self-confidence:

> The vigorous and unbroken expansion of the last 8 years is in dramatic contrast to the 30-month average duration of previous expansions. No longer is the performance of the American economy generally interpreted in terms of stages of the business cycle. No longer do we consider periodic recessions once every 3 or 4 years an inevitable fact of life.
>
> The forces making for economic fluctuations have been contained through the active use of fiscal and monetary policies to sustain expansion.[2]

Lyndon Johnson became president when John F. Kennedy was assassinated in November 1963. That year the US economy expanded by 4.4%. The year before, it had grown by 6.1%. Rather than raising taxes to cool down the economy and repay government debt, the Johnson administration cut taxes sharply in 1964 (an election year) and again in 1965. At the same time, government spending accelerated. Domestic discretionary spending, driven by Johnson's "Great Society" welfare programs, increased by 19% in 1964, 13% in 1965 and 18% in 1966. Defense spending was restrained during the first two years of Johnson's presidency, rising by 2.5% in 1964 and cut by 7% in 1965. But in 1966, as the Vietnam War heated up, it surged by

---

[2] Council of Economic Advisors, "Policies for Balanced Expansion". Chap. 2, *1969 Economic Report of the President*, pp. 73-74.

16%. With domestic discretionary and defense spending both growing fast, total government outlays leapt by 14% in 1966. Between lower taxes and increased spending, the economy boomed. GDP growth between 1964 and 1966 averaged 6.25% a year.

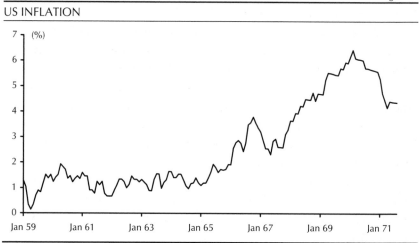

Figure 41

US INFLATION

Source: Bureau of Economic Analysis

Inflation, which had remained within an ideal range of 1–2% since 1958, moved above 2% in February 1966 and reached 3.8% in October. The Fed responded by tightening the effective federal funds rate from 4% in September 1965 to 5.75% in November 1966. Higher interest rates slowed economic growth to 1.0% during the first half of 1967, and that brought down the inflation rate. The Fed took the effective federal funds rate back down to 4% in April 1967, and the economy reaccelerated to a 4.5% growth rate in the second half of that year. Overall, GDP expanded by quite a respectable 2.5% in 1967. However, the economic slowdown put a significant dent in the government's tax receipts the following year.

Government outlays increased by 17% in 1967 (driven by a 22% increase in defense spending) and by 13% in 1968. Revenues, on the other hand, increased by 14% in 1967 and only 3% in 1968. As a result, the overall budget deficit jumped from 0.5% in 1966 to 1.0% in 1967 and to 2.8% of GDP in 1968, the worst shortfall since 1946.

By that time, the US economy was well overheated. GDP growth reaccelerated to 4.8% in 1968, and inflation, which had slowed to 2.3% in May 1967, ended 1968 at 4.7%, by far the worst level since 1951, during the Korean

War. When the inflation rate started moving up in 1966, the Dow Jones Industrial Average hit 1,000—a ceiling it would not break through for the next 16 years, until Fed chairman Paul Volcker crushed inflation in 1982.

Figure 42

US GDP GROWTH AND BUDGET BALANCE

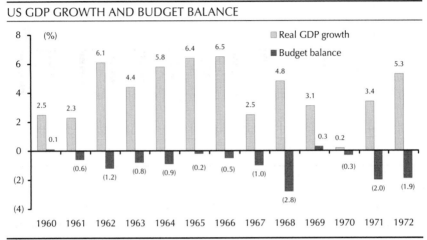

Source: Bureau of Economic Analysis

As a proportion of GDP, budget deficits during the 1960s—while still small by today's standards—were around twice those of the 1950s. The tax cuts and aggressive government spending during the Johnson administration not only triggered a serious bout of inflation, they also produced a dangerous balance-of-payments deficit. Throughout the 1960s, the United States still sold more to the rest of the world than it bought from abroad, so the trouble wasn't with the balance of trade. Rather, capital outflows were to blame. Heavy overseas investment by US corporations had produced a financial-account deficit. The amounts invested were large, but in light of the country's current-account surplus, they were sustainable. The destabilizing factor was US government's military grants to other countries. These plus the financial-account deficits greatly exceeded the current-account surplus and caused a significant shortfall in the overall balance of payments.

This overall imbalance meant that billions of dollars left the United States on a net basis each year. Many of those dollars accumulated in the nascent Eurodollar market (to be discussed later). Billions more came into the possession of central banks outside the United States when the dollars were converted into other currencies. These counted as US liabilities to foreign official agencies.

Figure 43

US BALANCE OF PAYMENTS

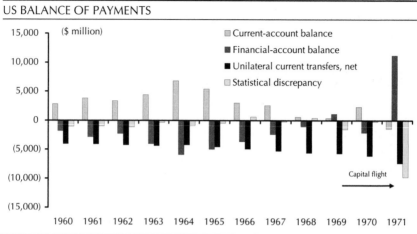

Source: Bureau of Economic Analysis

Under the Bretton Woods Agreement, US dollars were pegged to gold at a fixed rate of $35 an ounce, and the monetary authorities of other countries were free to convert their dollar holdings into gold at any time. Consequently, each year some fraction of the dollars going overseas returned to the United States and was exchanged for gold held by the US Treasury Department. It soon became clear to US government officials and monetary authorities around the world that gold was leaving the country at an unsustainable rate.

Figure 44

US GOLD RESERVES

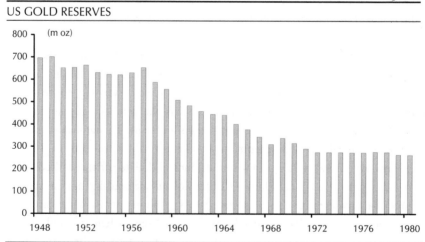

Source: IMF International Financial Statistics database

Between the start of the decade and 1968, the US lost nearly 250 million ounces of gold, roughly half of its official holdings.

This loss of gold, combined with the increase in the money supply, made it difficult for the Fed to meet its statutory requirements to maintain sufficient reserves of gold to back the dollars in circulation. The Federal Reserve Act had been amended in 1945 to reduce the ratio of gold to paper money and deposits from 40% (the level mandated when the Federal Reserve System was created in 1913) to 25%. In 1965, Congress had amended the Federal Reserve Act for a second time to eliminate the requirement for the Federal Reserve Banks to maintain any gold coverage ratio against their deposits, although they were still required to hold gold as reserves against Federal Reserve notes (i.e. the paper money in circulation).

In February 1968, President Johnson asked Congress to end that requirement as well:

> Our commitment to maintain dollar convertibility into gold at $35 an ounce is firm and clear. We will not be a party to raising its price. The dollar will continue to be kept as good as or better than gold.
>
> I am therefore asking the Congress to take prompt action to free our gold reserves so that they can unequivocally fulfill their true purpose—to insure the international convertibility of the dollar into gold at $35 per ounce.
>
> The gold reserve requirement against Federal Reserve notes is not needed to tell us what prudent monetary policy should be—that myth was destroyed long ago.
>
> It is not needed to give value to the dollar—that value derives from our productive economy.
>
> The reserve requirement does make some foreigners question whether all of our gold is really available to guarantee our commitment to sell gold at the $35 price. Removing the requirement will prove to them that we mean what we say.
>
> I ask speedy action from the Congress—because it will demonstrate to the world the determination of America to meet its international economic obligations.[3]

Congress obliged later that year. Therefore, by the end of 1968 the Fed no longer had any obligation to hold gold to back the money in circulation—although the Treasury was still obliged to exchange US gold for dollars presented by the monetary authorities of other countries.

This change at the Fed had no impact on the United States' ability to meet its international economic obligations, as President Johnson had suggested it would. To preserve the international monetary system, the US should have reduced government spending, increased interest rates and induced a recession.

---

[3] Council of Economic Advisors, 1968 *Economic Report of the President*, p. 16.

In other words, it should have replicated, through those measures, the automatic adjustment mechanism that was inherent in the gold standard. A recession would have caused prices to fall, making US exports more competitive. Higher interest rates would have made less credit available to finance imports. Consequently, the current-account deficit would have improved and dollars (and therefore gold) would have stopped flooding out of the country. If the government had also stopped or curtailed its military grants to its allies, the system could have been saved.

Decision time

By 1968, the United States had never been more prosperous. Nevertheless, government excesses had created imbalances that were beginning to destabilize the American economy, and with it the world economy. Policymakers in Washington were aware of the challenges they faced, as the following excerpts from President Johnson's Transmittal Letter for the 1968 Economic Report of the President make clear:

> Seldom can any single choice make or break an economy as strong and healthy as ours. But the series of interrelated decisions we face will affect our economy and that of the whole free world for years to come.
>
> In the coming weeks and months we must choose:
>
> Whether we will conduct our fiscal affairs sensibly; or whether we will allow a clearly excessive budgetary deficit to go uncorrected by failing to raise taxes, and thereby risk a feverish boom that could generate an unacceptable acceleration of price increases, a possible financial crisis, and perhaps ultimately a recession;
>
> Whether we will act firmly and wisely to control our balance-of-payments deficit; or whether we will risk a breakdown in the financial system that has underpinned world prosperity, a possible reversion toward economic isolationism, and a spiraling slowdown in world economic expansion."[4]

Belatedly, serious steps were taken in an attempt to regain control over the situation. Taxes were increased in 1968, and the growth in government spending was reduced from 13% in 1968 to 3% the following year. As a result, the budget swung from a deficit of 2.8% of GDP in 1968 to a small 0.3% surplus in 1969, the first surplus since 1960 (when it was an even smaller 0.1% of GDP). Monetary measures were even more aggressive. Between the beginning of 1968 and August 1969, the Fed doubled the effective federal funds rate to

---

[4] *Ibid*, pp. 3-4.

9.0%. Direct balance-of-payments measures were also imposed to restrain capital outflows. They included a mandatory program to restrain direct investment abroad and a Federal Reserve program to voluntarily constrain foreign lending by US banks. In other words, the US employed capital controls to improve its balance-of-payments position in 1968.

In combination, those measures worked. In 1969, US gold reserves actually increased for the first time since 1957. Had those policies been maintained for a number of years, the Bretton Woods system would have survived. Unfortunately, they weren't. The war had made President Johnson so unpopular he did not run for reelection in November 1968. Richard Nixon became the 37th president in January 1969.

The run on the dollar, 1971

In his first Economic Report of the President, dated 2 February 1970, President Nixon laid out the "seven basic principles" that would guide the management of economic policy under his administration. The first was that "the integrity and purchasing power of the dollar must be assured".[5] A little over a year and a half later, Nixon "suspended" the convertibility of the dollar into gold—and thereby destroyed the international monetary system. Since that day, the dollar has lost 96% of its value relative to gold.

Nixon could have held the Bretton Woods system together, but the harsh economic policies required to do so would have cost him reelection in 1972. Nixon was not prepared to make that sacrifice simply to preserve the value of the world's money.

The measures adopted in 1968 caused the booming 1960s to end on a negative quarter. GDP contracted by 1.9% in the last quarter of 1969, and by a further 0.7% in the first quarter of the new decade. After recovering over the next two quarters, GDP again contracted sharply, by 4.2%, in the fourth quarter of 1970, thanks to weak consumer spending and investment. Over the whole of 1969, the economy grew, but by a small 0.2%.

Rather than persisting with the tight fiscal and monetary policies needed to preserve the Bretton Woods system, Nixon stepped on the economic gas pedal. In 1970 his administration cut taxes and increased government spending. As a result, in 1971 tax revenues contracted by 2.9% while government outlays

---

[5] Council of Economic Advisors, *1970 Economic Report of the President*, p. 10.

increased by 7.4%. The resulting budget deficit, 2.0% of GDP, had been exceeded only twice during the previous 20 years. And the deficit remained high in 1972, at 1.9% of GDP.

Monetary policy under Nixon was equally disastrous. Arthur Burns replaced William Martin, Jr. as Fed chairman on 1 February 1970. During Burns's first year in office, the effective federal funds rate was slashed from 9% to 4%. Not surprisingly, the economy rebounded and was booming before the November 1972 election, when the President won a second term.

But the economic recovery that helped Nixon stay in power came at a high cost to the global economy. Once the fiscal and monetary stimulus began, America's balance-of-payments position quickly began to deteriorate. The overstimulated economy sucked in imports and threw the current account into a deficit of $166 million in the fourth quarter of 1970, the first since 1935. The United States had been the world's biggest exporter since World War II. During the 1960s, its current-account surplus had helped offset the country's capital outflows. So when the current account turned negative, the world began to doubt the adequacy of US gold reserves.

US economic policy had clearly become incompatible with the country's obligation to maintain the dollar's convertibility into gold. Concern grew that the dollar would be devalued, as sterling had been in 1967. In 1970, private capital outflows from the US surged to $6 billion, equivalent to roughly half of all the country's official reserve holdings. In the first quarter of 1971, another $3 billion flowed out. When the US current-account deficit skyrocketed to $812 million in the second quarter, a full-fledged run on the dollar began.

The United States' trading partners and military allies had been willing to hold large quantities of dollars as foreign-exchange reserves, rather than demanding their full conversion into gold. At the end of 1969, those US liabilities to foreign official agencies were roughly equal to the United States' entire official reserve assets—approximately $15 billion. When the Nixon administration launched its aggressive economic stimulus program in 1970, the overall balance-of-payments position deteriorated drastically, partly because of the weakening current account, but much more as a result of capital flight. By the third quarter of 1971, US liabilities to foreign official agencies had shot up to $46 billion, nearly four times the amount of US reserves, which by then had fallen to less than $12 billion. The conversion of even a quarter of those liabilities would have left the US with no gold reserves at all. Therefore, by the time Nixon suspended the convertibility of dollars into gold, he really had no alternative. The collapse of the Bretton Woods system had become inevitable the moment his administration decided to reflate the US economy with tax cuts and lower interest rates in 1970.

If there were a hell for economic-policy transgressors, Lyndon Johnson and Richard Nixon would spend eternity together in one of its small, dark chambers.

Floating money

Nixon's announcement of the suspension of dollar convertibility into gold on 15 August 1971 created panic throughout the world's financial markets. Dollar convertibility had been the cornerstone of the entire Bretton Woods system. When the dollar ceased to be convertible into gold, it called into question not only the value of the dollar itself, but the value of all the other currencies pegged to it.

Over the next four months, a series of high-level conferences and intense negotiations was held, culminating in the Smithsonian Agreement of December 1971. That meeting of the finance ministers and central-bank governors of the Group of Ten leading industrial nations, produced a 7.9% devaluation of the dollar relative to gold (i.e. the value of gold rose from $35 to $38 an ounce) and a corresponding upward adjustment of the currencies of other countries relative to the dollar. However, US officials would not agree to resume the convertibility of dollars into gold.

It was hoped that this general realignment would return the US balance of payments to equilibrium and allow the global economy to function within the Bretton Woods par-value system as before. Those hopes were short-lived. During 1972, the US current-account deficit continued to deteriorate sharply, further stoking anxieties about US economic policies. In February 1973, currency speculation and large cross-border capital flows forced a second devaluation of the dollar—only 14 months after the first. Combined, the two devaluations resulted in a 15.5% appreciation of the other OECD currencies relative to the dollar (23% if the Canadian dollar is excluded).

At that point the Bretton Woods par-value system disintegrated. The end came in early March, when Paul Volcker, then Under Secretary of the Treasury for Monetary Affairs, announced that the United States was prepared to accept a system of floating exchange rates. Leaders of the European Community, supported by the IMF's managing director, Pierre-Paul Schweitzer, fought to hold the par-value system together. They could not conceive of an international trading system in which the currencies of all countries were in constant flux relative to one another and to gold. Valéry Giscard d'Estaing, then the French Minister of Economy and Finance, characterized flexible exchange rates as "a sort of monetary LSD".[6]

Nevertheless, once it became clear that the United States had no intention of defending the par value of the dollar, talks collapsed. Six core countries of the European Community (Belgium, Denmark, France, Germany, Luxembourg and the Netherlands) reacted by agreeing to limit the fluctuations of their currencies relative to one another within a tight band, thus laying the foundations for eventual monetary union under the euro.

All hope of reestablishing the Bretton Woods system ended in January 1974, when the "ad hoc Committee of the (IMF) Board of Governors on Reform of the International Monetary System and Related Issues" abandoned the reform effort at its meeting in Rome. By that time the first oil shock, itself a consequence of the breakdown of the system, had made any near-term return to fixed exchange rates impossible.

Conclusion

The Bretton Woods system collapsed in 1971 because the United States refused to make the necessary economic adjustments to bring its balance of payments back into equilibrium. Instead, President Nixon closed the "gold window" at the US Treasury to stop the flood of US gold reserves leaving the country. That act simultaneously destroyed the international monetary system and severed the last real link between paper dollars and gold. A quarter of a century of stability and prosperity under the Bretton Woods system was over. Henceforth, money would be worth only as much as currency speculators determined it to be worth. In the post–Bretton Woods world, it gradually became apparent that there was no limit to how much money could be created. Moreover, as time went by, it also became clear there were fewer and fewer constraints on the number of financial entities that could create it. The new, volatile age of paper money had begun.

---

[6] The quote is taken from *The International Monetary Fund 1966-1971*, vol. 1: "Narrative", by Margaret Garritsen de Vries. She referenced "Statement by the Governor of the World Bank for France, Summary Proceedings, 1969, p. 60."

Chapter 6
The international debt crisis: Phases one through three

Neither a borrower nor a lender be;
For loan oft loses both itself and friend,
And borrowing dulls the edge of husbandry.

William Shakespeare, *Hamlet*

The loose-cannon credit crisis

Starting in the 1970s, international credit flows began to destabilize the global economy. One country after another was plunged into crisis as dollar-denominated credit from abroad produced short-term booms followed by longer-lasting busts. Each crisis threatened the solvency of the international financial system; and in each crisis the large international banks that had made the loans were bailed out from their mistakes by rescue programs directed from Washington. The United States not only tolerated those credit flows, it encouraged them by promoting capital-account liberalization in those countries where it could exert influence. By bailing out the banks each time, Washington rewarded imprudent risk-taking and thereby encouraged the next round of foolish lending. The sums at stake grew from one decade to the next, so that each successive crisis required a larger bailout than the one before.

The Latin American debt crisis, the Mexican peso crisis, the Asian crisis, and the contagion that subsequently spread to Russia and Brazil, are generally viewed as separate, compartmentalized episodes. In reality, they are all part of one long crisis caused by unregulated cross-border credit flows. In the mid-1970s, enormous amounts of dollar-denominated credit began sloshing around the world. Like a loose cannon on a ship, the credit would reel from one side of the world when economic conditions tipped one way—wreaking havoc all along its path—and then rocket back across the deck of the world economy in another direction, causing more chaos, when macroeconomic conditions began to tilt in a different direction. International credit broke loose in the 1960s owing to the failure of US policymakers to control the Eurodollar market and the US banks that dominated it. By the late 1970s, it had produced its first destabilizing economic boom, in Latin America.

Recycling the petrodollars

The Eurodollar market was well established by the time the Arab oil embargo in October 1973 set off the world's first oil shock. Oil prices, having traded between $2.82 per barrel and $3.56 per barrel for more than 20 years, rose to $10.10 per barrel by the beginning of 1974 and to $11.20 per barrel one year later. That threefold increase could not have been sustained under a fixed exchange-rate system that did not tolerate large-scale capital flows. In the oil-importing nations, gold outflows would have caused a contraction of the money supply, a severe recession and a collapse in demand for oil. Oil prices would have crashed in the ensuing glut.

But in the post-Bretton Woods world of fiat money and floating exchange rates, the Eurodollar market served as the conduit through which "petrodollars" were "recycled" from the oil-exporting nations to the oil-importing nations, allowing the balance of payments of both the surplus and the deficit countries to balance.

The economies of the oil-exporting nations were too small to absorb the riches that sky-high oil prices generated. Similarly, their banks were too small to intermediate deposits on that scale. As a result, dollar-denominated oil income began to flow into the Eurodollar market as deposits. Those inflows presented a challenge for the US banks that dominated the business. Deposits without borrowers were an unprofitable burden. The solution quickly became apparent: the petrodollars could be lent to the oil-importing nations, who were desperate for finance. Sovereign loans were viewed as safe—"nations don't go bankrupt," as Walter Wriston, head of Citibank, reportedly said. And so it was arranged: the oil exporters deposited their petrodollars into (mostly) US banks operating in the Eurodollar market in London, and those banks lent the money to oil-importing nations, primarily in Latin America. The capital inflows set off an economic boom. In 1980, the Mexican and Brazilian economies each expanded by more than 9%.

By 1982, the nine largest US banks had extended credit to Latin American nations equivalent to 177% of their capital.[1] That was the year Mexico defaulted. By 1984, every country in Latin America save Colombia and Paraguay had rescheduled its external debt.[2]

Phase 1: The Latin American debt crisis

The catalyst for the Latin American debt crisis was Fed Chairman Paul Volcker. In the early 1980s, when Volcker pushed US interest rates to crippling heights to crush inflation, he also crushed the countries that had borrowed petrodollars. High US interest rates caused a severe global recession, which in turn caused commodity prices around the world to drop. Developing nations were hit twice: once by high interest rates, and again by a plunge in their revenues from commodity sales. It simply was not possible for them to service their external debts. When these facts became known, foreign bankers took fright and ran for the exits, making it impossible for many countries to roll over existing loans.

The amounts involved were large and the threat they posed to the international financial system was very real. In 1982, the gross external liabilities of Mexico, Brazil and Argentina were $91 billion, $86 billion and $38 billion, respectively. Counterparty exposure meant that one bank failure could bring down many others in a domino effect. Therefore, once the Western banks had made the loans, it seemed their governments had no choice but to go in and clean up the mess if an economic disaster was to be averted.

---

[1] Harold James, *International Monetary Cooperation Since Bretton Woods* (Oxford University Press, 1996), p. 399.
[2] *Ibid*, 388.

Crises of that scale were not then an everyday occurrence, as they seem to have become today. In fact, the major US banks had not faced such a threat since the Great Depression. When Mexico announced on 18 August 1982 that it would no longer service its foreign-currency debt, a broad coalition was quickly assembled to provide assistance. The Federal Reserve provided Mexico with swap lines worth $700 million. The US Strategic Petroleum Reserve paid $1 billion in advance for oil. The US Department of Agriculture provided $1 billion in credit guarantees. And the US Treasury established a $1 billion credit line. The Bank for International Settlements kicked in $925 billion in short-term credit. France, Israel, and Spain provided $550 billion in swap lines. The IMF put in place a $3.75 billion extended arrangement. Finally, commercial banks were "bailed in", or pressured to provide an additional $5 billion in new loans. These arrangements were all completed before the end of 1982.[3]

Brazil came next, receiving a $5 billion facility from the IMF in November 1982 and $2.5 billion in support from foreign governments in 1984. Argentina entered an IMF arrangement for SDR1.5 billion in January 1983 (of which only SDR600 million was drawn). It also received $1.5 billion from foreign banks and another $1.4 billion from the IMF in December 1984.

The list of incapacitated debtor nations was long. By the end of 1984, 30 nations had begun to renegotiate their commercial bank debt.[4]

The rescue packages came with strings attached. The recipient nations were required to implement "structural adjustment" programs designed by the IMF. These typically included requirements to reduce the fiscal deficit, tighten monetary policy and liberalise trade and finance.

This Latin American debt crisis was not quickly resolved. It persisted through the 1980s and beyond. The IMF provided a number of other loans during the decade. In 1985, the Baker Plan attempted to structure a comprehensive solution. This involved a series of new loans from commercial banks and multilateral development agencies, to be combined with further structural adjustments on the part of the debtor countries. But the plan failed to resolve the crisis because it only added additional debt without restoring economic strength. It was not until 1989—when the US Brady Plan provided a mechanism for some debt relief by allowing banks to convert debts in

---

[3] James Boughton, *Silent Revolution: The International Monetary Fund 1979-1989* (IMF, 2001), p. 293.

[4] Harold James, *International Monetary Cooperation Since Bretton Woods* (Oxford University Press, 1996), p. 389.

developing nations into tradable securities—that the Latin American debt crisis began to abate.

Figure 45 provides a partial list of IMF loans from 1984 to 1989. These were supplemented by emergency support from many other sources.

Figure 45

IMF DISBURSEMENTS, 1984-89

(SDR MILLION)

1984		1987	
Brazil	1,370	Argentina	970
Chile	216	Chile	225
Hungary	297	Indonesia	463
Korea	504	Mexico	600
Mexico	903	Philippines	123
Yugoslavia	280	All countries	3,300
All countries	4,900		
1985		**1988**	
Argentina	984	Argentina	399
Chile	196	Brazil	365
Korea	136	Chile	150
Mexico	296	Hungary	165
Philippines	318	Mexico	350
Thailand	335	Philippines	70
Yugoslavia	225	Yugoslavia	122
All countries	4,000	All countries	2,700
1986		**1989**	
Argentina	473	Algeria	471
Chile	250	Argentina	184
China	598	Chile	139
Korea	120	Hungary	50
Mexico	741	Mexico	943
Philippines	229	Philippines	235
Thailand	111	Venezuela	759
Yugoslavia	135	All countries	3,500
All countries	3,800		

Source: IMF

During the second half of the 1970s, petrodollar loans set off an economic boom in the borrowing nations and generated impressive profits for the lenders. However, the bust that followed meant a "lost decade" for Latin America and a near-death experience for some of the world's largest banks. Excessive credit flows had dangerously destabilized both the debtors and the creditors, and large-scale emergency financing from industrialized nations was required to prevent a worldwide collapse of the financial sector and quite possibly a global depression. Very little seems to have been learned from the experience. The same series of events recurred twice during the 1990s. The

97

costs became greater with each round.

Phase 2: The peso crisis

The second round of the loose-cannon credit crisis began only five years after the Brady Plan had palliated the first. By the early 1990s, international banks had been able to reduce their exposure to the crisis countries to manageable levels. Considerable regulatory forbearance had given banks the time and considerable foreign-government-directed lending into Latin America had given them the means to extricate themselves. As Harold James put it: "It is difficult to avoid the conclusion that at least in some cases, commercial banks were being repaid from resources made available by creditor governments and multilateral institutions."[5]

When negotiations began in 1991 to establish a free-trade zone between Mexico, the United States and Canada, private-sector credit began flowing back into Mexico. Those inflows contributed to a deterioration in Mexico's current-account deficit. The Mexican government funded that deficit by selling government bonds, initially denominated in pesos. Later, however, as doubts emerged over the stability of the peso, the government sold *tesobonos*, short-term debt whose value was indexed to the dollar. By 1994, Mexico's current-account deficit had risen to 7% of GDP. Since every country's balance of payments must balance, inflows of foreign capital also amounted to 7% of Mexican GDP in that year.

During the second half of 1994, panic began to creep back into the hearts of foreign creditors. It became increasingly difficult for the government to arrange new loans or even to roll over existing debt. Moreover, the Mexican central bank had been forced to spend billions of dollars out of its foreign-exchange reserves defending the value of the peso, which had been stable at around three to the dollar since 1991. By the end of 1994, the central bank had only $6 billion left in reserves, with the prospect of $30 billion in foreign debt coming due in 1995— $10 billion in the first quarter alone.[6] Mexico was once again in crisis.

The peso crisis should not be viewed as entirely new and distinct from Mexico's crisis of the 1980s, however. After all, Mexico did not repay its last Brady bond until 2003. Rather, this crisis was merely a continuation of the

---

[5] *Ibid*, 398
[6] Robert E. Rubin, chap. 1 in *In An Uncertain World* (Random House, 2003).

earlier one—only now it was on a bigger scale and posed even greater danger to the global financial system. It also presented considerable political risks to the Clinton administration in the United States. The North American Free Trade Agreement (NAFTA), which had been forced on the American public against its adamant opposition, had gone into effect only at the beginning of 1994. Had Mexico defaulted on a very large amount of foreign debt just one year later, it would not only have embarrassed President Clinton but reduced the chances of further trade liberalization.

In his autobiography, Robert Rubin provides a frank and fascinating account of how he, as Treasury Secretary in the Clinton administration—with the support of Deputy Treasury Secretary Larry Summers, Deputy Treasury Assistant Secretary for International Monetary and Financial Policy Timothy Geithner and Fed Chairman Alan Greenspan, and with the full backing of President Clinton—defied US public opinion, the will of the Congress, and the leaders of other G7 nations to bail out Mexico in early 1995.

Direct support from the US government was required because it was feared that the IMF's resources were insufficient to resolve a crisis on the scale Mexico—and its creditors—were facing. Congress, however, refused to provide the funding. It had paid a high price in terms of popularity for passing NAFTA, and it was enraged by the whole fiasco. A *Los Angeles Times* poll found that 79% of the public was opposed to the rescue package.

When Congress could not muster the votes to pass the Mexican Stabilization Act, Rubin ignored it and drove through a $40 billion bailout without its consent. The United States put in $20 billion, the IMF provided $17.8 billion, and another $2.2 billion came in bits and pieces from here and there. For America's share, Rubin tapped the Exchange Stabilization Fund (ESF), which had been established to help stabilize the dollar when the Unites States devalued the dollar relative to gold during the Depression. When the use of the ESF was announced, according to Rubin's memoirs, "some in Congress were furious that we'd made the largest nonmilitary international commitment by the US government since the Marshall Plan without their consent". Sentiment on Wall Street was no doubt more supportive—given the massive losses the bankers would have suffered without it.

The package also required overcoming some resistance from the IMF, or, more accurately, the other shareholders of the IMF. Having more voting rights than any other country, the United States, through the Treasury Department, dominates the decision-making process at the IMF. In this case, the IMF had originally committed to make $7.8 billion in loans available to Mexico. Later, when the resources available for the total rescue package appeared too small to stem the capital flight, managing director Michel Camdessus promised to come up with another $10 billion, apparently without consulting representatives of the other industrialized countries on the IMF's board. Rubin explained:

> Because the decision was made when it was the middle of the night in Europe, we didn't have time to consult most of our Group of Seven (G-7) allies in advance of announcing our new proposal. The next day, they were furious at Camdessus for offering another $10 billion without consulting them, and very upset with us too.[7]

The following month, under pressure from his European directors, Camdessus attempted to back out of the commitment for the extra $10 billion, but Rubin pushed him into going ahead, and the funds were provided.

The bailout package did the trick. Mexico was able to repay its government debt that matured in 1995, foreign investors regained their nerve and stopped withdrawing credit lines, and the emergency loans were repaid by January 1997. This remarkable turnaround in Mexico's ability to pay its creditors had a great deal to do with the 70% devaluation of the peso relative to the dollar during 1994 and 1995. As a consequence of that collapse of its currency, Mexico's balance of trade with the United States flipped from a deficit of $1.7 billion in 1993 to a surplus of $15.8 billion in 1995 and $17.5 billion in 1996.

Figure 46

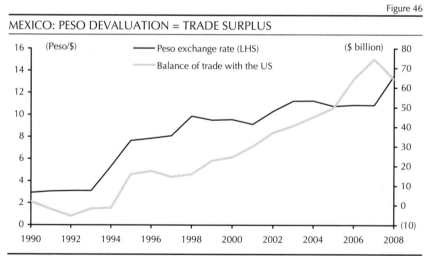

MEXICO: PESO DEVALUATION = TRADE SURPLUS

Source: IMF statistical databases, US Census Bureau trade statistics

Thus currency devaluations were a second crucial component of all the

[7] Ibid.

rescue efforts organized by Washington and executed by the IMF. Devaluations allowed the crisis-affected countries to repay their emergency loans by building up large trade surpluses with the United States. As time passed, the US trade deficit grew so large that it became the driver of economic growth for the world, not only for countries overcome by credit crises. Mexico serves as a case in point. In the years following 1995, the peso depreciated by a further 43% against the dollar, and in 2008 Mexico's trade surplus with the United States had grown to $64 billion.

Rubin justified the 1995 bailout on the grounds that a Mexican default could have caused international investors to withdraw credit from other developing countries. But that is exactly what should have happened. Time after time and in one country after another, experience demonstrated that a large influx of foreign credit produced a boom-bust-bailout sequence. Had Washington not intervened each time, reckless lenders would have suffered losses and become more responsible—or at least had less money left to lend. The bailouts encouraged and rewarded reckless lending. Rubin's Treasury Department recognized that it risked creating moral hazard by acting, but feared that if it failed to act, a new global debt crisis would erupt. Indeed, the Treasury believed that financial innovations during the preceding decade meant that a new crisis in the 1990s would be worse than the one in the 1980s. Yet by the same logic, how could it not have understood that the risk of collapse would become greater each year so long as credit flows and financial-product innovations were not restrained?

Phase 3: The Asian crisis and contagion

Well before the peso phase had been contained, the next phase of the international debt crisis had already become inevitable. Excessive inflows of dollar-denominated credit had begun to destabilize large parts of Asia during the second half of the 1980s. The pattern was the same as in Latin America. Too much dollar borrowing fuelled very rapid growth—the economies of Thailand, Indonesia and Korea grew by an average 6–8% a year from 1990 to 1996. But the foreign capital also created excess capacity, asset-price bubbles and worryingly large current-account deficits.

In this, the Asian-crisis phase, the catalyst that put lenders to flight was a devaluation of the Thai baht in July 1997. Initially, Washington was not particularly concerned about Thailand. A $17 billion bailout package was arranged in August but the United States did not contribute to it. The stakes rose considerably when the Indonesian economy collapsed next. Indonesia received a $23 billion bailout package to which the United States did contribute. When Korea broke down, the threat to the global financial system had undeniably become systemic. Korea had become the world's 11th-largest economy by borrowing aggressively from abroad to fund rapid industrial expansion. Credit flight brought Korea to the brink of default, and in December it received a $55 billion rescue package.

Figure 47

IMF DISBURSEMENTS, 1994-99
(SDR million)

1994		1997	
Argentina	612	Argentina	321
Bulgaria	233	**Indonesia**	**2,201**
Pakistan	123	**Korea**	**8,200**
Poland	640	Philippines	509
Russia	**1,078**	**Russia**	**1,467**
Turkey	235	**Thailand**	**1,800**
Ukraine	249	All countries	16,100
All countries	4,770		
1995		**1998**	
Argentina	1,559	**Brazil**	**3,419**
Mexico	**8,758**	**Indonesia**	**4,254**
Pakistan	134	**Korea**	**5,850**
Russia	**3,594**	**Russia**	**4,600**
Turkey	225	Philippines	538
Ukraine	788	**Thailand**	**500**
Zambia	652	All countries	20,600
All countries	16,967		
1996		**1999**	
Argentina	548	**Brazil**	**4,450**
Pakistan	107	**Indonesia**	**1,011**
Russia	**2,588**	**Korea**	**362**
Ukraine	536	**Mexico**	**1,034**
Venezuela	350	Pakistan	400
All countries	5,300	Philippines	253
		Russia	**471**
		Thailand	**200**
		Turkey	583
		Ukraine	467
		All countries	10,000

Source: IMF

These rescue packages were arranged by the IMF and came with the typical IMF strings attached. In order to bring about "structural adjustment" in the afflicted countries, the IMF imposed conditions on the loans it made available. The IMF "conditionality" demanded that recipient countries:

- ❑ Increase interest rates
- ❑ Tighten fiscal policy
- ❑ Close failed banks
- ❑ Stop directed lending
- ❑ Improve transparency
- ❑ Open the financial sector to foreign competition.

The consensus opinion now is that most of these measures made the Asian crisis worse rather than better. The Koreans, for instance, still refer to the 1998 economic collapse in their country as the "IMF crisis". And when the fourth phase of the international debt crisis overwhelmed the United States 10 years later, American policymakers forgot all about the conditions they had pressed the IMF to impose on the countries affected by previous crises, and addressed the US crisis with radically different measures.

Currency devaluations ended the Asian crisis by allowing an export-led recovery. During 1997, the Thai baht, the Indonesian rupiah and the Korean won were devalued by 46–50% relative to the dollar. As a result, between 1996 and 1998, Thailand's current-account balance swung from a deficit of 8% of GDP to a surplus of 13%; Indonesia's current account improved from a deficit of 3% of GDP to a surplus of 4%; and Korea's flipped from a 4% deficit to an 11% surplus.

But the crisis did not end in Asia. The contagion spread. Next, it struck Russia. In July 1998, the IMF arranged a $23 billion rescue package, but suspended it soon afterwards with only $5 billion disbursed. This was because the Russian government was unable to comply with the conditions set out in the loan agreement. When Russia defaulted on its foreign-held debt in mid-August, the crisis reached America for the first time. The Russian default had created a highly improbable "black swan" event in the bond market that inflicted such losses on Long Term Capital Management (LTCM) that its survival was in doubt. That hedge fund's extraordinary level of leverage and unfathomable derivatives positions meant its demise had the potential to annihilate much of Wall Street.

The vortex of the international credit crisis now shifted from the periphery of the global economy to the center. The crisis no longer merely involved small developing countries being overwhelmed by excessive credit inflows. From that time, the United States itself began to be overwhelmed by foreign credit. (The

North American debt crisis is the subject of Chapter 8.) The rest of this chapter considers the lessons that should have been learned from the first three phases of the international credit crisis.

A morally hazardous flow of funds

There are still debates as to whether these three crises were liquidity crises or structural economic crises. In reality, they were both: in each case, foreign liquidity came into the country and distorted the economy, then rushed out (in a panic of capital flight), leaving the economy in a bloated and unsustainable form, with excess capacity, imploding asset-price bubbles and ruined banks.

Each of the three crises followed the same pattern:

1. Foreign creditors lent money that created a short-term economic boom.

2. Capital flight began when it became clear those loans could not be repaid. At that point, the boom turned into bust and a balance-of-payments crisis arose.

3. The IMF and other foreign lenders (directed from Washington) extended emergency loans to the crisis countries that made it possible for the original lenders to withdraw their money.

4. The countries in crisis devalued their currencies and developed a large current-account surplus (most often with the United States) that allowed them to repay the emergency loans from the IMF.

So in the end, American consumers made everybody whole. The original lenders walked away with a profit; IMF staffers were well compensated for their hard work; the crisis countries were more competitive post-devaluation; and Americans ended up with a lot of new junk in their closets. And afterwards, the entire process began again in some other corner of the world.

The lessons the bankers learned through repeated experience was that they could lend money almost anywhere in the world without too much concern for any particular country's economic fundamentals, because the IMF would always be there to bail them out when the time came.

Unfortunately, after each round of the international debt crisis the US current-account deficit became larger, leaving the United States deeper and deeper in debt to the rest of the world. Eventually the global imbalances created by this process became so great they could no longer be sustained.

When they came unwound, the New Depression began.

Therefore, by intervening to prevent an international banking crisis in the 1980s and again in the 1990s, the IMF encouraged bankers and other creditors to continue their destabilizing cross-border lending. In other words, the IMF's bailouts created moral hazard. It therefore bears part of the responsibility for bringing about the current crisis in the global economy. Figure 48 shows how IMF lending grew from one round of the crisis to the next.

Figure 48

IMF: RESERVE POSITION IN THE FUND

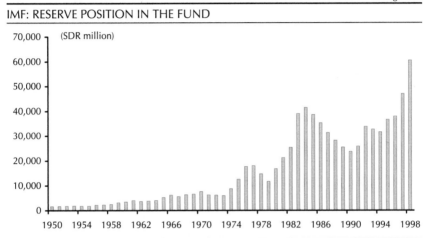

Source: IMF International Financial Statistics database

Conclusion

The crisis that began in Latin America in the 1980s, re-erupted in Mexico in 1994, engulfed Asia in 1997 and spread to Russia the next year, hit New York in September 1998. In its earlier phases, this loose-cannon credit crisis had posed serious medium-term threats (of fluctuating severity) to the solvency of the world's largest banks. But when genius failed at Long Term Capital Management,[8] the global financial system was confronted with the prospect of immediate and complete collapse. When US policymakers were forced to cut interest rates to avert the meltdown, they lost control over the US economy. Consequently, over the following decade the United States itself was to become

---

[8] Roger Lowenstein, *When Genus Failed* (Random House, 2000).

overwhelmed by foreign capital inflows, just as its smaller Latin American neighbors had been in the 1970s. Foreign capital blew the US economy into a bubble and in 2008 that bubble burst.

Unregulated cross-border credit flows, encouraged by moral-hazard-inducing IMF bailouts, were a key element behind the global economic disequilibrium that eventually produced the New Depression. Until international capital flows are bought under control, they are certain to continue destabilizing the global economy.

Chapter 7
The deficit decades:
The 1970s, 1980s and
1990s

Reagan proved deficits don't matter.

Vice President Dick Cheney[1]

When the link between the dollar and gold was severed in 1971, it marked such a break with the past that no one at that time could be certain what the consequences would be. In retrospect, it can now be seen that the triumph of paper money and floating exchange rates in the early 1970s radically changed the parameters within which the US economy operated. Four decades ago, the idea that the United States would accumulate trillions of dollars in budget and trade deficits over the course of the next generation would have appeared to be lunacy. But that is exactly what happened. By the mid-1970s, massive budget deficits had become the norm rather than the exception. Ten years later, equally shocking trade deficits

---

[1] Vice President Dick Cheney as quoted by Former Treasury Secretary Paul O'Neill in his memoirs by Ron Suskind, *The Price of Loyalty* (Simon & Schuster, 2004), p. 291.

developed. The emergence of those twin deficits has done incalculable harm to the US economy. This chapter traces their rise and impact across three decades as they brought the United States to the brink of ruin.

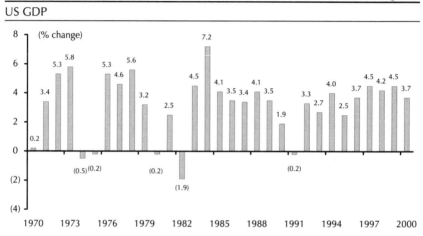

Figure 49

US GDP

(% change)

Source: Bureau of Economic Analysis

The inflationary 1970s

Following the breakdown of Bretton Woods, inflation and very large US budget deficits were the two economic issues that dominated the 1970s. Of the two, inflation was the more immediate threat. Ultimately however, budget deficits proved to be much more intractable and consequently much more pernicious.

Inflation

The United States experienced four waves of inflation between 1966 and 1980, each larger and more destabilizing than the one before.

The waves of inflation came in two phases. The two waves of the first phase were of the old-fashioned kind, where too much government spending caused the economy to overheat and created domestic bottlenecks in industrial capacity and labor availability that drove up prices. The first wave of inflation peaked at 3.9% in 1966. The second peaked in 1970, with an inflation rate of 6.4%.

Figure 50

US CONSUMER PRICE INDEX

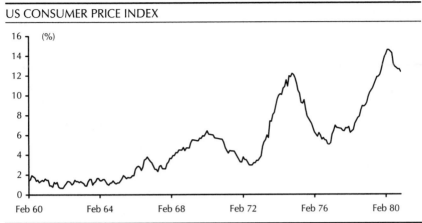

Source: Federal Reserve Bank of St. Louis

The second phase was driven by new and much more virulent forces. It had two new components. First, shortly after Bretton Woods collapsed, the dollar was devalued twice, in December 1971 and February 1973. It plunged again in 1977 (see Figure 51).

Figure 51

THE DOLLAR SINKS

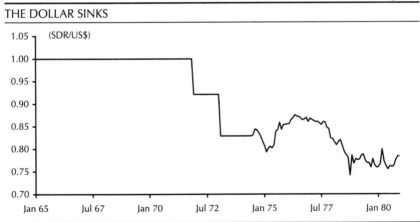

Source: IMF International Financial Statistics database

Each drop was a consequence of the deterioration in the US current account. The devaluations in 1971 and 1973 were discussed in Chapter 5. The sharp depreciation in 1977 was brought on by a current-account deficit that year that up until then was the largest seen in the 20th Century. These drops in the dollar caused a spike in global commodity prices (see Figure 52).

Figure 52

CRB COMMODITY PRICE INDEX

Source: Bloomberg

The second new component involved central banks. Capital flight out of the dollar, beginning in 1970, forced central banks outside the United States to print their own money and buy dollars to defend their currency pegs. This opened a new chapter in global monetary history, in which paper-money creation on a previously unimaginable scale would transform the world. That explosion of money creation can be seen in the increase in total foreign-exchange reserves (see Figure 53). It exacerbated the pressure on global commodity prices. Surging commodity prices, combined with domestic bottlenecks in the US economy, drove the US inflation rate into double digits. Thus, the third wave of inflation peaked at 12.2% in late 1974 and the fourth wave peaked at 14.6% in April 1980.

There is a tendency to blame the high rates of inflation during the 1970s on the decade's two oil shocks. Figure 52 demonstrates that this is misguided. After many years of price stability during the Bretton Woods era, commodity prices shot up after the end of 1971 when the dollar was first devalued. Oil prices did not rise until the Arab oil embargo during the Yom Kippur War of October 1973. Commodity prices again moved higher when the dollar fell in 1977, yet the second oil shock did not occur until 1979, after the overthrow of the Shah of Iran. The surge in oil prices certainly exacerbated inflation during the 1970s, but it did not cause it.

Next, consider the sevenfold increase in total foreign-exchange reserves during the decade (see Figure 53). Foreign-exchange reserves are held by central banks, which acquire foreign exchange by "printing" their own currency and using it to buy foreign currency, usually in order to prevent their own currency from appreciating.

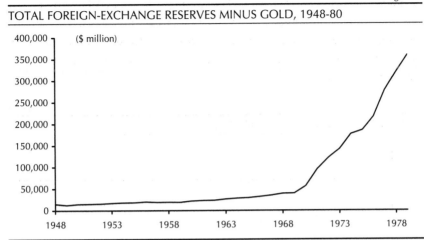

Figure 53

TOTAL FOREIGN-EXCHANGE RESERVES MINUS GOLD, 1948-80

Source: IMF International Financial Statistics database

During the final years of the Bretton Woods par-value system, capital flight out of the dollar put upward pressure on the value of many other currencies. That forced a number of central banks to buy dollars to keep their currencies pegged. To finance the acquisition of those dollars, they created paper money. Consequently, the amount of paper money rose sharply beginning in 1969. Paper-money creation on such a large scale was a complete break from the past. There can be no doubt that it played a significant role in the inflationary pressures that destabilized the world economy throughout that period.

But as extensive and unprecedented as it was, the paper-money creation of the 1970s gave only a hint of what was to come in the following decades. Foreign-exchange reserves would expand another twentyfold over the next 27 years, producing the "global savings glut" that inflated the worldwide economic bubble.

Budget deficits

During 1973, with US inflation accelerating fast, the Fed doubled the federal funds rate to 10.75%, which combined with fiscal constraint threw the country into its worst recession since the 1950s. GDP contracted by 0.5% in 1974 and by another 0.2% the following year. Tax revenues plummeted and the budget deficit shot up to 3.2% of GDP, the largest shortfall since World War II.

US budget deficits had exceeded 2% of GDP only three times since the war: in 1959, 1968 and 1971 (2.5%, 2.8% and 2.0%, respectively). After 1975, however, the budget deficit would fall below 2.5% of GDP only once during the next 20 years. Between 1975 and 1995, it averaged 3.5% of GDP a year. Budget deficits on that scale reflected a fundamental change in the management and the nature of the US economy. Over the following decades, the economy was transformed by government deficit spending and by the cumulative debt that spending brought about.

Figure 54

US BUDGET BALANCE AS A % OF GDP, 1960-80

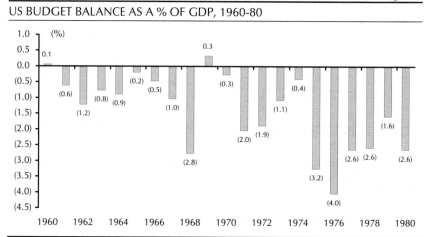

Source: Bureau of Economic Analysis (GDP), White House Office of Management and Budget (budget)

In 1975, however, no one would have expected the large budget deficits to persist for the simple reason that no one could imagine how such large deficits could be financed or how high rates of inflation could be avoided, given so much government spending. For instance, if the government borrowed 3.5% of GDP, that meant 3.5% of GDP was no longer available for the private sector to borrow. In other words, government borrowing would "crowd out" the private sector. It was understood that government borrowing on such a scale would inevitably push up interest rates, and that high interest rates would make private investment unprofitable. It was also understood that so much government spending would exacerbate the bottlenecks in the domestic economy, causing even more inflation.

That is how economists and policymakers understood the world in the 1970s. As a result, the outlook in the United States at the time seemed distinctly gloomy. Inflation and recessions were not supposed to occur simultaneously—yet during the 1970s they did. A sense of "malaise", as President Jimmy Carter described it, descended over the nation.

The 1980s: The end of crowding out

The American mood swung from malaise to mania during the 1980s. By flouting almost every aspect of economic orthodoxy, the Reagan administration created an economic boom in the United States that spread around the world. During the first half of the decade, the US current-account deficit exploded. Perversely, that was just what the economy needed (at least from a short-term perspective). Those trade deficits made it possible for the government to stimulate the economy through enormous budget deficits without pushing up prices. Two deficits—the twin deficits, as they were known—turned out to be much better than one. The policy of accepting twin deficits took the world quite some distance further down the road to ruin.

Crushing inflation

High inflation is a curse. It takes from those who save and gives to those who are in debt. Socially, it is destabilizing. And it feeds on itself. Once people expect prices to rise, they demand higher wages. Higher wages then drive prices higher. When US inflation moved into double digits in the 1970s, something had to be done about it. President Carter put the interest of his country ahead of his own and appointed Paul Volcker as Fed chairman a year before the next presidential election. Volcker crushed inflation by pushing bank prime lending rates above 20%. Unemployment rose to 11%, the economy withered, and Carter was not reelected. Inflation, however, ceased to undermine the foundations of American prosperity.

Figure 55

EFFECTIVE FEDERAL FUNDS RATE

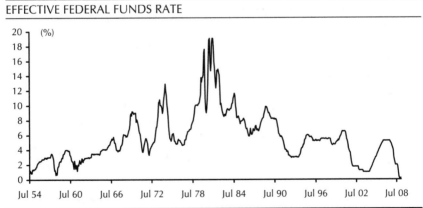

Source: Federal Reserve Bank of St. Louis

From a peak of 14.6% in April 1980, consumer price inflation plunged to 2.4% three years later.

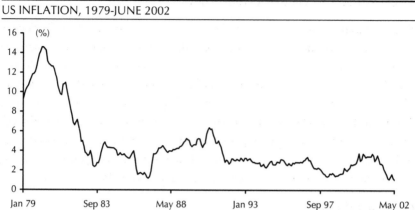

Figure 56

US INFLATION, 1979-JUNE 2002

Source: Federal Reserve Bank of St. Louis

The Fed's victory over inflation was a complete success. But there were unintended consequences. The high interest rates required to crush inflation attracted so much foreign money into US debt instruments that the dollar recovered all the ground it had lost since its first devaluation in 1971—and then some. Thus the cure for one crisis precipitated the next. High interest rates were necessary to kill inflation. But when the dollar shot up as a result, the overvalued currency made US industry uncompetitive in the global market. That set in train the deindustrialization of America.

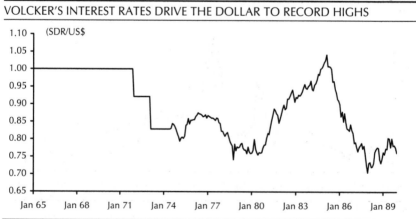

Figure 57

VOLCKER'S INTEREST RATES DRIVE THE DOLLAR TO RECORD HIGHS

Source: IMF International Financial Statistics database

Double deficits

The price for ending inflation in the United States was a severe recession. Unemployment soared to 11% and the economy contracted by 0.2% in 1980 and 1.9% in 1982—by far the worst economic showing since World War II. President Reagan did not interfere with the Fed's tight monetary policy. However, in 1981 his administration slashed taxes. Over the next five years, the economy revived thanks to a string of huge budget deficits: 3.9% of GDP in 1982, 5.9% in 1983, and an average of 4.9% between 1982 and 1986—the biggest peacetime deficits on record. President Reagan's "Morning in America" economic boom dawned as a result of a vast expansion of government debt.

Figure 58

US BUDGET DEFICIT AS A % OF GDP, 1970-90

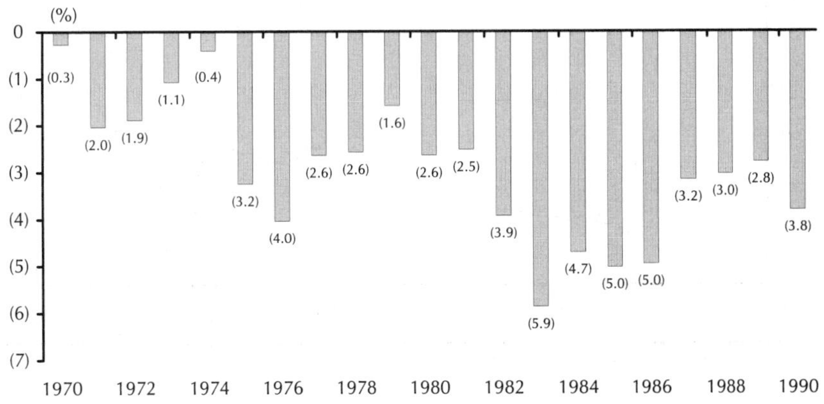

Source: Bureau of Economic Analysis (GDP), White House Office of Management and Budget (budget)

In an earlier, more orthodox age, such large budget deficits would have pushed interest rates even higher. They would also have ignited the next round of inflation as increased government spending encountered bottlenecks in the domestic economy. As it turned out, however, in the post–Bretton Woods era the economy was no longer constrained as it had been in the past. Foreign money funded the large budget deficits and foreign imports circumvented the domestic bottlenecks. That was a profound change.

Volcker's high interest rates attracted more than enough money from abroad to finance the massive budget deficits. At the same time, a surge in imports kept inflation in check. Between the first quarter of 1983 and the end of 1984, imports into the US jumped by 40%. Therefore, beginning in the early 1980s, a sharp jump in imports made it possible for the government to stimulate the economy with large budget deficits without worrying about inflationary consequences. It appeared to be a free lunch. The US could pay for its imports with dollars, and the dollars were no longer convertible into anything except more paper dollars. This created a new economic paradigm in which fiscal stimulus could be used aggressively to support employment and economic growth without hitting capacity constraints that would lead to higher inflation and higher interest rates. The government could now borrow freely without crowding out the private sector.

Figure 59

US IMPORTS VERSUS EXPORTS

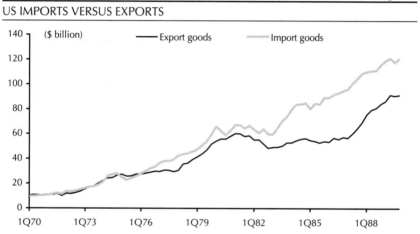

Source: Bureau of Economic Analysis

Any lingering concerns about the size of the US current-account deficit were set aside. Now that the United States did not have to redeem dollars for gold, the current-account deficit no longer seemed so important to US policymakers. And from 1983, it began to balloon. That year, the current-account deficit jumped to 1.1% of GDP. In 1984, it hit 2.4% of GDP. And it peaked in 1987 at the then unprecedented level of 3.4% of GDP, or $161 billion.

The ballooning US current-account deficit ushered in the age of globalization. The more the US imported, the more its trading partners benefited, and the more friends the United States made—or at least bought. Japan boomed. Korea and Taiwan were transformed. Even Thailand, Malaysia and Indonesia, the new Asian Tigers, took off by following a strategy of export-led growth.

Figure 60

US CURRENT-ACCOUNT BALANCE AS A % OF GDP, 1970-90

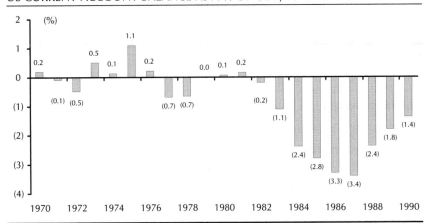

Source: Bureau of Economic Analysis

Within the United States, the surge in imports alleviated the bottlenecks that had caused the high rate of inflation. However, it also created winners and losers. Some segments of society and business benefited, while others suffered. The banking sector, globally competitive manufacturers, the US State Department and consumers all benefited. Labor and the large segment of US industry that could not compete with third-world wage rates suffered. Bankers benefited because the large current-account deficits had to be financed and bankers make money by arranging and providing credit. US industries that could compete in the global marketplace benefited because the more Americans imported, the more money the rest of the world had to buy their products. Those in charge of US foreign policy found that countries with very large trade surpluses with the United States were much more receptive to US foreign-policy initiatives. Finally, consumers benefited from the flood of cheaper foreign-made products, since wage rates in the developing world were up to 95% lower than in the US.

American labor unions, whose demands had become excessive, were devastated by foreign competition and went into terminal decline. Low-value-added manufacturers, such as textile and shoe makers, were gradually wiped out as the tariffs that had protected them were phased out. The benefits to consumers from cheaper imported products were offset by the lower wage rates imposed on labor.

Overall, while the groups benefiting from an increase in imports were more politically powerful than those who lost out, that did not mean that the country as a whole was better off—at least not in the long term. Beginning in the 1980s and accelerating in the 1990s, asset-price inflation in stocks and property underpinned Americans' purchasing power and more than offset the stagnation in US wage rates that resulted from globalization. Over time, rising asset prices became the foundation of US prosperity in place of manufacturing prowess. That transformation of the American economy was only beginning in the 1980s.

The Plaza Accord

The early 1980s were not that far removed from the time before 1971, when currencies were pegged to gold and when trade, by necessity, had to balance. So when the US current-account deficit exploded in the first half of the 1980s, policymakers around the world were horrified. US consumption and imports were causing too much growth and inflation in the rest of the world. US trade deficits meant trade surpluses everywhere else; and those surpluses translated into economic overheating that finance ministers and central bankers found difficult to contain.

Eventually, the massive trade deficits unnerved policymakers in Washington as well. Schooled in classical economic theory, they must have feared the consequences of such large trade imbalances. By 1985, it was universally agreed that something had to be done to rein in the destabilizing US trade deficits. In that year, economic and monetary officials from the five largest industrialized countries met at the Plaza Hotel in New York City. In the resulting Plaza Accord, they agreed that the dollar would be devalued to bring the US current account back closer to balance. Over the next two years, the dollar fell by 50% against the yen and the mark. The Plaza Accord achieved its goals. US import growth slowed, export growth accelerated very impressively from mid-1987, and by 1991 the US current account had returned to balance. The growth of household and financial debt slowed as the US property market turned down at the beginning of the 1990s, and the country experienced a mild recession. Government deficit spending increased to take up the slack. Overall, the US and global economies were more in balance in 1990 and 1991 than they have ever been since.

The 1990s: Crowding in

During the 1990s, US policymakers focused on reducing the budget deficit and expanding trade. They were astonishingly successful at both. By the end of the decade, the government's budget was in surplus and US goods exports had increased by 90% to $684 billion. Imports, however, had risen by 116% to

$1,032 billion. As the budget deficit shrank, the current-account deficit blew out to record levels. The consequences of this divergence between the improving budget deficit and the deteriorating trade deficit were disastrous. When the government stopped borrowing, the private sector was no longer crowded out; it was crowded in. As government debt growth slowed and then contracted, private-sector money that had been invested in the increasing pool of government bonds had to be redirected. That money went into stocks and property, igniting the NASDAQ bubble and the US property boom.

Trade liberalization

The global economy entered the 1990s in a slump. In the United States, the Fed had tightened monetary policy in 1988 in a belated attempted to rein in the decade's excesses. As a result, the overbuilt commercial property market experienced a severe adjustment that quickly caused the savings and loan industry to collapse. (Savings and loan associations, or thrifts—akin to building societies—accepted deposits and extended loans, mostly mortgages; their operations had been deregulated in the early 1980s.) The banks, which had still not fully recovered from their losses in the Latin American debt crisis, now found their domestic loan books badly impaired as well. Out of necessity, they stopped lending. The resulting "credit crunch" contributed to the economy sliding into a mild recession by the fourth quarter of 1990.

While the recession was mild, the recovery was muted. The unemployment rate rose from 5.4% at the beginning of 1990 to 7.8% by mid-1992. And when the economy did begin to revive, far fewer jobs were generated than in previous recoveries.

Against this background of considerable job insecurity, trade liberalization was a very contentious issue in the early 1990s. Both the Republican and the Democratic presidential candidates favored expanding "free trade", although labor unions and a very sizeable segment of the public opposed it. The Uruguay Round of the General Agreement on Tariffs and Trade (GATT) was ratified in 1993, and NAFTA, which created a free-trade zone between Mexico and the US and Canada, was approved by Congress the following year.

In retrospect, however, the gradual integration of China into the global economy from the early 1990s was much more consequential for world trade than either the Uruguay Round or NAFTA. During the 1980s, China's pragmatic new leader Deng Xiaoping had slowly shifted the country towards a market-oriented economic growth model tightly controlled by the Communist Party. Washington welcomed this change and encouraged it by allowing China to expand its trade surplus with the United States. The Cold War was over, and US policymakers must have hoped that a capitalist China might become a democratic China. In 1990, China's trade surplus with the United States was $10 billion. By 2000, it had grown to $84 billion, or roughly 7% of China's GDP that year.

After 2000, China would achieve a much larger trade surplus with the United States than any other country, but during the 1990s, it was just one of many nations that sold more to the Americans than it bought from them. After the Plaza Accord, the US current account steadily improved; in 1991, it briefly returned to a surplus. It soon deteriorated again, but it remained within a more-or-less manageable range, below 1.7% of US GDP, through 1997. Beginning in 1998, however, economic crises abroad and economic overheating at home caused the deficit to worsen again rapidly.

China devalued its currency by 31% in 1994. The following year, only a few months after NAFTA came into effect, the peso crisis led to a 30% devaluation of Mexico's currency. In 1997, the Asian crisis began. The Thai baht, the Malaysian ringgit, the Indonesian rupiah and the Korean won were devalued by between 35% and 50% that year. When Russia defaulted in 1998, the ruble was devalued by 71%. Finally, the contagion spread to Brazil, which devalued its real by 32% in January 1999.

Figure 61

US CURRENT-ACCOUNT BALANCE AS A % OF GDP, 1980-2000

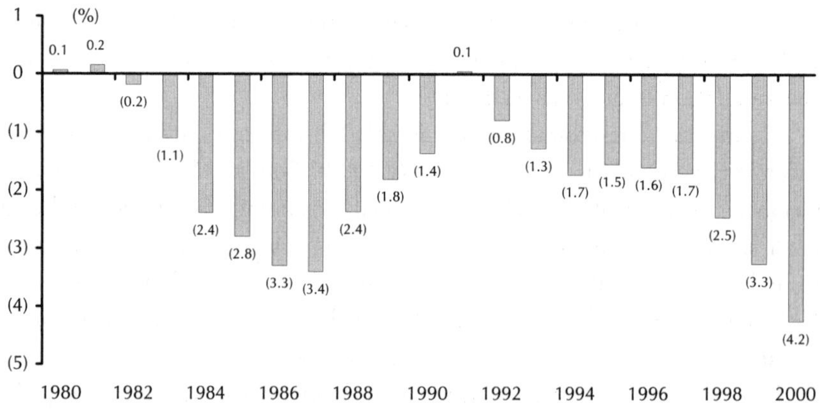

Source: Bureau of Economic Analysis

By the end of the decade, the United States found itself with a "strong-dollar policy", a term associated with Treasury Secretary Robert Rubin. As a result, the US current-account deficit deteriorated at a shocking pace, from 1.7% of GDP in

1997 to 2.5% in 1998 and 3.3% in 1999. The following year, the deficit blew out to 4.2% of US GDP, much worse than the previous record set in 1987. By the turn of the century, the gap between what the US imported and what it exported had become the most important driver of global economic growth.

The budget

Coincidentally, ironically and—as it turned out—very unfortunately, the explosion of the US trade deficit corresponded with the disappearance of the US budget deficit. During the 12 years the Republicans held the White House, from the beginning of 1981 to the end of 1992, the annual budget deficits had averaged 4.1% and government debt held by the public increased by $2 trillion, or 280%. And that was despite a tax increase initiated by President George H.W. Bush in 1991.

During his presidential campaign, Bill Clinton promised increased social spending, particularly in areas such as healthcare and education. As president, however, he adopted a quite different policy, one of fiscal restraint. That policy shift has been attributed to the influence of Robert Rubin, who served in the Clinton administration as Assistant to the President for Economic Policy from January 1993 to January 1995 and as Treasury Secretary from 1995 to 1999. Rubin persuaded Clinton that significantly reducing the US budget deficit would lead to substantially lower US interest rates that would set off an investment boom and restore the high economic growth rates of yesteryear. That advice was implemented—and it proved entirely correct.

Figure 62

US BUDGET BALANCE AS A % OF GDP, 1980-2000

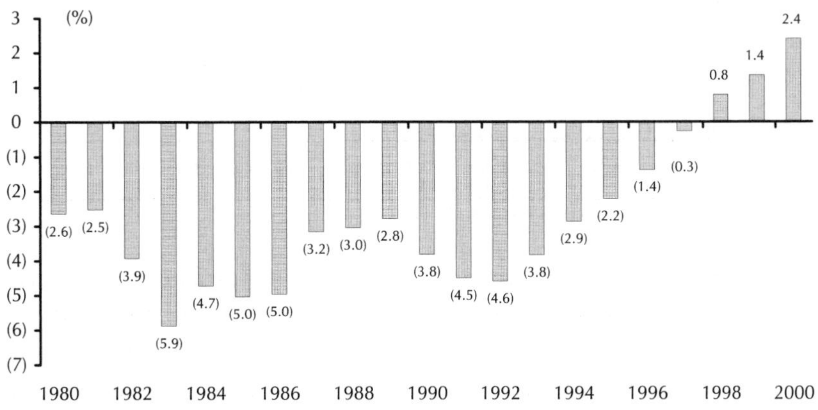

Source: Bureau of Economic Analysis (GDP), White House Office of Management and Budget (budget)

With the Omnibus Budget Reconciliation Act of 1993, Clinton signed into law a tax hike that took the top rate from 31% to 39.6%; the Bush tax increase had lifted it from 28% to 31% two years earlier. The combination of higher taxes and fiscal restraint had an extraordinary impact. It not only brought down interest rates and set off an investment boom, but also led to a frenzied investment bubble.

With taxes up and government spending curtailed, the budget deficit began contracting—from 4.6% of GDP in 1992 to 2.9% in 1994 and 1.4% in 1996. In 1998, Washington achieved its first budget surplus in almost three decades. The budget remained in surplus for four years, peaking at 2.4% of GDP in 2000.

The rationale for irrational exuberance

The last time the government's budget had balanced had been 1969. At that time the country's current account was also in balance. In the Reagan years, however, the United States began to run very large current-account deficits nearly every year. Its trading partners accumulated hundreds of billions of dollars as a result of their regular trade surpluses with the US. Figure 63 shows the expansion of their dollar stockpiles.

Figure 63

TOTAL FOREIGN-EXCHANGE RESERVES MINUS GOLD

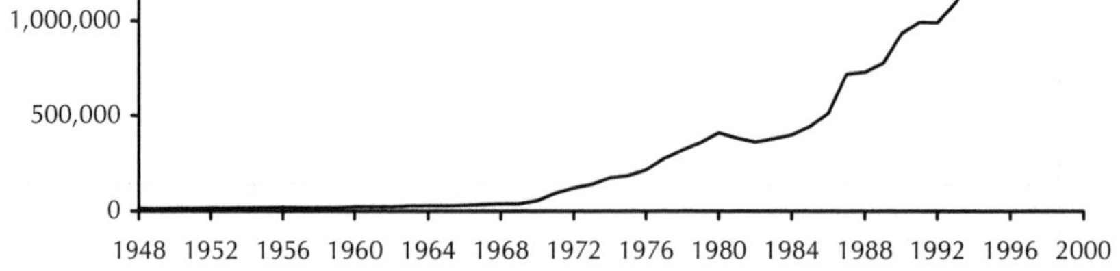

Source: IMF International Financial Statistics database

The central banks accumulating those dollar reserves preferred to invest them in the safest possible asset class: US Treasury bonds. Normally these were in plentiful supply. The United States' large annual budget deficits meant that the government sold enough new bonds each year to satisfy foreign and domestic demand. In 1996, that ceased to be the case. That was when the trouble began.

122

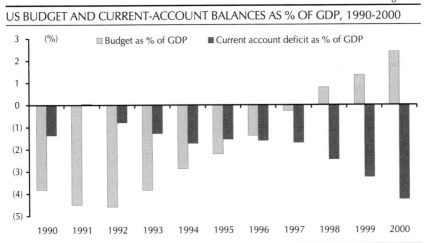

Figure 64

US BUDGET AND CURRENT-ACCOUNT BALANCES AS % OF GDP, 1990-2000

Source: Bureau of Economic Analysis (GDP and current account), White House Office of Management and Budget (budget)

In 1996, the current-account deficit exceeded the budget deficit as a percentage of GDP for the first time. Over the next four years, the current-account deficit worsened as the booming economy and Washington's strong-dollar policy pulled record imports into the country. Meanwhile, the budget swung from deficit to surplus. That meant the government stopped selling new Treasury bonds. It also started buying back (i.e. retiring) bonds it had sold in earlier years.

The swing from a budget deficit of 4.6% of GDP in 1992 to a surplus of 2.4% of GDP eight years later was quite extreme, and it profoundly disrupted the balance between the supply of dollar-denominated debt and the demand for that debt. When the government stopped selling new bonds, foreign central banks began buying up Treasury bonds that had been sold in earlier years. That pushed up the price of the bonds and drove down their yields. Between 1992 and 2000, the yield on 10-year Treasury notes declined from 7.7% to 5.0%. As the yield on government bonds plunged, investors, foreign and American alike, began to look elsewhere for yield. That was the beginning of many years of extraordinary capital misallocation. Some money went into debt issued by US government-sponsored enterprises (GSEs) such as Fannie Mae and Freddie Mac, some into corporate bonds, and a great deal into the stock market.

In December 1996, Fed Chairman Alan Greenspan coined the term "irrational exuberance" to describe investors' irrational enthusiasm for overvalued stocks. Over the following 26 months, the NASDAQ index rose another 100%. That was just the beginning. When LTCM imploded (see Chapter 6 and below), the Fed responded by throwing liquid fuel on the fire.

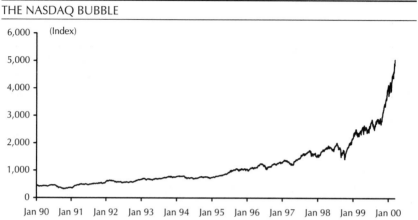

Figure 65

THE NASDAQ BUBBLE

Source: Bloomberg

LTCM

At the beginning of 1998, US policymakers were decidedly pleased with themselves. The economy had been expanding strongly for years, driven not by an ever-increasing budget deficit, as during the Reagan boom, but by investments in new technologies that were revolutionizing telecommunications and computing. Inflation and unemployment were low and the budget was on the brink of achieving its first surplus since 1969. The stock market was also roaring. So policymakers were completely broadsided when, in the third quarter, the US financial sector narrowly avoided systemic collapse.

When the Russian government defaulted on its debt, LTCM, one of the world's most prestigious hedge funds, blew up. When the magnitude of the financial industry's exposure to LTCM became known, panic spread through the financial markets. AAA-rated corporate bond spreads spiked and private-sector debt markets froze. The Dow and NASDAQ indexes plunged 18% and 30% respectively over the next two to three months. A sense of impending doom permeated the IMF/World Bank annual meetings in Washington that September.

The Fed intervened to prevent a financial-sector meltdown. The president of the New York Fed, William McDonough, convened a meeting of Wall Street's top bankers at his office and strongly urged them to resolve the matter. On 23 September a rescue was announced. Fourteen of LTCM's creditors would inject a total of $3.625 billion into the crippled firm in exchange for a 90% ownership stake. Bankers Trust, Barclays, Chase, Credit Suisse First Boston, Deutsche Bank, Goldman Sachs, Merrill Lynch, J.P. Morgan, Morgan Stanley, Salomon Smith Barney and UBS each contributed $300 million. Société Générale put in $125 million. Lehman Brothers and Paribas added $100 million each. Bear Stearns refused to cooperate.

Six days later on 29 September, the Fed cut interest rates by 25 basis points to 5.25%. On 25 October the Fed surprised markets with a second 25 basis-point cut, this one announced between the central bank's normally scheduled meetings. Rates were cut yet another 25 basis points at the next scheduled meeting on 17 November.

Those emergency rate cuts were not made in response to a weakening economy. GDP had expanded by 4.5% in 1997 and it would grow by 4.2% in 1998 and 4.5% the following year. Nor could the rate cuts be justified by concerns about the stock market. Although the Dow had fallen nearly 20% from 20 July to the end of August 1998, even at that low point it was still nearly 100% higher than it had been four years earlier.

In the midst of an economic boom and a stock market bubble, the Fed had been forced to cut rates three times in seven weeks to prevent the collapse of the global financial system—a crisis brought on by rampant speculation and reckless lending gone wrong. For the Fed to have to choose between accepting an immediate systemic collapse or creating an even greater speculative boom is a predicament that would have warranted sympathy—had the Fed's chairman not been a cheerleader for the kinds of financial innovations and practices that had produced the crisis in the first place. But by failing to regulate the creditors and by opposing those who would have tightened regulatory standards, the Fed bore a good part of the blame for this narrowly averted meltdown.

The three rate cuts at the end of 1998 threw fuel on the fire of an overheated economy and an already out-of-control NASDAQ tech bubble. Moreover, the episode confirmed what the financial community had long strongly suspected: the Fed would come to their rescue no matter how outrageous their antics.

Over the next two years, exuberance swelled into mass ecstasy. As stock prices climbed ever higher, speculation became America's favorite sport. The Dow rose another 69% between Greenspan's "irrational exuberance" speech and the end of the decade. NASDAQ, however, was the main event. The NASDAQ index began the decade at 459. When Netscape went public in August 1995, it hit 1,005. By the time Pets.com listed in February 2000 it had reached 2,553, joining the Tulip Mania of 1637 and the South Sea Bubble of 1720 as one of the most extraordinary speculative bubbles in history.

Conclusion

During the last three decades of the 20th Century, the United States' deficits shaped economic events not only in the United States, but around the world. During the 1970s, when trade was balanced, large budget deficits led to domestic bottlenecks, high rates of inflation and stagnation as government borrowing crowded out the private sector.

During the 1980s, a jump in imports into the US circumvented the domestic bottlenecks, held inflation in check and caused large trade deficits even as President Reagan ramped up the US economy with a string of extraordinary budget deficits. Although patently unsustainable, at that time two deficits seemed to work better than one.

When the directions of the deficits diverged during the 1990s, with the budget deficit flipping into surplus while the trade deficit reached unprecedented heights, the private sector was "crowded in". With not enough new government debt to go around, the private sector bought up previously issued government debt instead. That pushed up its price and drove down its yield—and lower yields fuelled an extraordinary economic boom.

The United States thus ended the 1990s with a budget surplus, a booming economy, a stock market bubble and a trade deficit on a scale never before seen. By then, the imbalances in the US and global economies had become so great that the global depression that took place during the following decade had already become unavoidable.

Chapter 8
The North American debt crisis

At that period, I felt we were pretty close to a global financial meltdown.

Ben Bernanke[1]

The crisis that eventually overwhelmed the United States in 2008 was in reality no more than an extension of the loose-cannon credit crisis that had begun rolling around the developing world in the 1970s. Like the Latin American debt crisis, the peso crisis and the Asian crisis, The North American debt crisis was caused by foreign capital entering the country and creating an economic bubble.

Between 2000 and 2008, the US economy went from boom to bust, to bigger boom, to catastrophic bust. This chapter describes how the US current-account deficit and the foreign credit that financed it destabilized the economy and led to the New Depression.

---

[1] Fed Chairman Ben S. Bernanke, interview on *60 Minutes*, 15 March 2009.

The NASDAQ crisis

In mid-2000 the NASDAQ bubble popped, as every bubble eventually does. The NASDAQ index fell nearly 80% from peak to trough. Hundreds of overleveraged internet and telecommunications companies disappeared, and dozens of serious corporate scandals came to light. Business investment collapsed.

Overall, however, the resulting recession was quite mild. In fact, US GDP still managed to expand by 0.8% that year. But that gentle outcome disguised the true danger posed by the stock market crash. The reality is that in 2001–02, the global economy only very narrowly escaped falling into a depression.

Private-sector debt and debt-driven asset-price inflation had become the engines of economic growth in the United States during the second half of the 1990s. Economic growth around the rest of the world was largely a function of the extraordinary surge in American imports. When the US equity bubble burst, household net worth took a serious hit, causing imports to contract by 6% in 2001. The rate of global economic growth slowed by half to less than 2%, and global commodity prices fell by 20%.

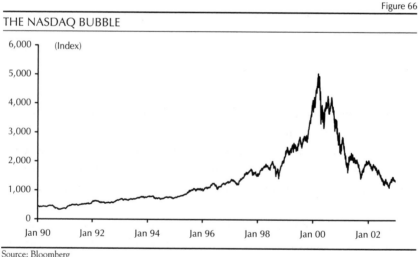

Figure 66

THE NASDAQ BUBBLE

Source: Bloomberg

With household net worth dropping, unemployment rising and business investment in freefall in the United States—and much of the rest of the world in even worse shape—the outlook for the global economy was alarming. US policymakers were particularly concerned that deflation would take hold in the United States as it had in Japan during the 1990s and in the United States during the Great Depression. Therefore, the policy response to the NASDAQ crash was particularly aggressive.

The administration of President George W. Bush cut taxes, sent out tax refund checks and increased government spending. As a result, the federal budget swung from a surplus of 2.4% of GDP in 2000 to a deficit of 3.4% of GDP in 2003. At the same time, the Fed cut the federal funds rate to 1.0% and held it there for 12 months.

That combination of aggressive fiscal and monetary stimulus sustained the consumer—directly at first, as the government mailed money to Americans, and less directly later by creating an enormous property bubble. Consumption typically accounts for about 70% of GDP. During 1999 and 2000, at the peak of the NASDAQ bubble, consumption had increased by 5.1% and 4.7%, respectively. During the recession of 2001, it still managed to increase by 2.5%. In 2004, its growth rate had reaccelerated to 3.6%.

Still, the danger of a double-dip recession, or even the possibility of a much more significant downturn, persisted for some time. The economy did not gain any real traction until mid-2003, and the threat of deflation persisted for nearly another year after that.

In July 2003, Federal Reserve Chairman Alan Greenspan told Congress: "there is an especially pernicious, albeit remote, scenario in which inflation turns negative against a backdrop of weak aggregate demand, engendering a corrosive deflationary spiral."[2] During the recession of 1990–91, the Fed had reduced interest rates to a 28-year low of 3.0%. In the NASDAQ recession, the Fed slashed the federal funds rate to 1.0%; and when the market began to worry that with rates so low the Fed was "out of bullets", Fed Governor Ben Bernanke let it be known that the Fed was prepared to print money and buy government bonds to push interest rates down further out the yield curve. "We have a technology called the printing press," he said[3].

In the event, the Fed was not required to print money and buy up debt to reflate the economy; that would come later. Holding the federal funds rate at or below 2% for three years was sufficient to rekindle asset prices. By the time the Fed pushed rates up to 2.25% at the end of 2004, the US property market was on fire. As a creator of wealth, a font of financing and a driver of global economic growth, America's property bubble was to put the NASDAQ bubble to shame.

---

[2] Fed Chairman Alan Greenspan, testimony before the Committee on Financial Services, US House of Representatives, 15 July 2003.

[3] Fed Governor Ben S. Bernanke, "Deflation: Making Sure 'It' Doesn't Happen Here" (remarks before the National Economists Club, Washington, DC, 21 November 2002).

Fannie and Freddie issue $3 trillion of debt

The housing boom in the United States had actually begun in the late 1990s. Its origins were similar to those of the stock market bubble. As discussed in Chapter 7, when the US government began running budget surpluses in the late 1990s, instead of crowding out private-sector investment by selling large amounts of Treasury bonds each year, the effect was to crowd the private sector's investments into other kinds of assets. The principal beneficiaries of this "crowding in" were Fannie Mae and Freddie Mac.

When the US government budget went into surplus in 1998 and the government began buying back its debt for the first time in living memory, it created a shortage of AAA-rated debt. The two housing-finance giants were quick to fill the void. Since their debt was understood to implicitly have the full backing of the US government, their bonds were rated AAA and considered the next best thing to Treasury bonds. There was no shortage of buyers.

Figure 67

ANNUAL CHANGE IN DEBT OUTSTANDING FOR GOVERNMENT AND GSES

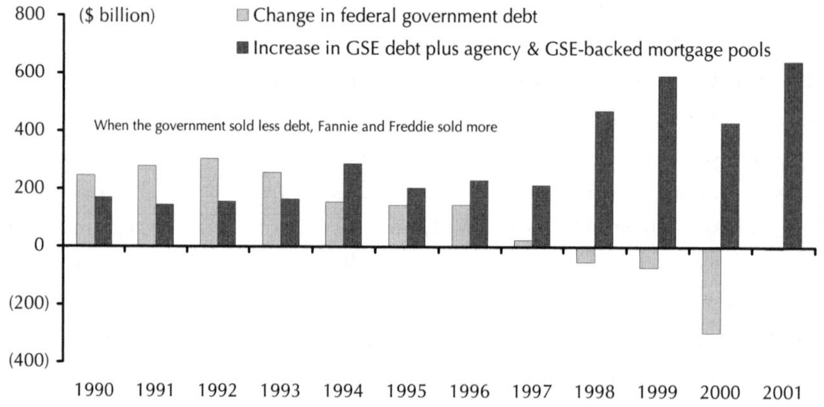

Source: Federal Reserve Flow of Funds

Beginning in 1998, Fannie Mae, Freddie Mac and other GSEs went on a borrowing binge. Between 1998 and 2003 they issued $3 trillion in debt. To put this into perspective, the entire amount of US government debt held by the public at the end of 2003 was $3.9 trillion.

Finding it so easy to grow their liabilities, Fannie and Freddie rushed to grow the asset side of their balance sheets as well by buying up or guaranteeing mortgages originated by banks or other financial institutions. While Fannie and Freddie's debt was considered to be backed by the US government, the compensation packages of

130

their senior management were in no way limited by a government pay scale. The larger Fannie and Freddie became, the more profits they generated; and the more profits they generated, the greater the bonuses paid out to management.

The bonanza at Fannie and Freddie began to come to an end when the federal budget, after four years in surplus, fell back into a large deficit in 2002. When the NASDAQ bubble popped and the economy went into recession, tax revenues fell and fiscal stimulus increased. By 2003, the budget deficit had risen to $378 billion, or 3.4% of GDP. At that point, the US Treasury Department realized that in seeking buyers for its bonds, it was competing with Fannie and Freddie. They were all selling bonds to the same investors, US institutions and foreign central banks.

The government must have also recognized that Fannie and Freddie were causing the housing market to overheat. In February 2004, Chairman Greenspan testified before Congress that the Fed was worried about the impact the two were having on the broader economy. Working together, the Treasury Department and the Fed eventually brought the GSEs back under control. An investigation by the Office of Federal Housing Enterprise Oversight, Fannie's regulator, uncovered "accounting irregularities" involving the use of derivatives at both institutions. Fannie and Freddie were stopped from growing their balance sheets further until their accounts had been cleaned up. Their top executives were forced out and the Office of Federal Housing Enterprise Oversight detailed 101 charges from 1998 to 2004 against Franklin Raines and two other former Fannie executives; requesting $100 million in penalties and $115 million in return of bonuses.

Between 1998 and 2003, however, the $3 trillion increase in the balance sheets of Fannie Mae and Freddie Mac had an extraordinary impact on the US and global economy by driving up property prices in America. Rising property prices sustained the American consumer during the post-NASDAQ recession. After contracting by 6% in 2001, imports into the US began expanding again the following year. By the time the recovery fully took hold in 2004, the US current-account deficit was 50% larger than it had been four years earlier when the NASDAQ peaked. At $625 billion, the current-account deficit was equivalent to 5.3% of US GDP that year.

The huge current-account deficit created an uncontrollable dynamic as it was reinvested in the US economy. America's trading partners were inundated with dollars as a result of their trade surpluses. The central banks of those countries intervened to prevent an appreciation of their currencies by printing money and buying dollars in order to hold their exchange rates at very competitive levels. In consequence, central bank dollar holdings, i.e. foreign-exchange reserves, soared. As described elsewhere, this was paper-money creation on a scale that had never before occurred in peacetime.

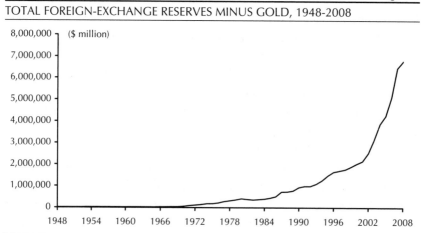

Figure 68

TOTAL FOREIGN-EXCHANGE RESERVES MINUS GOLD, 1948-2008

Source: IMF International Financial Statistics database

Nearly all the dollars accumulated by the central banks of the United States' trading partners were reinvested in dollar-denominated assets in order to generate a return. Every country's balance of payments must balance. So, the bigger the US current-account deficit became, the more dollars flowed into the United States through its financial-account surplus. By necessity, the current-account deficit and the financial-account surplus are practically mirror images of one another.

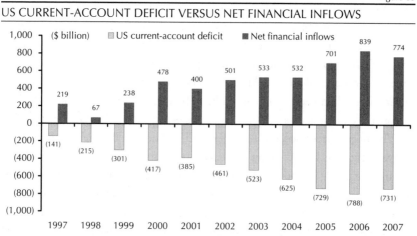

Figure 69

US CURRENT-ACCOUNT DEFICIT VERSUS NET FINANCIAL INFLOWS

Source: Federal Reserve Flow of Funds

How the Fed lost its mojo

By the middle of the decade, the risk of deflation in the United States had receded. Large capital inflows and low interest rates were quickly leading to a new round of economic overheating. When Chairman Alan Greenspan and his colleagues at the Fed began to apply the brakes, they discovered they had lost control over interest rates. Try as they might, they could not make the 10-year bond yield rise.

When the Fed first increased its funds rate from 1.0% to 1.25% in June 2004, the yield on the 10-year Treasury bond was 4.73%. Over the next 21 months, the Fed hiked rates 14 more times to 4.75%, but the 10-year bond yield did not move. Not until April 2006 did the yield begin to move higher. And even when the tightening cycle ended in June 2006—following two more rate hikes that took the federal funds rate to 5.25%—the 10-year yield had still only reached 5.11%. Thus, between June 2004 and June 2006, the Fed ratcheted up the federal funds rate 17 times by a total of 425 basis points, but over the same period, the yield on the 10-year government bond rose only 38 basis points. The "long end" of the yield curve seemed to entirely ignore the Fed's efforts to push rates up from the "short end".

Since the long end of the yield curve determines mortgage rates, the Fed's inability to push up the interest rate that mattered meant it could not slow down the housing boom or cool down the economy. As early as February 2005, Greenspan told the Senate: "For the moment, the broadly unanticipated behavior of world bond markets remains a conundrum." [4]

This was a dangerous state of affairs. The property market was bubbling, the US economy was overheating, the global economy was going gangbusters, and the Fed had lost control over interest rates. How had this happened? The explanation for the so-called "conundrum" is to be found in the US trade deficit. The astronomically large trade deficit brought equally large inflows of capital into the United States (the current-account deficit being the mirror image of the financial-account surplus). The inflow of credit from abroad drove up US bond prices and drove down bond yields—and there was nothing the most powerful central banker in the world could do about it. Alan Greenspan had lost control over interest rates. In his autobiography, he wrote, "I would place the US current account far down the list" (of imbalances to worry about). [5] That was another important thing he was wrong about.

---

[4] Fed Chairman Alan Greenspan, testimony before the Committee on Banking, Housing, and Urban Affairs, US Senate, 16 February 2005.

[5] Alan Greenspan, The *Age of Turbulence: Adventures in a new world* (The Penguin Press, 2007), p. 347.

Global boom

By 2004, the property market was already a bubble and the US economy had become severely distorted by it. Americans had come to view their homes as automated teller machines from which they could extract equity at will. Home-equity extraction averaged $520 billion in 2003 and 2004 or approximately 4-5% of GDP in each year.[6] As homeowners borrowed money against the rapidly inflating value of their homes, they spent it. Consumption fuelled the economy and pulled imports into the United States in extraordinary amounts, creating a worldwide economic boom. In 2004, the US current-account deficit broke through 5% of GDP for the first time. In 2006, it exceeded 6%. During those years, powered by debt-financed consumption in the United States, the global economy grew at its fastest pace in 30 years.

Figure 70

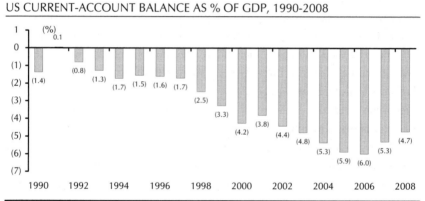

US CURRENT-ACCOUNT BALANCE AS % OF GDP, 1990-2008

Source: Bureau of Economic Analysis

The US economy expanded by an average of 3.1% between 2004 and 2006, causing a surge in tax revenues. By 2007, the federal budget deficit was back down to only 1.2% of GDP. This created a new problem. The government was no longer issuing much new debt, and Fannie and Freddie were issuing even less, but the current-account deficit was throwing off nearly $800 billion a year into the global economy. Those dollars were being accumulated by central banks, and not enough Treasury debt or government-backed debt was being issued to absorb it all. Again, as in the late 1990s, foreign central banks were forced to buy US government bonds that

---

[6] Alan Greenspan and James Kennedy, *Estimates of Home Mortgage Origination, Repayments, and Debt on One-to-Four-Family Residences* (Federal Reserve Board Finance and Economics Discussion Paper 2005-41).

had been issued in earlier years, thus raising their prices and lowering their yields. Depressed interest rates only made the US property market hotter.

Figure 71

FEDERAL BUDGET BALANCE AS % OF GDP, 1990-2007

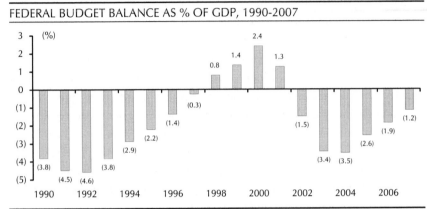

Sources: Bureau of Economic Analysis (GDP), White House Office of Management and Budget (budget)

Central banks outside the United States were inundated with dollars and needed dollar-denominated AAA bonds to invest them in. After Fannie and Freddie were reined in, the private sector stepped forward. Between 2003 and 2005, private-sector issuance of asset-backed securities (ABS) quadrupled to $800 billion. Just as the GSEs were able to expand when the government stopped issuing debt at the end of the 1990s, now, when the GSEs had all but ceased issuing debt, the private sector took over.

Figure 72

ANNUAL CHG IN DEBT OUTSTANDING: GOVT, GSEs & PRIVATE-SECTOR

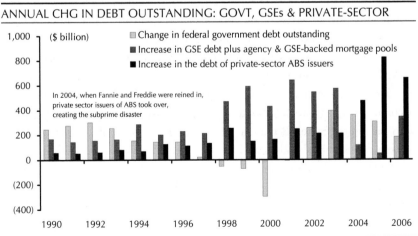

Source: Federal Reserve Flow of Funds

Figure 72 shows very clearly that Fannie and Freddie greatly expanded their debt issuance to satisfy the demand for AAA-rated debt when the US budget went into surplus in 1998; and, similarly, that when both the government and Fannie and Freddie reduced their debt issuance in 2004 and 2005, the private sector ramped up its debt issuance to meet that demand.

With US interest rates very low, yield-starved investors were quick to move into the ABS market, where yields were more attractive. Between 2004 and 2006, ABS issuers sold $2 trillion of debt. As they grew their liabilities, they had to grow their assets to generate profits. To do so, they hired tens of thousands of mortgage brokers to call up people with poor credit records and encourage them to borrow money. Subprime mortgages were handed out by the loan originators with little concern about the borrowers' ability to repay them. The originators had no intention of holding the loans to maturity. They "securitized" them, paid the credit-rating agencies to give them AAA ratings, and sold them off to gullible investors around the world. And for a few years, subprime was sublime. Subprime loans rose from 7% of the total mortgage market in 1997 to 21% in 2004.

Like Mexico, Brazil, Thailand and Korea before it, the United States was now being overwhelmed by the inflow of foreign credit. But it was not a small developing country. It generated a quarter of global GDP, and US demand had long been the main driver of growth in the other three-quarters of the world as well.

The combination of low interest rates and the large quantity of cheap mortgages being thrust on low-income earners drove US property prices to dizzying heights in 2006. And as a direct result, the global economy was on fire. Commodity prices soared and oil approached $150 a barrel. The boom wrapped around the world, from primary commodity producers in Latin American and even Africa, to the property market in Moscow and London. US goods imports peaked at $2.1 trillion in 2008, allowing the United States' trading partners to buy a record amount of US goods exports as well ($1.3 trillion). China was becoming a superpower thanks to a quarter-trillion-dollar-a-year trade surplus with the United States. Economic miracles had also materialized in countries as unexpected as Ireland and Iceland.

And then it all went wrong. The boom of the 1990s had been described and justified as a "new paradigm". Perhaps the boom that peaked in early 2007 should be known as the subprime paradigm. The underpinnings of the latter boom were even less credible than the very dubious ones of its predecessor. It is extraordinary that anyone could have bought into them for a single minute.

Figure 73

COMMODITY PRICE INDEX, 1996-MAY 2009

Source: Bloomberg

The North American debt crisis

...credit and investment flowed into economies that still had many shortcomings. These shortcomings included some traditional macroeconomic problems, such as overvalued exchange rates that were effectively fixed to the US dollar and inappropriate fiscal or monetary policy. But they also involved structural weaknesses, such as underdeveloped and poorly regulated financial systems, serious governance and corruption issues in some countries, lack of financial transparency, and various counterproductive regulatory, labor, and trade regulations. Excessive inflows into countries with serious vulnerabilities are an accident waiting to happen.[7]

Former Treasury Secretary Robert Rubin wrote those lines about the countries afflicted by the Asian crisis. But the crisis that began in 2008 revealed that the US economy shared all the same shortcomings. Moreover, the weaknesses Rubin referred to yielded the same "accident" when combined with excessive inflows of credit. In fact, the North American debt crisis should demonstrate beyond reasonable doubt that no country—no matter how theoretically sophisticated or technologically advanced—can withstand the large-scale inflow of foreign credit. Financial regulators around the world have been unable to prevent credit flows from devastating their financial sectors—not the Japanese, not the Thais, not the British, and perhaps most shamefully of all, not the Americans.

---

[7] Robert E. Rubin, *In An Uncertain World* (Random House, 2003), p. 217.

The American crisis proves that any country can be (and most now have been) overwhelmed by loose-cannon credit.

The policy response to the American crisis was analyzed in Chapter 1. Here, however, it should be pointed out that US policymakers adopted nearly all of the policies the IMF had forbidden in the other countries overwhelmed by great inflows of foreign credit. IMF "conditionality" generally demanded that governments receiving assistance:

❏ Increase interest rates

❏ Tighten fiscal policy

❏ Close failed banks

❏ Stop directed lending

❏ Improve transparency, and

❏ Open the financial sector to foreign competition.

In contrast, since the beginning of its crisis, the United States has cut interest rates to zero and begun printing money to prop up asset prices; approved a $1.6 trillion (with a *t*) budget deficit for Year 1; propped up the failed banks, which comprise the great majority of the financial sector; and increased directed lending by the Fed, by Fannie and Freddie and, most probably, by many other lenders. In fact, the only bit of the standard IMF "advice" that Washington has followed is to allow foreign competition in the financial sector. But in this case, the accounts of US banks are so impaired and opaque that none of the few global institutions that are still solvent dares to make an American acquisition.

Conclusion

Eventually, every credit bubble implodes. Eventually, asset prices become so inflated that society simply cannot earn enough money to service the interest on its debt—the debt that drove up the asset prices in the first place. The financial sector makes every effort to roll over the debt so borrowers can avoid default. But sooner or later, panic sets in. Then the game is up. It becomes clear that the economic fundamentals are so poor the credit can't be repaid. Then no more credit can be extended, and the economic structure built on a seemingly unlimited supply of credit collapses. Debtors default. Creditors fail. So it was in the United States in 2008.

Once the US government abandoned fiscal rectitude and sound money, the course toward disaster may have been unalterably set. When policymakers in Washington also accepted massive trade deficits, it certainly was. Globalization financed with debt denominated in a fiat currency never had a chance of succeeding over the long term. By the mid-1990s, it was too late to restore balance. The economy had become too distorted and the political process too corrupted by deficits and debt. Having long since lost sight of the guiding principles of economic orthodoxy, policymakers were forced to become crisis managers, with debt and currency-debasement as their only tools.

Chapter 9 Deregulation, derivatives and the threat of mass destruction

...derivatives are financial weapons of mass destruction, carrying dangers that, while now latent, are potentially lethal.

Warren Buffett[1]

A quadrillion of anything must be dangerous. The global derivatives market grew in size from $10 trillion in 1990 to $760 trillion in June 2008—equal to the value of everything produced on earth during the previous 20 years. If its growth had continued at that rate, it would have topped a quadrillion dollars ($1,000,000,000,000,000) in 2010 and $1 quintillion (add three more zeros) before 2020. Instead, the derivatives market imploded, triggering a systemic

---

[1] Warren Buffett, Bershire Hathaway Inc. 2002 Annual Report, p. 15.

crisis throughout the world's financial industry. Derivatives are largely unregulated, and 90% of all transactions trade over the counter. Forget about global warming: our civilization is at much greater risk of being wiped out by these financial instruments of mass destruction than by melting polar ice caps. This chapter describes how deregulation of the financial industry undermined the global economy by dismantling the safeguards put in place after the Great Depression. It also explores the possibility that the derivatives market may be history's greatest Ponzi scheme.

Losing control over credit creation

Over the course of the past 50 years, the financial system of the United States has changed beyond recognition. At the beginning of that period, the Fed held a tight grip on credit creation, and the banking and securities industries were firmly regulated. By the middle of this decade, the Fed had completely lost control over credit creation and the financial industry had become very loosely regulated. In fact, by 2005 it had become difficult to determine whether the government was regulating the banks or the banks were regulating the government.

In 2008, a systemic crisis engulfed the US financial sector as a consequence of deregulation. The government was forced to nationalize a large part of the industry and to inject capital or provide loan guarantees for most of the rest in order to prevent the industry's complete annihilation. So far the worst has been averted, but almost all of the industry's vulnerabilities remain.

Financial-product innovation and industry deregulation circumvented and then destroyed the laws enacted to ensure sound banking after the calamity of the early 1930s. Greed, hubris and corruption all played a part in driving the financial sector toward excess and, ultimately, self-inflicted ruin. This section addresses those developments in chronological order.

Watershed: the Eurodollar market

From the late 1960s, the Eurodollar market in London began to undermine US monetary policy by making a pool of largely unregulated dollar liquidity available to corporate borrowers with operations outside the United States. During the 1950s and 1960s, a combination of US government aid and US corporate investment abroad had produced a pool of dollars held outside the country—primarily in London—and beyond US jurisdiction. Those dollars were subject to neither reserve requirements nor interest-rate caps, and they were held by both non-US banks and the foreign subsidiaries of US banks. Money was created in the Eurodollar market as funds were borrowed and redeposited, just as money was created in the US banking system through the process of fractional reserve banking. In the Eurodollar market, however, there were no regulators to set the reserve ratio. This meant the amount of money that could be created was only limited by the bankers' own willingness to keep sufficient reserves on hand to meet their depositors' demands for cash. In this way, US dollars (or, more precisely, dollar-denominated deposits and loans) were created without the consent—or even the knowledge—of the monetary authorities in the United States.

As the Eurodollar market grew (from $1.5 billion in 1959 to $46 billion in 1970[2]), it began to interfere with the US government's attempts to fine-tune the economy. By the second half of the 1960s, for example, the Eurodollar market was hampering government attempts to cool down the economy by increasing interest rates, since US corporations could simply borrow dollars in the Eurodollar market in London at interest rates over which the Fed had no control.

Short-term capital flows originating in the Eurodollar market also began to destabilize currency markets during the late 1960s. Ultimately, the fixed-exchange-rate regime that was a cornerstone of the Bretton Woods international monetary system collapsed under an onslaught of currency speculators funded out of the Eurodollar market. The unwillingness or inability of the US government to bring the Eurodollar market under regulatory control must be seen as a watershed. Afterwards, the US government lost control not only over credit creation but also over its own currency, its balance of payments and its ability to control the domestic economy.

Disintermediation and the loss of control over credit

By 1971, when the Bretton Woods system collapsed, not only had the dollar become a purely fiat currency, but the Fed had lost its monopoly on the ability to create dollars, thanks to the rapid growth of the unregulated Eurodollar market. Moreover, once all attempts to reestablish a fixed-exchange-rate regime were abandoned in 1973, US monetary authorities no longer had the ability to control the value of the dollar relative to other currencies or gold.

The large government budget deficits during the second half of the 1960s bear most of the blame for bringing about the loss of control over money and

---

[2] Harold James, *International Monetary Cooperation Since Bretton Woods* (Oxford University Press, 1996), p. 180.

credit during these years. The unwillingness of the Johnson and Nixon administrations to prevent government spending from exceeding government revenues overstimulated the US economy and led to high rates of inflation.

Inflation exacerbated the Fed's loss of control over the credit system by ushering in the age of disintermediation. When inflation pushed up government bond yields and the yield on other market-determined interest rates, depositors began to take their funds out of banks (where interest rates were capped) and invest them in higher-yielding credit instruments. The rapid growth of mutual funds also played an important role in this process. Mutual funds attracted large amounts of money by offering investors the possibility of higher returns than they could get by depositing the money in a bank. Between 1964 and 1972, mutual-fund assets doubled to $59 billion.[3]

The loss of deposits caused by disintermediation threatened the stability of the banking sector, forcing the Fed to liberalize and eventually phase out altogether the Regulation Q interest-rate ceilings on bank deposits. In 1970 the ceilings on three-month negotiable certificates of deposit (CDs) were eliminated, and in 1973 the ceiling on longer-term CDs was also removed. This change meant that banks could effectively bid for funding by offering interest rates on CDs that were significantly higher than the rates the Regulation Q restrictions permitted on deposits. This allowed banks to attract as much funding as they desired through the credit markets. By significantly broadening the banks' funding sources, the removal of interest-rate ceilings on CDs made it more difficult for the Fed to constrain bank lending by controlling the cost and availability of deposits.

Until then, the Fed had been able to restrict lending through open-market operations that pushed up the cost of deposits and made them less plentiful. From the early 1970s, however, the banks were able to access funding not only from their traditional deposit base but also from the entire credit market. This made the Fed's task much harder. It was no longer possible to restrain lending by controlling the supply of deposits. The whole credit market was now open to the banks as a source of funds, and the Fed did not have the tools to effectively control the quantity of credit on offer there, particularly given the growth of the Eurodollar market. The Fed's subsequent open-market operations had to be directed at controlling the rate of interest throughout the credit market rather than only the rate of interest at which banks lent federal funds to one another.

---

[3] Board of Governors of the Federal Reserve System, *Flow of Funds Accounts of the United States*.

In practice that proved to be anything but easy, not least because the credit market was becoming larger and much more complex all the time.

Rolling back New Deal banking regulation

Developments during the 1980s made it even more difficult for the Fed to control credit. A decade of high inflation had effectively bankrupted the savings and loan (S&L) industry. The industry was threatened with insolvency because the yield on its assets (primarily 30-year fixed-rate mortgages, dating from the 1950s and 1960s) earned far less than its very high cost of funds, which had risen with inflation. Congress intervened to save the S&Ls by passing the Depository Institutions Deregulation and Monetary Control Act of 1980. This was followed by the Garn-St. Germain Depository Institutions Act of 1982. Between them, the Acts phased out the Regulation Q interest-rate ceilings on time deposits and eliminated the ban on paying interest on current accounts. This was the first important rollback of the banking laws that had been passed in the New Deal era. The two Acts also deregulated the savings and loan industry. Previously, S&Ls were restricted to mortgage lending; now they were allowed to have up to 50% of their assets in commercial real estate and up to 30% in consumer loans, commercial paper and corporate debt. They were also permitted to issue credit cards and offer check accounts. Those measures had disastrous consequences and ultimately cost taxpayers $125 billion between 1986 and 1996, according to the US General Accounting Office. However, the S&L crisis did not drastically affect the US financial sector as a whole. At the peak, the S&Ls accounted for only about 5% of all loans in the banking sector. Nevertheless, the consequences of the deregulation of the S&L industry did presage the fate of the system as a whole following the deregulation of the banking industry at the end of the century.

The removal of the Regulation Q interest-rate restrictions gave the banks much greater control over the liabilities side of their balance sheets. The development of securitization produced an equally great revolution on the assets side.

Securitization refers to the process by which loans are turned into tradable securities. Securitization dramatically changed the banking business. Previously, when banks made loans they had to hold them to maturity. They also had to hold regulatory capital against those assets. If the loan went bad, the bank took the loss. Securitization freed banks from many of their traditional concerns. It allowed them to originate a loan, package it with a great number of other loans, split that pool of loans into various tranches with differing degrees of risk and then sell the tranches to outside investors. Through this process, banks generated "origination" fees and sometimes "servicing" fees if they continued to collect the interest payments before passing them on to the securities' new owners. Furthermore, it freed the banks from both the credit risks associated with those loans and the need to maintain regulatory capital against them.

Mortgages were the first products to be securitized, beginning in the 1970s. The technique quickly spread to many other asset classes. Credit-card receivables, car-purchase loans and even student loans were all securitized on a very large scale (at least until 2007).

As the supply of these new products grew, so did the market for them. Mutual funds, money-market funds, banks, pension funds and insurance companies in the US and overseas were all attracted by the higher rates of interest they offered. By the late 1990s, the world was awash with dollars as a result of the very large US trade deficits; and those dollars were hungry for yield.

Repealing Glass-Steagall

As described in Chapter 6, in the early 1980s the US banking industry had become caught up in a very serious crisis stemming from imprudent lending to Latin America. By the end of the decade, thanks to the IMF, this crisis no longer seriously threatened the industry's solvency. However, by then the banks had become overextended by lending in the US commercial property market as well. When the excesses there began to correct, a mild recession took hold in 1990–91, and the banks needed some time to repair their balance sheets. They did this with the help of a steep yield curve engineered by the Fed.

From the mid-1980s onward, however, the real action was in the equity and bond markets, from which the banks were barred by Glass-Steagall. After having been rangebound between 600 and 1,000 for 16 years, the Dow Jones Industrial Average broke decisively through the 1,000 level in 1983 and never looked back. Notwithstanding a 23% one-day plunge in October 1987, the Dow ended the decade at 2,752.

By 1990, disintermediation was threatening to make banks obsolete. Corporations raised most of their funds directly from the market; mortgages, credit cards, car loans and student loans could all be originated, financed and distributed without any help from banks. Between their growing obsolescence and the mergers and acquisitions boom underway on Wall Street, it is not surprising that the banks lobbied Congress and the Federal Reserve hard to be allowed to conduct more underwriting business, which Glass-Steagall had specifically forbidden. In 1987, the Federal Reserve Board approved the application of three bank holding companies to engage, through subsidiaries, in underwriting and dealing in commercial paper, certain types of mortgage-backed securities and municipal-revenue bonds, so long as they limited their underwriting and dealing income from those securities to 5% of the total gross income of the affiliate. That limit was raised to 10% in 1989 and 25% in 1997.[4]

In April 1998, Travelers, one of the world's biggest insurance companies, and Citicorp, one of the world's biggest banks, announced their merger—at the time, the largest in history. Given that Glass-Steagall legally banned banks, insurance companies and investment banks from having the same owners or managers, the proposed merger seemed to face certain regulatory challenges, all the more so since Travelers had already acquired Salomon Smith Barney, a leading investment bank. However, in September that year the Fed green-lighted the deal, although its press release did caution that its approval was subject to conditions: first, "that Travelers and Citigroup conform the activities of its companies to the requirements of the Glass-Steagall Act and the Board's related orders and interpretations thereunder, including the Board's revenue test." And, more specifically:

> ...that Travelers and the combined organization, Citigroup Inc., take all actions necessary to conform the activities and investments of Travelers and all its subsidiaries to the requirements of the Bank Holding Company Act in a manner acceptable to the Board, including by divestiture as necessary, within two years of consummation of the proposal.[5]

As luck—and a very expensive lobbying campaign—would have it, "within two years of consummation" was more than enough time. In November 1999, only 14 months after the implosion of LTCM had nearly destroyed the global financial system, Congress felt the time was right to repeal what was left of Glass-Steagall. The Gramm-Leach-Bliley Act of 1999, also known as the Financial Services Modernization Act, did just that—though by then, little remained of Glass-Steagall anyway.

The Regulation Q interest-rate ceilings on deposits had been removed in the 1970s and early 1980s; and the separation of commercial banking and investment banking had been whittled down to near irrelevance over the preceding dozen years as commercial banks had been allowed to reenter the underwriting business. Alan Greenspan wrote in his autobiography that he felt these changes were long overdue: "Years in the making, the Financial Services Modernization Act finally did away with the Glass-Steagall Act, the Depression-era law that limited the ability of banks, investment firms, and

---

[4] Federal Reserve, "Permissible Activities by Board Order (Underwriting and Dealing)", section 3600.21, *Bank Holding Company Manual*, December 2000, pp. 1-2.

[5] Federal Reserve press release, 23 September 1998.

insurance companies to enter one another's markets."[6] The *New York Times* would later describe Gramm-Leach-Bliley as "the most significant financial-services legislation since the Depression".[7]

Thus, after 65 years, bankers were brokers and brokers were bankers again. Lobbyists for the banking industry had persuaded Congress that "modernization" was needed to counter the threat to the financial industry from foreign "universal" banks, presumably those based in Japan and Germany. Moreover, for some time a rethink had been underway regarding the causes of the Great Depression. Many influential academics had come to believe that bankers were not to blame for the collapse of the banking industry in the early 1930s; instead, they argued, the Fed had been at fault for not increasing the money supply sufficiently to prevent the collapse. In any case, lawmakers were convinced that lessons had been learned and that modern central-banking practices meant a financial-sector collapse could never recur. Rather than being alarmed by the LTCM crisis of the previous year, Congress was apparently reassured by it, since it had been handled so well. Finally, banks, bankers and the lobbyists representing them were among Congress's largest campaign contributors.

The Financial Services Modernization Act did not address the longstanding muddle in the US financial regulatory regime. If anything, it made it worse. The act:

> ...split up oversight of conglomerates among government agencies. The Securities and Exchange Commission, for example, would oversee the brokerage arm of a company. Bank regulators would supervise its banking operation. State insurance commissioners would examine the insurance business. But no single agency would have authority over the entire company.[8]

America's system of regulating its financial sector, long fragmented, had been left far behind by the rapid changes in the industry. The need for a complete overhaul of the system had been recognized for years. But reform had been blocked by aggressive opposition from stakeholders within the system who stood to lose power in a unified regulatory body, and from many in the financial industry who found that a fragmented system allowed them to shop around for a lighter regulatory touch, a pursuit known as "regulatory arbitrage". The following paragraph from the 2005 FDIC Banking Review sheds considerable light on just what a mess oversight of the financial sector had become in the years immediately before the collapse:

---

[6] Alan Greenspan, *The Age of Turbulence* (The Penguin Press, 2007), pp. 198-199.

[7] Eric Lipton and Stephen Labaton, "Deregulator Looks Back, Unswayed", *The New York Times*, 17 November 2008.

[8] *Ibid.*

The current system for regulating and supervising financial institutions is complex. At the federal level, commercial banking organizations are regulated and supervised by three agencies—the Office of the Comptroller of the Currency (OCC), the Federal Reserves System (Federal Reserve), and the Federal Deposit Insurance Corporation (FDIC). Thrifts are regulated and supervised by the Office of Thrift Supervision (OTS) and credit unions by the National Credit Union Administration (NCUA). The federal regulatory system also includes regulation of the securities industry by the Securities and Exchange Commission (SEC) and the Commodities Futures Trading Commission (CFTC), regulation of Fannie Mae and Freddie Mac by the Office of Federal Housing Enterprise Oversight (OFHEO), regulation of the Federal Home Loan Banks (FHLBs) by the Federal Housing Finance Board, regulation of the farm credit system by the Farm Credit Administration, and regulation of pension funds by the Employee Benefits Security Administration in the Department of Labor and by the Pension Benefit Guaranty Corporation. The Departments of the Treasury (Treasury), Justice (DOJ), and Housing and Urban Development (HUD) and the Federal Trade Commission (FTC) play ancillary roles. Noticeably absent at the federal level is regulation of the insurance industry, which is performed exclusively by the states. In addition, each of the states regulates financial services providers which are chartered or licensed in their jurisdictions.[9]

Deregulating derivatives

The Commodity Exchange Act of 1936 required that all futures and commodity options be regulated and traded on organized exchanges. The purpose of that law was to ensure transparency and to prevent the manipulation of commodity prices. In the late 1990s, the Act came under attack.

In November 1999, a report of the President's Working Group on Financial Markets recommended that the Act be amended to allow derivatives to trade over the counter and to free them from the regulatory jurisdiction of the Commodity Futures Trading Commission. The report, titled "Over-the-Counter Derivatives Markets and the Commodity Exchange Act", was signed by Fed Chairman Alan Greenspan, Treasury Secretary Larry Summers, Securities and Exchange Commission Chairman Arthur Levitt, and William Rainer, Chairman of the Commodity Futures Trading Commission.[10] The introduction to the report stated:

> The Working Group has concluded that under many circumstances, the trading of financial derivatives by eligible participants should be excluded from the [Commodity Exchange Act]. To do otherwise would perpetuate legal uncertainty or impose unnecessary regulatory burdens and constraints upon the development of these markets in the United States.

---

[9] Rose Marie Kushmeider, "The US Federal Financial Regulatory System: Restructuring Federal Bank Regulations", *FDIC Banking Review* vol. 17, no. 4 (2005).

[10] *Report of The President's Working Group on Financial Markets, Over-the-Counter Derivatives Markets and the Commodity Exchange Act*, November 1999.

...Although this report recommends the enactment of legislation to clearly exclude most OTC financial derivatives transactions from the CEA, this does not mean that transactions may not, in some instances, be subject to a different regulatory regime or that a need for regulation of currently unregulated activities may not arise in the future.

The following year, Congress passed the Commodity Futures Modernization Act of 2000 (CFMA), which revised the Commodity Exchange Act to allow many types of financial derivatives to legally trade over the counter. It also removed such over-the-counter derivatives transactions from the jurisdiction of the Commodity Futures Trading Commission, leaving them largely unregulated. CFMA was the last piece of legislation required to set the stage for the Great Meltdown of 2008. The bill was signed into law by President Clinton on 21 December 2000.

Figure 74

TOTAL OVER-THE-COUNTER DERIVATIVES CONTRACTS

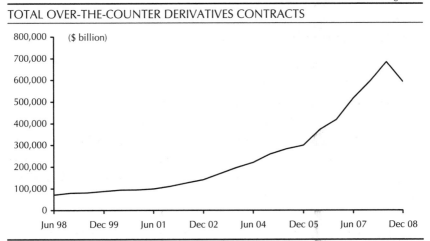

Source: *BIS Quarterly Review*, June 2009

Greenspan, Summers, Levitt and Clinton are all intelligent men. Given that unregulated derivatives trading nearly destroyed the world fewer than eight years later, how could they all have made such a terrible mistake in supporting its deregulation? These comments by Greenspan shed light on the question:

It should come as no surprise that the profitability of derivative products has been a major factor in the dramatic rise in large banks' noninterest earnings and doubtless is a factor in the significant gain in the overall finance industry's share of American corporate output during the past decade. In short, the value added of derivatives themselves derives from their ability to enhance the process of wealth creation.[11]

---

[11] Fed Chairman Alan Greenspan, "Financial derivatives" (remarks before the Futures Industry Association, Boca Raton, Florida, 19 March 1999).

That quote was from a speech made way back in March 1999, when the derivatives market was a mere $100 trillion in size. Between the passage of CFMA and the systemic financial-sector crisis, that market would become eight times larger.

Of course, that is only the notional amount. The actual amount of money at risk is a much smaller figure—at least so long as none of the counterparties go bankrupt. Unhappily, in 2008 numerous large counterparties either went bankrupt or would have done so, had the government not propped them up with capital injections or outright nationalization. Problems with subprime loans may have been the spark, but derivatives were the combustible material that incinerated the global financial system. It is naïve to think otherwise.

The age of derivatives

By 2008, only around 10% of all derivatives traded on exchanges. The other 90% ($684 trillion) traded over the counter. The average daily turnover of the 10% that were exchange-traded amounted to $4.2 trillion in April 2007 (the most recent data available). The turnover of the remaining 90% of derivatives that trade over the counter is unknown. It may or may not have been nine times greater (in proportion to its relative size), but if it were, then the average turnover of the entire derivatives market each day would have been $42 trillion, or the equivalent of about 75% of what the earth produces each year.

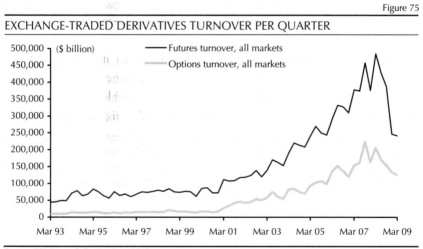

Figure 75

EXCHANGE-TRADED DERIVATIVES TURNOVER PER QUARTER

Source: *BIS Quarterly Review*, June 2009

The financial community generates fees for trading derivatives as well as for creating and "structuring" them. These fees vary, and no official statistics on the totals are available. But it seems fair to assume that the aggregate fees earned from a $760 trillion market turning over as much as $42 trillion a day would range between mindblowing and astronomical. Derivatives explain why the financial sector's share of corporate profits became so much greater than normal after CFMA was passed.

Figure 76

CORPORATE PROFITS: FINANCIALS VERSUS NON-FINANCIALS

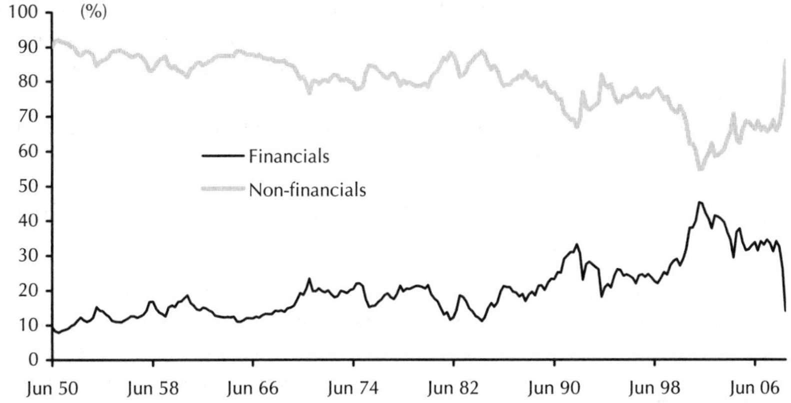

Source: Bloomberg

Greenspan finds a flaw

Why are 90% of derivatives traded over the counter, rather than through exchanges? Exchanges impose transparency and security. Counterparty risk is eliminated or at least very considerably reduced when trades are conducted on exchanges and settled through clearing houses, because the exchange itself is a counterparty to each trade. The exchange requires traders to maintain minimum margin requirements that are always sufficient to cover any potential losses. If the position moves against a trader, reducing his margin, the exchange demands that he put up additional margin. If he fails to do so, then the exchange closes out the position before it results in a loss that exceeds the margin (for if the loss did exceed the margin, the exchange could have to bear that loss).

Chairman Greenspan was an enthusiastic proponent of derivatives. He saw them as "an increasingly important vehicle for unbundling risks. These instruments enhance the ability to differentiate risk and allocate it to those investors most able and willing to take it". [12] However, Greenspan had considerable reservations about the desirability of government regulation. Given the tremendous influence he wielded during his reign as the longest-serving Fed chairman, his views on these issues warrant consideration in some depth.

Greenspan's views on regulation were particularly peculiar for a central banker. They also turned out to be particularly dangerous. For instance, he told an audience from the Futures Industry Association:

> The greater use of [over-the-counter] derivatives (as opposed to exchange-traded ones) doubtless reflects the attractiveness of customized over standardized products. But regulation is also a factor; the largest banks, in particular, seem to regard the regulation of exchange-traded derivatives, especially in the United States, as creating more burdens than benefits. As I have noted previously, the fact that the OTC markets function quite effectively without the benefits of the Commodity Exchange Act provides a strong argument for development of a less burdensome regime for exchange-traded financial derivatives. [13]

Two years earlier, in a talk entitled "Government regulation and derivative contracts", he had explained:

> A second imperative, once public policy objectives are clearly specified, is to evaluate whether government regulation is necessary for those purposes. In making such evaluations, it is critically important to recognize that no market is ever truly unregulated. The self-interest of market participants generates private market regulation. Thus, the real question is not whether a market should be regulated. Rather, the real question is whether government intervention strengthens or weakens private regulation. If incentives for private market regulation are weak or if market participants lack the capacity to pursue their interests effectively, then the introduction of government regulation may improve regulation. But if private market regulation is effective, then government regulation is at best unnecessary. *At worst, the introduction of government regulations unavoidably involves some element of moral hazard* [author's emphasis]—if private market participants believe that government is protecting their interest, their own efforts to protect their interest will diminish to some degree.

> Whether government regulation is needed, and if so, what form of government regulation is optimal, depends critically on a market's characteristics. A "one-size-fits-all" approach to financial market regulation is almost never appropriate. The degree and type of government regulation needed, if any, depends on the types of instruments traded, the types of market participants, and the nature of the relationships among market participants.

> Recognizing that a one-size-fits-all approach is seldom appropriate, it may be useful to offer transactors a choice between seeking the benefits and accepting the burdens

---

[12] *Ibid.*
[13] *Ibid.*

of government regulation, or forgoing those benefits and avoiding those burdens by transacting in financial markets that are only privately regulated. In such circumstances, the privately regulated markets in effect provide a market test of the net benefits of government regulation. Migration of activity from government-regulated to privately regulated markets sends a signal to government regulators that many transactors believe the costs of regulation exceed the benefits. When such migration occurs, government regulators should consider carefully whether less regulation or different regulation would provide a better cost-benefit tradeoff without compromising public policy objectives.

Later in the speech, he observed that

Institutional participants in the off-exchange derivative markets also have demonstrated their ability to protect themselves from losses from fraud and counterparty insolvencies....[They] also have demonstrated their ability to manage credit risks quite effectively through careful evaluation of counterparties, the setting of internal credit limits, and the judicious use of netting agreements and collateral. Actual losses to institutional counterparties in the United States from dealer defaults have been negligible.

Thus, there appears to be no need for government regulation of off-exchange derivative transactions between institutional counterparties.[14]

Had the speaker been an investment banker, such opinions might not have been all that surprising. But for the world's most powerful central banker to make the case for "private market regulation" of financial markets over government regulation was peculiar indeed. Did he really say "*the introduction of government regulations unavoidably involves some element of moral hazard*"? And did he really propose giving market participants a choice as to whether they would be regulated or not?

When private market regulation was put to the test following the passage of the CFMA, the consequences were catastrophic. A systemic crisis overwhelmed the financial sector and the economy spiraled down toward depression. That collapse eventually led Greenspan to the realization that his world view was flawed. On 23 October 2008, he admitted to the House Oversight Committee, "I made a mistake in presuming that the self-interest of organizations, specifically banks and others, were such that they were best capable of protecting their own shareholders and their equity in the firms."[15]

---

[14] Fed Chairman Alan Greenspan, "Government regulation and derivative contracts" (remarks at the Financial Markets Conference of the Federal Reserve Bank of Atlanta, Coral Gables, Florida, 21 February 1997).

[15] Excerpts from the *Washington Times* transcript of the exchange on 23 October 2008 between Alan Greenspan and House Oversight and Government Reform Committee Chairman Henry Waxman.

He was not let off lightly. In close questioning, Congressman Henry Waxman, the panel chairman, gave the former Fed chairman the opportunity to elaborate on his mistaken presumptions:

> *Rep. Waxman:* Dr. Greenspan, I want to start with you. You were the longest-serving chairman of the Federal Reserve in history, and during this period of time you were perhaps the leading proponent of deregulation of our financial markets. Certainly you were the most influential voice for deregulation. You have been a staunch advocate for letting markets regulate themselves.

> Let me give you a few of your past statements. In 1994, you testified at a congressional hearing on regulation of financial derivatives. You said there is nothing involved in federal regulation which makes it superior to market regulation. In 1997, you said there appears to be no need for government regulation of off-exchange derivative transactions. In 2002, when the collapse of Enron led to renewed congressional efforts to regulate derivatives, you wrote the Senate: "We do not believe a public policy case exists to justify this government intervention." And earlier this year, you wrote in the *Financial Times*: "Bank loan officers in my experience know far more about the risks and workings of their counterparties than do bank regulators."

> And my question for you is simple: Were you wrong? Would you be sure the mike is turned on?

Later:

> *Mr. Greenspan:* I made a mistake in presuming that the self-interest of organizations, specifically banks and others, were such that they were best capable of protecting their own shareholders and their equity in the firms.

And later:

> *Rep. Waxman:* Dr. Greenspan, I'm going to interrupt you just—the question I have for you is, you had an ideology, you had a belief that free, competitive—and this is your statement—"I do have an ideology. My judgment is that free, competitive markets are by far the unrivaled way to organize economies. We've tried regulation. None meaningfully worked." That was your quote.

> ...Do you feel that your ideology pushed you to make decisions that you wish you had not made?"

> *Mr. Greenspan:* Well, remember that what an ideology is, is a conceptual framework with the way people deal with reality. Everyone has one. You have to—to exist, you need an ideology.

> The question is whether it is accurate or not.

> And what I'm saying to you is, yes, I've found a flaw. I don't know how significant or permanent it is. But I've been very distressed by that fact. But if I may, may I just answer the question—

> *Rep. Waxman:* You found a flaw in the reality—

> *Mr. Greenspan:* Flaw in the model that I perceived as the critical functioning structure that defines how the world works, so to speak.

Rep. Waxman: In other words, you found that your view of the world, your ideology was not right. It was not working.

Mr. Greenspan: Precisely. That's precisely the reason I was shocked, because I had been going for 40 years or more with very considerable evidence that it was working exceptionally well.

Excerpts from a speech Greenspan gave in London in September 2002 illustrate how extreme his ideology was—and, perhaps, how gullible the public was to accept it:

But let us consider now another aspect of market regulation efforts: transparency. There should not be much dispute that markets function best when the participants are fully informed. Yet, paradoxically, the full disclosure of what some participants know can undermine incentives to take risk, a precondition to economic growth.

Greenspan then gave an example of a property developer who would not be able to buy land at a price that would make his project profitable if the landowners were fully aware of the returns he expected to earn if he could get the land cheaply. Greenspan went on:

An example more immediate to current regulatory concerns is the issue of regulation and disclosure in the over-the-counter derivatives market. By design, this market, presumed to involve dealings among sophisticated professionals, has been largely exempt from government regulations. ... But regulation is not only unnecessary in these markets, it is potentially damaging, because regulation presupposes disclosure, and forced disclosure of proprietary information can undercut innovation in financial markets just as it would in real estate markets.

To require disclosure of the structure of the innovative product either before or after its introduction would immediately eliminate the quasi-monopoly return and discourage future endeavors to innovate in that area. The result is that market imperfections would remain unaddressed and the allocation of capital to its most-productive uses would be thwarted. Even requiring disclosure on a confidential basis solely to regulatory authorities may well inhibit such risk-taking. Innovators can never be fully confident, justly or otherwise, of the security of the information."[16]

By the way, Greenspan was in London to receive an honorary knighthood from Queen Elizabeth II in recognition of his contribution to global economic stability. Really.

As shown above, Alan Greenspan had virtually led a crusade to persuade the public that derivatives should be allowed to trade over the counter and with as little regulatory oversight as possible. After much of the financial system had collapsed, he found a flaw in his free-market ideology. How much better it

---

[16] Fed Chairman Alan Greenspan, "Regulation, Innovation, and Wealth Creation" (remarks before the Society of Business Economists, London, UK, 25 September 2002).

would have been if he had found it sooner—or if he had never been Federal Reserve chairman at all, so he would not have been in the position to disseminate his flawed ideology with such damaging effect.

What lies beneath?

The exchange between Congressman Waxman and Greenspan, then aged 82, suggests it is never too late to confess a mistake or abandon a false ideology. However, by the time the former Fed chairman saw the light, a great deal of (possibly irreparable) damage had already been done. More than $600 trillion-worth of derivatives contracts are still being traded in an unregulated, completely opaque over-the-counter market. That market's size has made all its major participants too big to fail. Its fragility has required the US government to intervene in myriad unprecedented ways and on a previously unimaginable scale to prevent the world's entire financial superstructure from disintegrating. Who can say—who dares imagine—what losses may still be concealed within it?

The consumer protection group Public Citizen has charged that the unregulated electronic trading of energy futures made legal by the CFMA allowed Enron to manipulate the energy market in California and was responsible for the rolling blackouts and price spikes that occurred in that state during 2001. If that is true, could over-the-counter derivatives not also be used to manipulate the price of other commodities, such as oil?

In the opening paragraph of a report entitled *Blind Faith: How deregulation and Enron's influence over government looted billions from Americans*[17], Public Citizen rightly points out: "The three principles of *transparency*, *accountability* and *citizen oversight*—all removed under deregulation—are necessary elements for a market system to function properly." Nowhere can those principles be more lacking than in the derivatives markets. With contracts measured in trillions of dollars anonymously changing hands daily, are there any markets that could not be manipulated? Who can say?

Credulity must now give way to angry mistrust. Common sense and recent experience both strongly recommend that the entire derivatives industry be treated with a great deal of skepticism and fear. AIG had to be nationalized because one of its divisions had written $440 billion worth of credit default swaps (CDS) and its failure to pay would have threatened the solvency of many

---

[17] Public Citizen, "Blind Faith: How Deregulation and Enron's Influence Over Government Looted Billions from Americans", December 2001.

of the counterparties to those trades. As Fed Chairman Bernanke explained on *60 Minutes*:

> I understand why the American people are angry. It's absolutely unfair that taxpayer dollars are going to prop up a company that made these terrible bets, that was operating out of the sight of regulators, but which we have no choice but to stabilize, or else risk enormous impact, not just in the financial system, but on the whole US economy.[18]

In other words, the government was forced to take financial responsibility for AIG's CDS losses in order to prevent a derivatives Armageddon. So far, $182 billion of taxpayers' money has been made available to AIG, and $15.7 billion has been paid out to the top 10 CDS counterparties as follows: Société Générale, $4.1 billion; Deutsche Bank, $2.6 billion; Goldman Sachs, $2.5 billion; Merrill Lynch, $1.8 billion; Calyon, $1.1 billion; Barclays, $0.9 billion; UBS, $0.8 billion; DZ Bank, $0.7 billion; Wachovia, $0.7 billion; and Rabobank, $0.5 billion.

Looking beyond AIG, there is no reason for optimism that the threat posed by derivatives has even been contained. The potential for losses in that market far exceeds the losses the financial industry has reported thus far on nonperforming loans. A 1% loss ratio on the $700 trillion worth of derivatives contracts that trade over the counter would amount to $7 trillion; a 10% loss ratio, $70 trillion. There is a terrifying possibility that the entire industry is a Ponzi scheme on a scale that would make Bernie Madoff look like a small-town rascal.

The derivatives industry must be investigated and controlled

Derivatives were one of the main causes of the New Depression and they continue to pose an enormous threat to society. An in-depth public investigation is required to shine a spotlight on this unregulated can of worms. In the United States, a citizens' committee that excludes bankers, lobbyists and government officials should be empowered to hold hearings and determine the answers to the following questions:

- ❑ Were derivatives the principal cause of the US financial sector's systemic collapse?
- ❑ What percentage of derivatives is used for hedging and what percentage is used for speculation?

---

[18] Fed Chairman Ben Bernanke, interview on *60 Minutes*, 15 March 2009.

- ❏ Which activity—hedging or speculation—has cost US taxpayers more to clean up so far?
- ❏ Who are the top 500 speculators?
- ❏ What benefits are derived from speculation in derivatives?
- ❏ What are the costs and the potential costs?
- ❏ Who receives the benefits and who pays the costs?
- ❏ Is there any good reason all derivatives should not be made to trade on regulated exchanges, with all transactions settled through clearing houses?
- ❏ If all the current outstanding derivatives contracts were cleared through an exchange, would that reveal illegal activities such as accounting fraud or securities manipulation? Would it reveal a Ponzi scheme in which new derivatives are regularly created to manipulate the value of derivatives created earlier?
- ❏ Are over-the-counter-traded derivatives being used to manipulate commodity prices or other markets in the same way Public Citizen has charged that energy futures were used to manipulate the energy market in California?
- ❏ Did the sixfold increase (to $8 trillion) in the notional amount of commodity derivatives outstanding between 2004 and 2007 explain the spike in commodity prices during that period? When the 2008 crisis erupted and trading in these contracts fell, commodity prices crashed. When trading recovered, prices picked up even though demand remained depressed and, in the case of oil, excess capacity remained very high.
- ❏ Approximately $41 trillion in credit default swap contracts remain open. Who is exposed? Are they capable of bearing the losses?
- ❏ How much profit do derivatives generate for the financial industry to structure? To sell? To trade?
- ❏ What percentage of the industry's profits does that account for?
- ❏ How dependent has the United States become on the "wealth" generated by the financial sector's derivatives business, or, as Greenspan put it, "their ability to enhance the process of wealth creation"?[19]

---

[19] Fed Chairman Alan Greenspan, "Financial Derivatives" (remarks before the Futures Industry Association, Boca Raton, Florida, 19 March 1999).

- ❑ If the United States imposed strict regulations governing derivatives speculation, would the industry move offshore? If so, what measures could the United States take to ensure that US companies did not participate in offshore derivatives markets?
- ❑ Was the deregulation of the derivatives market the consequence of the financial sector's undue influence over the government? If not, was it simply an honest mistake, or was there some other reason that the government has not made public why it allowed such a dangerous market to develop with practically no regulatory oversight? There is surely some less imbecilic explanation than that a quadrillion dollars worth of unregulated derivatives makes the world a safer place by spreading the risk around "to those investors most able and willing to take it".[20]
- ❑ Should the CFMA of 2000 be repealed so that all derivatives must be regulated and trade through exchanges? If so, who should regulate derivatives?

Until the derivatives industry is brought under control, and preferably made very much smaller, it will represent a contingent liability to the government of the United States—possibly one so large that not even the US government could honor it.

Conclusion

The deregulation of the financial industry has been one of the gravest policy mistakes in the history of the United States. It caused the Federal Reserve to lose control over credit creation and brought the country to the brink of a derivatives-induced financial Armageddon, where it still teeters today. As a consequence, dozens of financial institutions are now too big to fail but too leveraged to survive without government support. Deregulation allowed a few thousand individuals to amass great fortunes, but its ultimate cost to the taxpayers is very likely to be reckoned in the trillions—possibly even tens of trillions. Finally, as Chapter 10 will show, financial-sector deregulation gave rise to a culture of credit in the United States and contributed to the deindustrialization that has debilitated the nation.

---

[20] *Ibid.*

Chapter 10
America doesn't work

It is incumbent on every generation to pay its own debts as it goes. A principle which if acted on would save one-half the wars of the world.

Thomas Jefferson[1]

Over the last quarter-century, the United States has pursued a disastrous economic policy that has left it deindustrialized and heavily in debt. Now only trillions of dollars in additional government debt can stave off a collapse on the scale of the Great Depression. This chapter explains why the American economy is simply not viable as it is currently structured, and how it came to be this way.

A new economic paradigm

Since the 1980s, a culture of debt has arisen in the United States. That change was the consequence of a misguided trade policy that gave rise to a current-account deficit of unprecedented size. Between 1982 and 2008, the United States imported $7.4 trillion more than it exported. It financed the shortfall on credit. That credit transformed the structure of the US economy.

---

[1] Thomas Jefferson to A.L.C. Destutt de Tracy, 1820.

As has been noted, every country's balance of payments must balance. Thus, between 1982 and 2008, $7.4 trillion in foreign capital entered the United States to finance that deficit. That amount was considerably more than the entire amount of US government debt held by the public at the end of 2008—$5.8 trillion. As the money flowed in, it created a credit-fuelled economic bubble—just as foreign capital inflows blew Latin America into an economic bubble in the 1970s and the Asian Crisis countries into economic bubbles in the 1990s.

In the process, the structure of the US economy changed. The manufacturing sector was decimated when exposed to ultra-low-wage foreign competition, while the service sector came to dominate the economy and employment as credit-driven asset-price inflation created the wealth that made many of those services profitable.

Consequently, over less than three decades as the US trade deficit grew to previously unimaginable levels, the country's economic growth model became one of credit-financed consumption that depended on ever-increasing amounts of credit each year to sustain it. In 2008, when the private sector could no longer bear the burden of so much debt, that model fell apart.

That paradigm of debt-fuelled consumption can never be resuscitated. The US economy is now on government-funded life support that cannot be paid for over the long run. The limited nature of government resources makes it inevitable that a new economic paradigm will emerge over the next five to ten years. The future of the United States—and the rest of the world—will be determined by the form that new paradigm takes.

Birth of the debt culture

Once US dollars ceased to be convertible into gold at the beginning of the 1970s, there was no longer any constraint on the amount of dollar-denominated debt that could be created by the Federal Reserve system or the Treasury Department, or, for that matter, the private sector. For the next decade, fear of inflation and the Fed's still relatively tight control over the financial sector kept credit growth relatively constrained. Beginning in the early 1980s, however, a flood of imports into the United States began to profoundly affect the economy. By circumventing many of the domestic bottlenecks that had caused high rates of inflation, this influx kept prices in check. It also quickly created a large trade deficit that was funded by foreign capital inflows, which loosened credit conditions in the United States. As these changes were taking place, the deregulation of the banking industry was significantly reducing the Fed's control over credit creation. When imports continued to surge, the stage was set for an explosion of credit.

Since the end of World War II, Washington had consistently pursued a policy of global trade liberalization. Five rounds of trade liberalization under the auspices of the GATT had been successfully completed before the end of the 1960s. During that period the expansion of international trade occurred within the framework of the Bretton Woods system, which was structured to ensure that trade between nations balanced. It was only after the Bretton Woods system broke down in the early 1970s, therefore, that the global imbalance that eventually destabilized the world began to take shape.

The United States continued to promote international trade liberalization even after Bretton Woods collapsed. The Tokyo Round of GATT was completed in 1979 and the Uruguay Round in 1993. From the early 1980s, however, the United States' trade policy underwent a very important change, as American policymakers became willing to tolerate very large current-account deficits for the first time. Until then, the economically orthodox view had been that trade must balance, or else—in the case of a trade deficit—the economy would suffer deflationary consequences as resources left the country to pay for that deficit. In the first half of the 1980s, however, it became clear that the United States could run very large trade deficits and finance them with dollar-denominated debt.

Policymakers in the Reagan administration seem to have embraced this new post-Bretton Woods reality. Imports appeared to help keep domestic inflation in check by opening up foreign sources of supply. Moreover, Americans did believe that "free trade" ultimately worked to everyone's advantage. Their mistake was to assume that the expansion of world trade would produce the same benefits within an international monetary system based on fiat money as it had within a system based on the gold standard.

Unlike the gold standard or the Bretton Woods system, however, the post-Bretton Woods international monetary system had no mechanism for preventing large and persistent trade imbalances. In the mid-1980s, the US current-account deficit grew to 3.5% of GDP; two decades later, following the entry of China and other low-wage countries into the global economy, the deficit reached 6.0% of GDP.

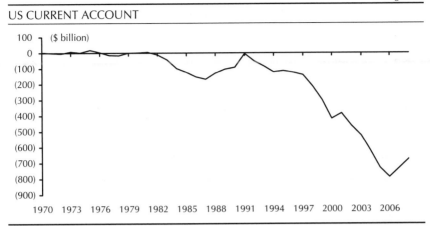

Figure 77

US CURRENT ACCOUNT

Source: Bureau of Economic Analysis

By then, what was understood to be "free trade" had actually become something very different: debt-financed trade. The debt that financed that trade, and the imbalances that built up around the world because of it, destabilized the global economy. Ultimately, when that debt could not be repaid, the global financial sector spiraled into systemic crisis and international trade collapsed. Had the Bretton Woods system remained in place, with its corollary of balanced trade, the global economy would have expanded at a much slower pace over the past 30 years than it has done. On the other hand, the global economy would not now have collapsed into depression. The high rates of economic growth during the 1980s, 1990s and most of the 2000s were great while they lasted, just as the Roaring Twenties must have been. Now that the global economy that boom created has broken down, we may not know for decades whether the boom years were worth their eventual price. The Roaring Twenties were certainly not worth the price paid during the 1930s and 1940s.

The debt culture

In the early 1980s, credit became a driver (and, eventually, *the* driver) of economic growth in the United States, expanding considerably faster than the economy as a whole. The ratio of debt to GDP had remained quite close to 150% from the end of World War II up through the end of the 1970s. Then it began to rise sharply, increasing from 168% in 1981 to 228% in 1987. By 2007, it topped 350%.

Figure 78

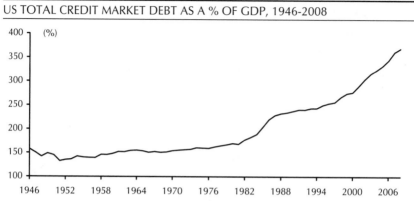

US TOTAL CREDIT MARKET DEBT AS A % OF GDP, 1946-2008

Source: Federal Reserve Flow of Funds (debt), Bureau of Economic Analysis (GDP)

The growing reliance on credit began to change the structure of the US economy by pushing up asset prices, promoting the growth of the financial and real-estate industries and generally creating more purchasing power than would have existed on a cash-payment basis.

Government debt

The debt buildup began with the government sector. The Reagan tax cuts of 1981 produced budget deficits that averaged 5% of GDP over the next five years. Figure 79 shows the annual increase in the federal government's debt alongside the corresponding increase in nominal GDP.

Figure 79

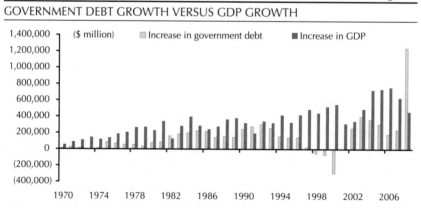

GOVERNMENT DEBT GROWTH VERSUS GDP GROWTH

Source: Federal Reserve Flow of Funds (debt), Bureau of Economic Analysis (GDP)

Figure 80 presents the increase in government debt as a percentage of the increase in nominal GDP. It makes the relationship between debt and GDP somewhat easier to grasp than Figure 79, but it tends to exaggerate the significance of credit growth during recession years (as in 1982 and 1991), when nominal GDP growth is depressed. But both graphs make clear the extraordinary shift in the government's finances from a large deficit to a large surplus during the 1990s.

Figure 80

RATIO GOVERNMENT DEBT GROWTH TO GDP GROWTH

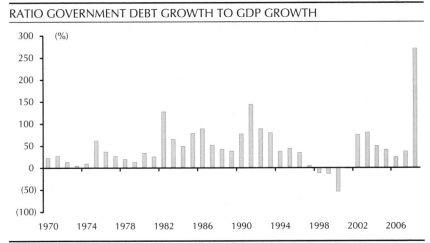

Source: Federal Reserve Flow of Funds (debt), Bureau of Economic Analysis (GDP)

The increase in government debt drove most of the growth during President Reagan's "Morning in America" economic boom of the mid-1980s. It also kept the economy out of a serious recession in the early 1990s and again in 2002 and 2003 following the implosion of the NASDAQ bubble. With the exception of those periods, government debt had never grown significantly faster than GDP until 2008, when enormous government spending was required to prevent the annihilation of the US financial sector and the collapse of the global economy that would have accompanied it. In 2008, the increase in government spending was more than two-and-a-half times the increase in GDP.

The large government budget deficits of the early 1980s led to the large current-account deficits of the mid-1980s by stimulating domestic demand and pulling in imports. In turn, the current-account deficits created a new credit dynamic in the United States as foreign capital flowed into the country to finance the growing trade shortfall. From that time, credit growth accelerated throughout the private sector.

Household-sector debt

Traditionally, GDP grew more than household-sector debt by a considerable margin. But in 1985 and 1986, household debt growth outstripped GDP growth for the first time. During the next decade, the increase in household debt averaged 78% of the increase in GDP. It accelerated again in the late 1990s. Between 2002 and 2007, household debt grew much faster in absolute dollar terms than the GDP did. During those six years, it increased by an average of $1 trillion a year, while GDP increased by only $600 billion a year. In addition to supporting the rise of the service sector, much of the spending by US households also fuelled economic growth in other countries via imports.

Figure 81

HOUSEHOLD DEBT GROWTH VERSUS GDP GROWTH

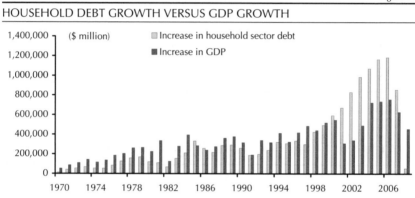

Source: Debt Federal Reserve Flow of Funds (debt), Bureau of Economic Analysis (GDP)

Figure 82

RATIO OF HOUSEHOLD DEBT GROWTH TO GDP GROWTH

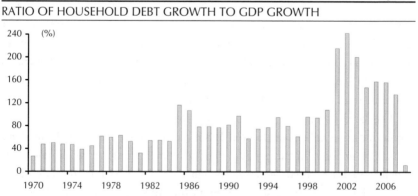

Source: Federal Reserve Flow of Funds (debt), Bureau of Economic Analysis (GDP)

Corporate and financial-sector debt

The corporate and financial sectors followed the same trend as the household sector.

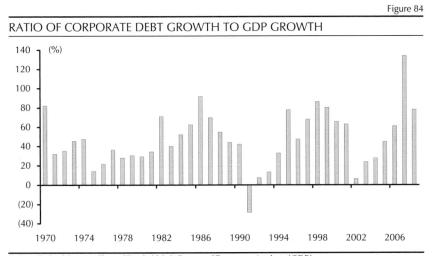

Figure 83

CORPORATE DEBT GROWTH VERSUS GDP GROWTH

($ million)   ▨ Increase in corporate debt   ■ Increase in GDP

Source: Federal Reserve Flow of Funds (debt), Bureau of Economic Analysis (GDP)

Figure 84

RATIO OF CORPORATE DEBT GROWTH TO GDP GROWTH

(%)

Source: Federal Reserve Flow of Funds (debt), Bureau of Economic Analysis (GDP)

The financial sector, being the main culprit in this crisis, is also the most interesting.

Figure 85

FINANCIAL-SECTOR DEBT GROWTH VERSUS GDP GROWTH

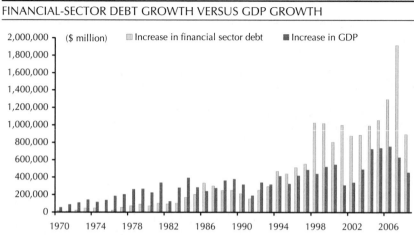

Source: Federal Reserve Flow of Funds (debt), Bureau of Economic Analysis (GDP)

Figure 86

RATIO OF FINANCIAL-SECTOR DEBT GROWTH TO GDP GROWTH

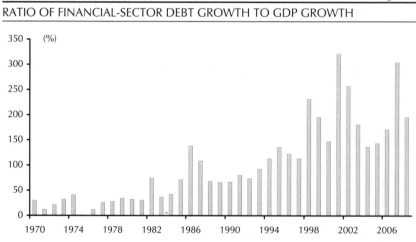

Source: Federal Reserve Flow of Funds (debt), Bureau of Economic Analysis (GDP)

Until the banking-sector deregulation of the early 1980s, GDP always expanded much more than financial-sector debt. During 1986 and 1987, the increase in the financial sector's debt exceeded the growth in GDP for the first time. The sector slowed its debt expansion in the late 1980s as problems in the formerly booming property market impaired banking-sector assets. However, in 1994 the increase in financial-sector debt outstripped GDP growth once again.

In 1998, the year Travelers merged with Citibank in anticipation of the repeal of Glass-Stegall the following year (see Chapter 9), financial-sector debt grew twice as fast as GDP. Over the following decade, its debt grew by an average of $1.1 trillion a year, while GDP grew by an average of $540 million a year. The figures for financial-sector debt are taken from the Fed's Flow of Funds statistics and it is unclear whether these fully account for the banks' off-balance-sheet entities or for the credit lines the banks extended. But they certainly do not incorporate the financial sector's exposure to the derivatives market, which by 2008 was rapidly approaching $1 quadrillion in size.

Total credit-market debt

Aggregating the debt-growth data for all sectors of the economy illustrates how out of control the US credit bubble ultimately became. In 2007, total credit-market debt in the United States expanded by $4.5 trillion—seven times more than the growth in nominal GDP.

Figure 87

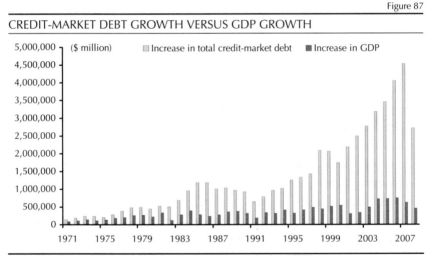

CREDIT-MARKET DEBT GROWTH VERSUS GDP GROWTH

Source: Federal Reserve Flow of Funds (debt), Bureau of Economic Analysis (GDP)

It is easy to understand how rapid credit growth fuels economic growth. Credit finances investment and consumption, which generate jobs and purchasing power. Credit expansion at twice the rate of nominal GDP growth (as occurred in the 1960s and 1970s) would already have been a very powerful force for expansion—although even then the difference between the two would be bound to raise doubts about the long-term stability of the banking sector. A ratio of credit growth to GDP growth of 300% should have set off alarm bells during the 1980s. For this ratio to have averaged more than 500% a year over the past decade is mind-boggling.

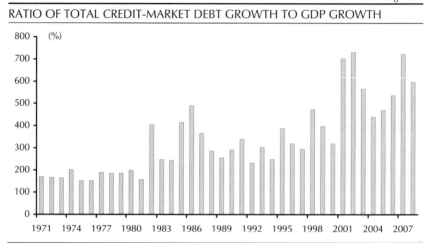

Figure 88

RATIO OF TOTAL CREDIT-MARKET DEBT GROWTH TO GDP GROWTH

Source: Federal Reserve Flow of Funds (debt), Bureau of Economic Analysis (GDP)

It appears that more and more debt was required each year to sustain an acceptable level of economic growth. So long as credit growth continued to accelerate, the economy continued to prosper. In that respect, the economy began to resemble a Ponzi scheme.

The explosion of credit caused the economy to expand in two ways: directly, by making credit available to consumers and businessmen to spend; and indirectly by fuelling asset-price inflation. This latter effect can be seen most clearly through changes in household net worth.

Household net worth increased markedly in the second half of the 1970s as a result of high rates of inflation. But it continued to increase even after inflation was tamed in the early 1980s. Its growth rate accelerated again in the late 1990s as the ratio of total credit growth to GDP growth approached 400% and produced the NASDAQ bubble. Household net worth fell when the NASDAQ bubble burst. However, the policy response to that crisis quickly created a property bubble that sent household net worth rising more steeply than ever in 2003. How? By generating even more credit growth.

Figure 89

US HOUSEHOLD NET WORTH

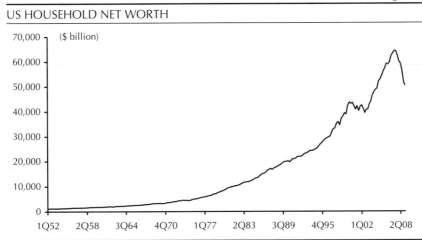

Source: Federal Reserve Flow of Funds

Home-equity extraction

Rising property prices allowed American home-owners to treat their houses as automated teller machines. As home prices rose, a large percentage of home-owners remortgaged their homes based on the reappraised, higher value. This enabled them to withdraw part of the increased value of the home and to spend it.

In 2005, Fed Chairman Greenspan published a paper estimating that "home-equity extraction" amounted to as much as 7% of disposable income in 2004, or the equivalent of 5% of GDP.[2] As home-equity extraction became more widespread, consumer spending increased from its normal range of 67–68% of GDP to 71% of GDP.

Low interest rates drove up asset prices, and asset-price inflation created the collateral that supported new debt. This dynamic fuelled US consumption and created an economic boom domestically and globally. Debt-financed consumption fuelled the service-oriented economy at home and the export-oriented economies of the United States' goods-producing trading partners abroad.

[2] Alan Greenspan and James Kennedy, *Estimates of Home Mortgage Origination, Repayments, and Debt on One-to-Four-Family Residences* (Federal Reserve Board Finance and Economics Discussion Paper 2005-41).

Figure 90

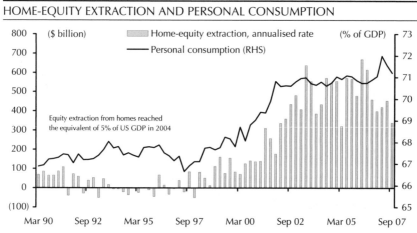

HOME-EQUITY EXTRACTION AND PERSONAL CONSUMPTION

Source: Bureau of Economic Analysis, UBS

The economy transformed

The combination of rising imports and rapid credit growth completely changed the structure of the American economy. At the end of World War II, the United States was the global manufacturing powerhouse. For the next 25 years, US exports consistently exceeded imports by a wide margin.

Figure 91

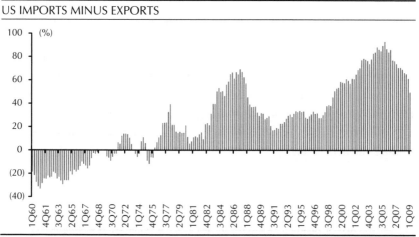

US IMPORTS MINUS EXPORTS

Source: Bureau of Economic Analysis

During that time, manufacturing contributed more than 25% of economic output and nearly a third of all jobs. When the US trade balance flipped into deficit at the end of the 1960s, however, the deindustrialization of America got under way.

Figure 92

MANUFACTURING-SECTOR CONTRIBUTION TO GDP

Source: Bureau of Economic Analysis

The manufacturing sector's contribution to GDP fell below 25% in 1969. By 1980, it was less than 20%. The more the United States imported from abroad, the less it manufactured at home. The sector's contribution to GDP fell below 15% in 2000, and by 2008 it amounted to only 11%. Similarly, manufacturing-sector employment fell from 29% of all jobs in 1947 to 10% in 2007.

Figure 93

PLAYING WITH FIRE: MANUFACTURING AND FINANCE AS A % OF GDP

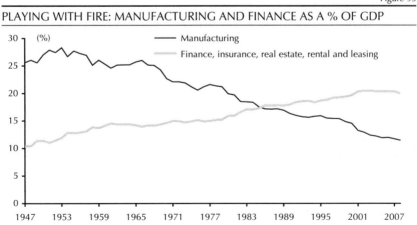

Source: Bureau of Economic Analysis

173

As the goods-producing industries shrank, the services-producing industries expanded. The finance, insurance, real estate, rental and leasing industries (FIRE) grew particularly rapidly. Business in the FIRE category expanded rapidly during the 1950s and then stabilized at around 15% of GDP during the 1960s and 1970s. When the debt culture began to take hold in the early 1980s, FIRE's share of the economy began to expand significantly again. By 2001, it accounted for more than 20% of GDP. Employment in these industries grew much less than output, however—from 3% of total employment in 1948 to 6% in 2007. Employment grew faster in other parts of the services sector, notably healthcare and professional and business services.

The following tables provide a complete breakdown of the changing composition of US economic output and employment over the past 60 years.

Figure 94

VALUE ADDED TO GDP BY INDUSTRY				
(%)	1947	1948	2007	2008
Agriculture, forestry, fishing and hunting	8	9	1	1
Mining	2	3	2	2
Utilities	1	1	2	2
Construction	4	4	4	4
Manufacturing	**26**	**26**	**12**	**11**
Wholesale trade	6	6	6	6
Retail trade	9	9	6	6
Transportation and warehousing	6	6	3	3
Information	3	3	4	4
Finance, insurance, real estate, rental and leasing	**10**	**10**	**20**	**20**
Finance and insurance	2	2	8	7
Real estate and rental and leasing	8	8	12	13
Professional and business services	4	4	12	13
Professional, scientific and technical services	1	1	7	8
Administrative and waste-management services	1	1	3	3
Educational services, healthcare and social assistance	2	2	8	8
Educational services	0	0	1	1
Healthcare and social assistance	2	2	7	7
Arts, entertainment, recreation, accommodation and food services	3	3	4	4
Arts, entertainment and recreation	1	1	1	1
Accommodation and food services	3	2	3	3
Accommodation	na	na	1	na
Food services and drinking places	na	na	2	na
Other services, except government	3	3	2	2
Federal	8	7	4	4
State and local	4	4	9	9

Source: Bureau of Economic Analysis

The contribution of the manufacturing sector to GDP collapsed from 26% in

1947 to 11% in 2008. Agriculture, forestry, fishing and hunting declined even more, from 8% of GDP to 1%. On the other hand, the FIRE sector doubled its contribution to 20%. Professional and business services also expanded sharply, from 4% of GDP to 13%. And healthcare and social assistance jumped from 2% of GDP to 7%. The federal government's share of GDP halved, while that of state and local governments more than doubled, leaving government's total share roughly unchanged.

In light of the events of 2008—the bankruptcy and/or nationalization of much of the financial sector and the collapse of the property market—it is necessary to question the real contribution of the FIRE industries to GDP. It is fair to conclude that in reality their contribution was far less than these official statistics indicate.

Figure 95

EMPLOYMENT BY INDUSTRY				
(% of all full- and part-time employees)	1948	1949	2006	2007
Agriculture, forestry, fishing and hunting	5	5	1	1
Mining	2	2	0	0
Utilities	1	1	0	0
Construction	5	4	6	5
Manufacturing	**29**	**27**	**10**	**10**
Wholesale trade	5	5	4	4
Retail trade	9	9	11	11
Transportation and warehousing	6	6	3	3
Information	3	3	2	2
Finance, insurance, real estate, rental and leasing	**3**	**4**	**6**	**6**
Finance and insurance	2	3	4	4
Real estate and rental and leasing	1	1	2	2
Professional and business services	3	3	13	13
Professional, scientific and technical services	1	1	5	6
Administrative and waste-management services	1	1	6	6
Educational services, healthcare and social assistance	3	3	13	13
Educational services	1	1	2	2
Healthcare and social assistance	2	2	11	11
Arts, entertainment, recreation, accommodation and food services	5	5	9	9
Arts, entertainment and recreation	1	1	1	1
Accommodation and food services	4	4	8	8
Accommodation	na	na	1	1
Food services and drinking places	na	na	7	7
Other services, except government	7	7	5	5
Federal	8	9	4	4
State and local	8	8	13	13

Source: Bureau of Economic Analysis.

Employment in manufacturing collapsed between 1948 and 2007; the total number of workers in that industry peaked at 20 million in 1979 and fell to 14 million in 2007. Employment in agriculture, forestry, fishing and hunting also fell very significantly, but less importantly in terms of the numbers of people employed—2.5 million at the peak in 1948, and just 1.4 million in 2007.

On the other hand, employment in professional and business services, in healthcare and social assistance, and in food and drink services increased most significantly. Employment in state and local government also rose notably. By 2007, 13% of the US workforce was employed in professional and business services, 11% in healthcare-social assistance, 11% in retail trade, and 7% in food services and drinking places (as against 10% in manufacturing, down from 29% in 1948). A further 17% of workers were employed by federal, state or local government.

Employment in the goods-producing industries had fallen to 16% of all jobs in 2007, while employment in the service industries had risen to 67% of the total.

Figure 96

GOODS-PRODUCING VERSUS SERVICE INDUSTRIES

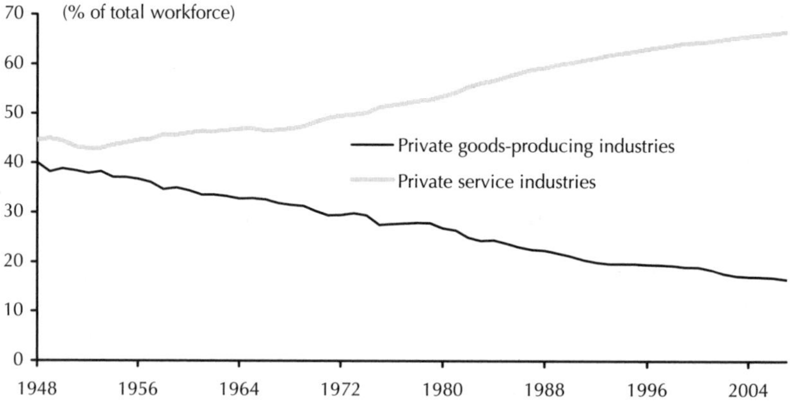

Source: Bureau of Economic Analysis

So long as the credit bubble in the United States continued to inflate each year, the growth of the service sector was hailed as the natural, even inevitable, path for a modern, "developed" economy. But the implosion of the financial sector and the property market under the weight of too much debt has discredited the United States' debt-fuelled consumption paradigm. The rise of the services sector stands exposed as neither natural or inevitable, and certainly not sustainable.

The reality is that the United States has deindustrialized to the point where it is incapable of producing the goods it consumes. And without access to increasing amounts of consumer credit, Americans can no longer afford to consume the "services" around which the economy is now built and which now employ 67% of the workforce. In 2009, the United States' $14 trillion economy is being held together only by a $1.6 trillion government budget deficit and a $1 trillion increase in the Fed's balance sheet. So far at least, these have prevented an economic collapse that could well have resembled that of the Great Depression.

This disaster occurred because the United States was unwilling to live within its very considerable means. From the 1960s onward, the country's leaders, having failed in their duty to keep the government's budget in balance, progressively debased the national currency and allowed the United States to become dependent on imported goods financed on credit. It must be acknowledged that a political system that would permit politicians to flout every tenet of economic orthodoxy must itself be flawed and badly in need of reform.

Conclusion

Since 1982, the United States has bought $7.4 trillion more from the rest of the world than the rest of the world has bought from the United States. It has financed the difference on credit. That trade deficit has destabilized not only the United States but the entire world, by creating a large imbalance between the world's expanded production capacity and its ability to afford the goods that capacity can produce. Just as excessive credit expansion during the 1920s created excess global capacity and caused the Great Depression when that credit could not be repaid in the early 1930s, the United States' credit-financed spending spree of recent years has created enormous excess capacity around the world today. Now that the credit cannot be repaid, governments, with Washington rightly in the lead, are compelled to incur and spend trillions of dollars of additional debt to absorb the excess capacity in order to prevent—or at least stave off—a collapse on the scale of the Great Depression. This catastrophe was caused in large part by the confusion of policymakers, who mistook debt-financed trade for free trade.

Part 3: The future

What must be done

Misguided economic policies, combined with the forces of globalization, have produced global imbalances on an extraordinary scale. Inherently unsustainable, that disequilibrium began to come unwound in 2008, threatening the world with a New Great Depression. A multi-trillion-dollar, multinational intervention has halted, for the moment, the downward spiral in economic output, trade and asset prices by preventing market forces from restoring balance in the global economy—balance at a much lower level of output and employment. However, governments cannot afford to keep the world on fiscal and monetary life support forever. The means must be found to rebalance the global economy through growth rather than contraction. Part 3 explores how that might be achieved.

The lack of American competitiveness in the global economy, and the United States' ability, until now, to finance its massive trade deficits with dollar-denominated debt, are at the core of the global disorder. US policymakers must implement a strategy that restores the country's competitiveness before the American public votes for protectionism. Chapter 11 draws on lessons from Japan's Great Recession and builds on Keynesian analysis to outline such a strategy. Chapter 12 discusses the budgetary, monetary, regulatory and political reforms necessary in the United States to rebuild the foundations for sustainable prosperity.

The United States has been the world's engine of economic growth for more than six decades. Its economy represents a quarter of global economic output. Decoupling was a myth. This New Depression began in the United States, but it spread to every corner of the world. If that country's structural crisis is not resolved, every country will suffer. There would be no winners from America's demise. For all these reasons, this global crisis cannot be resolved until the structural economic crisis in the United States is overcome.

Chapter 11
Restructuring America

The state of the economy calls for action, bold and swift, and we will act—not only to create new jobs, but to lay a new foundation for growth. We will build the roads and bridges, the electric grids and digital lines that feed our commerce and bind us together. We will restore science to its rightful place, and wield technology's wonders to raise healthcare's quality and lower its cost. We will harness the sun and the winds and the soil to fuel our cars and run our factories. And we will transform our schools and colleges and universities to meet the demands of a new age. All this we can do. All this we will do.

President Barack Obama[1]

In order to restructure the economy and return the country to the path of sustainable growth, the US government should implement a new industrial policy that invests heavily in 21st Century industries. Think Apollo, but on a much greater scale and with much more than a space race at stake.

Lessons from the Great Depression and Japan's Great Recession suggest that Washington could easily finance a $3 trillion national industrial restructuring program over the next 10 years. An investment on that scale in the industries of the future would create technological miracles that would

---

[1] President Barack Obama, inaugural address, 20 January 2009.

permanently end the US trade deficit, raise enough tax revenues to balance the budget, and end the nation's debilitating dependence on credit. A trillion-dollar investment in solar technology would yield limitless cheap energy. A trillion-dollar investment in genetic research and biotechnology could extend the human life span by 20 years or more. There is a real possibility that this economic crisis could be turned into an unprecedented opportunity to advance humanity's wellbeing.

Since the 1960s, a string of disastrous policy mistakes has left the United States economy unviable, while the forces of globalization are expediting its deterioration. The country's industries are not globally competitive. The private sector has grown dependent on debt that it can no longer service. Government finances are on course for bankruptcy. A continuation of the status quo is almost certain to end very badly.

The choice, then, is between economic restructuring and potentially irreversible decline. A little more debt and some of America's vaunted ingenuity could lock in another American Century. This opportunity should not be allowed to pass. There may not be another.

Too socialist?

In the United States today, a great debate is raging as to whether the country is becoming "too socialist". The Republican Party, having increased the national debt by 70% ($2.4 trillion) during the eight years of President George W. Bush's administration, has concluded since losing office that government is getting too big. The Democrats are finding it difficult to respond, having inherited an economic crisis that only massive government spending can prevent from turning into a new Great Depression. Politically entertaining though this debate may be, it is hindering the nation's ability to formulate a strategy for overcoming the structural crisis that confronts it. It's too late now to discuss the kind of economic system the United States will have in 2010. The fact is, the United States has had a "managed economy" since 1942. By itself, that is regrettable. What makes it truly tragic is that America's managed economy has been very poorly managed.

Before 1930, the United States did have a capitalist economy. In that year, government outlays amounted to 3% of GDP, meaning that of every $100 spent in the economy, the government spent $3. Government spending rose as high as 11% of GDP during the Great Depression. In 1942, the first full year after the US entered World War II, it jumped to 24% of GDP, and the following year to 43%. After the war it declined to 12% (in 1948), but during the Korean War it rose again to 20% and remained at roughly that level until 2008. Any time the economy became too weak, the government spent more. When it boomed—or bubbled, as in 2000—the government spent a bit less (as a percentage of GDP). But overall, for more than half a century, the government has spent $20 of every $100 spent in the United States "fine-tuning" the economy in an attempt to spare it from recession. Ultimately, that has not worked out so well. In 2008 the economy collapsed. In 2009, the government was forced to spend $26 of every $100 spent in the country to prevent the economy from breaking down altogether. And for every $26 the government spent, it increased its debt by $11. That amount excludes the $1 trillion created and spent by the Federal Reserve.

Figure 97

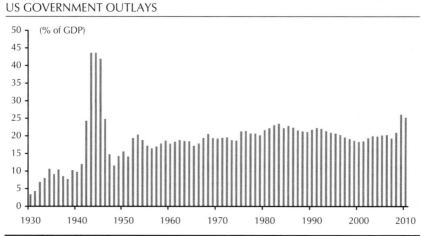

US GOVERNMENT OUTLAYS

Source: CBO

So now the US economy is on government life support. The CBO expects government outlays to total 25% of GDP in 2010 and to average 23.4% over the next ten years. Even on the basis of those projections—which rest on very optimistic assumptions—at the end of that period in 2019, US government debt will amount to $14.3 trillion or 68% of GDP, up from $5.8 trillion or 41% of GDP in 2008.

After that, the outlook becomes much worse. According to CBO projections, government outlays will reach 27% of GDP in 2035, 32% in 2050 and 44% in 2080. Meanwhile, the national debt will climb to 79%, 128% and 283% of GDP in those three years, respectively. Rising Medicare costs account for much of the projected increase in outlays and debt in the years after 2020. Based on the CBO projections, the annual interest expense on the government's debt will amount to 12% of GDP by 2080.

Therefore, while it is possible that the United States may be able to limp along on government life support as a badly managed economy for quite a number of years into the future, that path will eventually bankrupt the country and open the door to a crisis that could extend well beyond economics.

What it really takes

These projections are terrifying. But the future is not set in stone. Policies can be changed. Disaster can be averted. First, however, it is necessary for the public to understand and for policymakers to acknowledge that the economic crisis now underway is not simply a severe recession but a breakdown of a failed economic paradigm. It will not be enough merely to "get the credit flowing again". This crisis was caused by too much flowing of credit, which blew the economy into a balloon. That balloon is now full of holes. Pumping more credit into it is not going to make it viable again. If the financial sector provided the household sector with another trillion dollars of fresh credit in 2010, households would spend it and the economy would enjoy a growth spurt. But in 2011 the households would default again, GDP would contract and the financial sector would need another bailout. The debt-fuelled consumption paradigm has come to a dead end. Americans don't earn enough money to be able to take on any more debt. It is crucial for everyone to understand that.

Figure 98

US HOUSEHOLD-SECTOR DEBT AS A % OF GDP

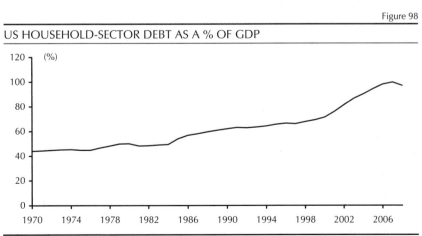

Source: Federal Reserve Flow of Funds

Creating a bigger credit bubble did not work after the NASDAQ bubble popped and it won't work now that the property bubble has popped. Some other approach is needed to restore the economy to sustainable growth.

To find a policy that works, it is first necessary to make an honest assessment of the economy's failings.

The harsh truth about the American economy can be summarized as follows: it is not viable as it is currently structured; it is in crisis because the country consumes much more than it produces; and there are no known tools in the existing policy tool kit that can correct that situation without provoking a depression. The country has lost much of its manufacturing base and continues to deindustrialize because its wage rates are up to 40 times higher than those of low-wage countries. Over several decades, the service sector, underwritten by rapid credit expansion, swelled to become the dominant part of the US economy, only to collapse when the private-sector debt burden became unbearable. The government has intervened with a multi-trillion-dollar "rescue package" to prevent the collapse in aggregate demand from the private sector from plunging the economy into a new Great Depression. However, the government's response is not sustainable. Moreover, it has not targeted the causes of the crisis, much less resolved them. In fact, there is every reason to expect that globalization will continue to deindustrialize America, making it even less able to produce as much as it consumes in the years ahead.

Policymakers must devise a permanent solution to this predicament before the government's ability to support the economy through deficit spending is depleted. To be effective, the solution must bring the country's trade back into balance; it must bring the government budget back into balance; and it must wean the country off its dependence on credit growth as the driver of economic growth. In other words, the solution must entail restructuring the US economy to make it self-sustaining; and this must be accomplished in a manner that does not provoke a global depression.

How can this be done?

Lessons from the past

The Great Depression of the 1930s and Japan's Great Recession, which began in 1990, were both caused by credit bubbles very similar to the one responsible for the current crisis in the United States. Policymakers failed to find a cure for the Great Depression, which did not end until World War II utilized or destroyed all the excess capacity that had been created by too much credit during the Roaring Twenties. Similarly, policymakers in Japan have not yet managed to end their Great Recession (although they do deserve credit for preventing the economy from collapsing into a depression as bad as that of the 1930s). Still, those two calamities have been analyzed in great depth, and some useful conclusions can now be drawn.

In his 1936 book *The General Theory of Employment, Interest and Money*, John Maynard Keynes argued that during a depression, governments should carry out large-scale deficit spending to put to work the underused resources of the economy. Exasperated by the reluctance of the British government to act to support the economy, he wrote:

> If the Treasury were to fill old bottles with banknotes, bury them at suitable depths in disused coalmines which are then filled up to the surface with town rubbish, and leave it to private enterprise on well-tried principles of laissez-faire to dig the notes up again, there need be no more unemployment and, with the help of the repercussions, the real income of the community, and its capital wealth also, would probably become a good deal greater than it actually is. It would, indeed, be more sensible to build houses and the like; but if there are political and practical difficulties in the way of this, the above would be better than nothing. [2]

The *General Theory* came too late to have much impact on the way governments dealt with the Great Depression. Later however, Keynes' theories became so widely accepted that by the 1960s economic policymakers came to believe government deficit spending could be used to iron out even small ripples in the business cycle. Although Keynesian economics (as distinct from Keynes himself) became somewhat discredited during the stagnation of the 1970s, the $1.6 trillion budget deficit in 2009 is nothing if not a very aggressive Keynesian response to the New Depression. Massive government deficit spending has prevented the bottom from completely dropping out from under the economy as it did during the 1930s. This result strongly supports Keynes's analysis. However, as his theories were not tested during his lifetime, Keynes did not offer a strategy for weaning an economy off government life support once the emergency had passed. That question is one of the greatest challenges facing policymakers today.

Japan is a more recent case in which massive fiscal stimulus was applied to support aggregate demand following the collapse of a credit bubble. After the Japanese economic bubble burst in 1990, the country went on government life

---

[2] John Maynard Keynes, *The General Theory of Employment, Interest and Money* (The Macmillan Press, 1936), p. 129.

support. Over the past 20 years, the budget deficit of the Japanese government has averaged 4.6% a year (6.3% annually over the past decade), and the ratio of Japanese government debt to GDP has increased from 69% to more than 200%. While massive government spending never managed to resolve the crisis— Japan's nominal GDP is no higher now than it was in 1993—it did prevent a depression. Unemployment has remained quite low and the Japanese standard of living has remained very high.

Japan's experiment also offers a number of lessons. Perhaps most importantly, it suggests that it is possible for an advanced industrial nation to borrow much more than would have been considered possible twenty years ago. Moreover, Japan was able to finance that debt without resorting to paper-money creation by the central bank for the purpose of buying government debt. In other words, the Bank of Japan did not monetize the government's budget deficits. It is also important to note that massive government borrowing did not "crowd out" the private sector by pushing up the cost of borrowing. The yield on 10-year government bonds is less than 1.4% today. Richard Koo has written two important books detailing some of the lessons from Japan's "balance-sheet recession".[3]

Japan's experience gives hope that the US government will be able to continue to support its failed economy for a number of years into the future without resorting to monetizing the debt, which would risk creating hyperinflation. On the other hand, Japan has not solved its economic crisis. And it is not yet clear how the Japanese experiment ends. Will the country be able to continue growing its government debt to support the economy? Up to what level? Then what? There are real reasons for concern that such high levels of government debt could eventually have a very damaging impact on the Japanese economy and society.

The Japanese government has faced a great deal of criticism for spending the stimulus money on wasteful projects such as unwanted bridges to nowhere. If Japanese policymakers had known in 1990 that the government would end up spending the equivalent of more than 150% of GDP to stimulate the economy over the following two decades, wouldn't they have spent the money in a different way? It seems certain that they would have.

That may be the most important lesson US policymakers can learn from the Japanese experiment: not to waste the stimulus money on bridges to

---

[3] Richard C Koo, *Balance Sheet Recession* (John Wiley & Sons, 2003) and *The Holy Grail of Macroeconomics* (John Wiley & Sons, 2008).

nowhere. They should consider carefully the possibility that to keep the economy afloat, the government may have to keep spending vast sums for the next decade or more. If the US post-bubble experience follows that of Japan, the US government could end up spending trillions of dollars more than even the worst-case scenarios currently anticipate. For instance, if US government debt expands by the equivalent of 150% of GDP, as happened in Japan, that would amount to $21 trillion (in current dollars) in deficit spending. (Current CBO projections suggest that the ratio of US government debt to GDP will be 68% in 2019.) In that case, or even in the case where US government debt rises to 100% of GDP, it would be better for the government to spend the money in a rational, far-sighted manner with the aim of generating the maximum possible returns for society, rather than wasting the money on a long series of pork-barrel projects that accomplish little or nothing for the betterment of the nation.

The current baseline

The CBO's Baseline Budget Outlook projects that the United States budget deficits will amount to $7.1 trillion over the next 10 years (2010 to 2019). Those projections are likely to prove far too optimistic. A $10 trillion deficit over 10 years is the best that can be realistically hoped for.

Figure 99

BUDGET DEFICIT PROJECTIONS

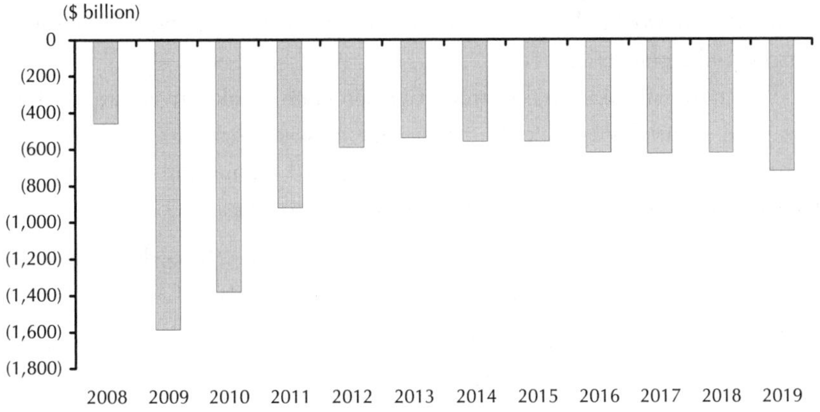

Source: CBO

187

Trillion-dollar annual deficits for the next decade may keep the United States from collapsing into a severe depression, just as very large annual budget deficits have kept Japan out of depression. But they would do nothing to restore the economy's long-term viability. In 2020, the economy would still be dependent on debt. More trillion-dollar budget deficits would be needed to support it in the years that followed. The trade deficit would still be massive, and the process of deindustrialization would be much closer to completion. The country would continue to consume much more than it produced as long as other countries continued to accept its IOUs. But with each year that passed, structurally the economy would become increasingly rotten at its core. Eventually, it would all end very badly in one of any number of "you get what you deserve" scenarios.

American ingenuity

There is a much more attractive alternative future, in which the United States remains the world's dominant superpower with a revitalized, self-sustaining economy. That alternative requires a national industrial-restructuring program, in which the government would invest in 21st Century technologies with the goal of establishing an unassailable American lead in the industries of the future. That goal could be achieved at the cost of $3 trillion over 10 years. It would leave the United States government $20 trillion in debt in 2019, rather than $17 trillion, as appears likely otherwise. But it would make the country a technological superpower, with a quarter-century lead over its closest competitor. It would also yield technological marvels that would enrich every person on the planet.

The national industrial-restructuring program could invest in a dozen advanced technologies or only a few. But it would have to be designed to reshape the US economy so that it once again becomes self-sustaining and, therefore, capable of meeting the following three criteria:

1. The United States must be able to produce enough goods or services to pay for what it consumes, in order to eliminate its trade deficit;

2. The economy must generate enough tax revenues to balance the government's budget; and

3. The economy must be able to expand while the ratio of credit to GDP is kept constant, in order to kick its destabilizing debt habit.

Consider, for example, a scenario in which the government invested $1 trillion each in solar energy, nanotechnology, and genetic engineering and biotechnology. The investments in sustainable energy would bring energy independence. Investments in biotechnology would yield medical miracles. Investments in nanotechnology would restore the United States' industrial dominance in world markets. New industries would bring in new taxes that would return the government's budget to surplus. New technologies would generate exports and ensure a trade surplus for decades to come. And unlike much of the service sector today, these industries would not boom or bust depending on credit growth. They would produce real goods, real profits and real jobs.

It is far beyond the scope of this book to explore in detail the scientific possibilities of the 21st Century. But an investment program on the scale outlined above could not fail to generate wide-ranging benefits.

Solar energy

A $1 trillion investment in solar energy could perfect photovoltaic energy generation, cover the Nevada desert (which is already government owned) with solar panels, and replace the electricity grid from one end of the country to the other to accommodate direct current. The many benefits would include:

- ❑ Energy: Cheap, clean and in limitless supply.
- ❑ Trade: Roughly 40% of the US trade deficit can be attributed to energy imports. Eliminating these would be tremendously helpful in removing the global imbalances destabilizing the world.
- ❑ Government budget: Revenues would be expanded by taxing the domestically produced energy. Expenditures would be cut, as it would no longer be necessary to militarily secure foreign oil supplies.
- ❑ Enhanced national security.
- ❑ Domestic job creation.

Genetic engineering and biotechnology

A $1 trillion investment here would very likely yield a genetic revolution with consequences as great as those produced by the Industrial Revolution. The medical benefits should be enormous. In agriculture, a new Green Revolution could be anticipated. Benefits would include:

- ❑ Education: Large government grants to US universities would increase their global dominance.

❑ Trade: The development of new products, including life-saving drugs, would bring US trade back into balance.

❑ Government revenues: New industries would bring in new taxes that would quickly repay their cost of development and much more.

Nanotechnology

A $1 trillion investment in nanotechnology would develop industrial processes and molecular-engineered materials that would restore the United States' competitive advantage in many types of manufacturing. Benefits:

❑ Education: The government investment in nanotech would advance US universities' capabilities in physics.

❑ Trade: The development and sale of completely new products would help resolve the country's structural economic crisis and balance its trade.

❑ Government revenues: New industries would yield new sources of revenue, making it possible for the government to recover its development costs.

The financing

During a bubble, so long as the credit keeps flowing, the economy expands. More factories are built, more businesses are opened and production capacity grows. Large profits are generated, causing investment capital and bank deposits to swell. When the borrowed money can't be repaid, the economy stops expanding because supply outstrips demand. Then the excess capacity weighs on the economy. It can't be used. With no need for more capacity, new investment is anemic. That produces excess financial capacity as well. No viable investment opportunities exist to absorb the profits created during the boom. The economy is mired in a liquidity trap with no demand for loans (no matter how low interest rates go) and high rates of unemployment. Thus the nation's resources—physical as well as financial—are left idle. Eventually they deteriorate and are destroyed.

Keynes argued that governments, rather than standing by while the economy rots, should borrow and spend in a depression to take up the excess capacity and put idle resources to use. Japan has followed his advice since its bubble burst in 1990, and the United States is doing the same today now that its credit bubble has popped. The result has been a great improvement on the economic management of yesteryear. US unemployment is only 10%—not 25%, as it was during the Great Depression.

But now that Keynes's advice has been put fully to the test, policymakers are discovering an unanticipated complication. It is not clear how they can withdraw support for the economy without causing it to slump back into depression. It is equally unclear how the government can continue financing this economic life support over the long term. In other words, there is no exit strategy.

Keynes is dead (as he knew he would be in the long run). He has brought us this far. Now we are on our own. We must find the exit. We do have some advantages that Keynes did not have, however. We are much more familiar with post-bubble depressions than he was. He only saw the Great Depression, and there is no evidence that he ever really understood what caused it. We, on the other hand, have not only the Great Depression to refer to but also the New Depression and all the smaller credit-bubble crises—Latin American, peso, Asian—as well as the ongoing Great Recession in Japan.

Keynes did not have enough data to determine what caused the Depression. Today's economists do not have that excuse. It is perfectly clear that all these crises were caused by an explosion of credit after the collapse of a hard-money regime. In each case, the credit distorted the economy by fuelling a boom; and the boom ended in a bust characterized by excess industrial *and financial* capacity.

What our generation must learn is that this excess financial capacity can be used not only to absorb the economy's excess capacity, but also to put the economy back on a sustainable course. The Japanese government's debt exceeds two times GDP, yet its 10-year bond yield is 1.4%. The 10-year US Treasury note yields only 3.5% despite a $1.6 trillion budget deficit, equivalent to 11% of US GDP.

There is a very large pool of money available in this post-bubble world that, if used intelligently, could restore the United States to economic viability while generating technological miracles as a bonus. That money is available only to the government, since most of the private sector is not creditworthy. But that is just as well in this case, because only the government is large enough to carry out the kinds of investment programs needed to remake the American economy into a going concern.

The money is available now, but it won't be forever. According to the Federal Reserve's Flow of Funds statistics, the size of the dollar-denominated credit market is $53 trillion. If the government does not borrow and invest, much of that liquidity will be destroyed in the poor post-bubble investment environment. Over time, if the government sticks to its current strategy of keeping the economy on life support (without curing its disease) with trillion-dollar-a-year deficits from now to eternity, then most of the remaining liquidity will be squandered, probably on bridges to nowhere, and this unique opportunity will be lost.

In other words, this is a "use it or lose it" situation. The better alternative is to use it. The Great Depression was not solved by economists, it was ended by generals. Japan's Great Recession continues, but the prognosis is not good. There is a better way. Bold investment in economic restructuring is the exit strategy.

Objections

Countless objections will be raised to the implementation of an industrial policy in the United States. Here, a few are considered.

Objection: The government makes a mess of things, and the money would just be wasted. Business should be left to the private sector.

Response: It is certainly very regrettable that government policy mistakes led to the debilitation of the US economy and the New Depression. At this point, however, only the government is large (and creditworthy) enough to carry out investments on the scale needed to restructure the economy. If the government does not act, the money will end up being squandered on wasteful government life-support programs in any case.

Objection: An industrial policy would transform the United States into a socialist country.

Response: The United States already has a managed economy, which is mismanaged. It is not managed equitably enough to be termed socialist, and it is not managed efficiently enough to avoid severe economic decline unless changes are made. Any attempt to go cold-turkey and return to pre-1930 capitalism would result in economic collapse as soon as the government life support was withdrawn. The only viable option left is much more intelligent management. Only after the country reestablishes a viable, self-sustaining economic structure will the United States have a hope of returning to a free-market economy functioning within an

192

economically orthodox framework. But that is certainly not the economic system the country has today.

Objection: A $3 trillion investment program could not be financed.

Response: It could easily be financed. Adding $3 trillion to the $10 trillion that the government is likely to have to borrow to fund its deficits over the next 10 years would leave the ratio of government debt to GDP at less than 100%. Japan's ratio of government debt to GDP will hit 225% in 2010. Moreover, after the US government's $1 trillion investment in biotechnology and genetic engineering yields a cure for cancer, it will not take long to pay off the entire government debt. The only real threat that could make an investment program on this scale unaffordable would be a derivatives-induced meltdown of the financial sector that could cost the government trillions or tens of trillions of dollars to clean up. Should that occur, it would be better to sacrifice the financial industry than to abandon the economic restructuring plan. Finance is a sunset industry.

Objection: $3 trillion would not be enough.

Response: A trillion dollars is an enormous amount of money, even in today's world. Three trillion would produce miracles. However, if that sum failed to make the US economy self-sustaining, double it: $6 trillion certainly would. There is every reason to believe that even $6 trillion could be easily financed.

Objection: Other countries would oppose a large-scale investment program by the US government.

Response: That is very likely. Nevertheless, the world is dependent on exporting to the United States. The rest of the world will benefit from a healthy American economy. There will be no winners if the US economy goes into terminal decline.

Objection: Government ownership of such important industries would make government too powerful and would pose a threat to democracy.

Response: True. The investments in those industries would have to be managed as national trusts with very carefully thought out management structures involving checks and balances to prevent the abuse of power. This is a concern not to be dismissed lightly.

Conclusion

An aggressive application of Keynesian deficit spending appears to have prevented the collapse of the United States' failed economic paradigm from plunging the world into a 1930s-style depression—at least for the time being. But since none of the causes of this crisis have been corrected, the outlook for the global economy remains alarming.

The opportunity exists to build on Keynesian analysis and resolve this crisis of global imbalances at its core. It is not enough for the government to borrow and spend just to keep the economy on life support. The government must borrow and spend to cure the economy's disease. The money is available. Only the will is lacking.

The alternative to restoring the viability of the US economy through a multi-trillion-dollar government investment program is a continuation of the status quo of economic degeneration, from which the United States may not be able to recover.

The United States did not win World War II by relying on the private sector and the invisible hand of the market. Instead, the government took complete control of every aspect of the economy, determining output, prices and interest rates. The structural economic crisis confronting the United States today does not pose as imminent a threat to the survival of the nation as the two-front world war of the 1940s, so the government's response to it need not be so extreme. But if the United States fails to reverse its structural economic decline, the damage could soon become irreversible. A national industrial-restructuring program is required to address this national emergency. There is no reason to fear it would not succeed.

Chapter 12
A call for reform

Finally, in our progress toward a resumption of work we require two safeguards against a return of the evils of the old order; there must be a strict supervision of all banking and credits and investments; there must be an end to speculation with other people's money, and there must be provision for an adequate but sound currency.

President Franklin D. Roosevelt[1]

The divergence of US economic policy from sound economic practice over the past 50 years has ended in a New Depression that is worldwide in scope. A multi-trillion-dollar emergency intervention has prevented the unprecedented disequilibrium in the global economy from coming unwound for the moment, but no permanent solution to the crisis has been found. Befuddled policymakers, lost in the rubble of a failed belief system, have only begun to grasp the enormity of the challenges confronting them.

If economic breakdown is to be averted, it will be necessary to recreate a macroeconomic environment in which stable and self-sustaining economic growth is possible. Experience demonstrates that such an environment can only exist within a framework of balanced budgets, balanced trade, sound money that

---

[1] President Franklin D. Roosevelt, first inaugural address, 4 March 1933.

governments cannot create or debase, and a tightly constrained financial industry. Those conditions existed in the United States as recently as 50 years ago. This chapter considers whether there is any possibility that they could be reestablished.

In the early 1950s, the leaders of the United States believed in balanced budgets, dollars were backed by gold, the Federal Reserve had tight control over credit creation, and international trade was roughly in balance. If those conditions had persisted, the global economy would have grown much more slowly than it did during the decades that followed. However, it is very unlikely that the world would be now battling to stave off a new Great Depression, with little prospect of returning to self-sustaining growth within the foreseeable future.

Perhaps everything will work out for the best. Perhaps a quick and permanent fix can be found to the crisis that has now overwhelmed the global economy. In that case, all will have been for the best in the best of all possible worlds. Unfortunately, that Panglossian outcome seems highly unlikely. The more realistic prognosis is considerably more dire. A 1930s-style depression with 1940s-like repercussions cannot be ruled out. The emergency policies adopted to avoid that result have set the global economy on an uncharted course. Rather than just hoping for the best, it would be wiser to find a way back to a stable system bound by something much more closely resembling 1950s (or 1890s) economic orthodoxy. But is there any way back? In truth, the obstacles blocking meaningful reform are so numerous and difficult that there may not be.

If the US government were to cut spending or raise taxes to balance its budget over the next few years, the US—and therefore, the global—economy would collapse into severe depression, since the private sector is debilitated by debt and incapable of supporting itself. Nor is there any way to restore balanced trade in the near term without provoking a global depression. If Washington imposed trade tariffs, it would cause mass unemployment across the rest of the world and most probably lead to destabilizing rates of inflation in the United States. There is no obvious way to return to a gold standard. There is not enough gold in the world to support the magnitude of global commerce today; and even if there were, it is not distributed evenly enough to make international trade possible. It would be possible to regain control over the financial sector, but that would require political reform as a prerequisite. The following sections take each of these subjects in turn, examining what would be the ideal outcome, the impediments to such an outcome, and then other, second-best but potentially more feasible solutions.

Balanced budgets

In an ideal world, an amendment to the constitution requiring the federal budget to balance would be passed this year and the government would live within its means forever afterwards. In the real world, however, there is no possibility of that happening. In 2010, the US budget deficit is expected to be 10% of GDP. If the government were to cut its spending and raise taxes to ensure that the budget balanced, the economy would be at least 10% smaller in 2010 than current forecasts suggest. In all probability, the contraction would be much greater than that, as government spending has a multiplier effect. Most probably, GDP would contract by at least 10–15%, unemployment would rise toward 20% and the financial sector (in the absence of massive government bailouts, which a balanced budget would not permit) would collapse under the weight of nonperforming loans. The situation would deteriorate further in 2011 and 2012. The outcome, in short, would be a replay of the Great Depression.

The reality is that the US economy is on government life support, and trillion-dollar annual budget deficits are likely for as far as it is possible to forecast. The government will not be able to maintain such large deficits indefinitely using traditional sources of financing. Eventually, if current policies remain in place, the Federal Reserve will have to print money and buy Treasury bonds to finance the deficits. In other words, the Fed would have to monetize the debt. Over time, that practice would generate very high rates of inflation and destroy the value of the dollar, greatly reducing the worth of all dollar-denominated debt instruments, including Treasury bonds, corporate bonds, mortgages and bank deposits. Barring a derivatives-market meltdown, that process will not take place immediately, but it quite possibly could within the next 25 years.

If balancing the budget now will lead to immediate economic collapse, and doing nothing will lead to economic collapse in the not-too-distant future, some other, out-of-the-box approach is well worth a try. The case for a multi-trillion-dollar program to restructure the US economy by investing in 21st Century industries was made in Chapter 11. If the government is going to avoid destroying the currency to finance its deficits, it will have to develop new industries to tax. If government laboratories were to invent a cure for cancer, the sales proceeds from that vaccine would not simply bring the government budget back into balance; they would eliminate the entire national debt in the space of only a few years.

Balanced trade

The United States' current-account deficit created the global credit bubble that led to the New Depression. During 2009, that deficit improved very sharply (relative to its peak of nearly $800 billion in 2006). When US households were cut off from additional credit, imports into the United States plunged. That improvement will not last long, however. When the United States imports less from the rest of the world, it does not take long before the rest of the world imports less from the United States. Also, when government life support stabilizes the economy, shopping will resume and imports will reaccelerate much more quickly than exports, as was the case following the NASDAQ-bubble recession. Most importantly, because the wages of US factory workers are up to 40 times higher than those in developing countries like China, the US manufacturing base is being hollowed out. If current trends continue, the United States will have no manufacturing industries at all within 25 years. But it is inconceivable that the current trend would be allowed to continue for that long. A protectionist backlash would almost certainly forestall it.

Over the long run, trade must balance. No country, not even the United States, can continue buying much more than it sells without eventually running out of credit. That is just common sense. However, the US trade deficit is not going to simply correct itself. American wages make American industries uncompetitive in the global market, and currency manipulation by many of the country's most important trading partners prevents the dollar from depreciating to a level at which US industries would be competitive. (There is no ambiguity about whether a country is manipulating its currency. Any country that has a rapid buildup in foreign-exchange reserves is manifestly doing so.) How, then, can trade be made to balance?

Protectionism would be one of the worst ways of restoring balanced trade. If the United States were to erect extensive trade tariffs, its trading partners would retaliate and US exports would decline. However, since the United States imports so much more than it exports, the rest of the world would suffer more—or at least suffer more directly—than the United States. The industrial capacity of the countries with large surpluses with the US would go unused and unemployment would skyrocket, with socially destabilizing consequences. Those countries would respond aggressively not only with trade barriers of their own, but also by fanning geopolitical flames to damage US foreign-policy interests. No one should underestimate the amount of geopolitical goodwill the United States has bought with its massive trade deficits. The US would also suffer indirectly as tariffs pushed up prices and drove up inflation and interest rates. Protectionism should be the last resort. But unless some alternative solution to America's deindustrialization is found, it will not take too many years of double-digit unemployment in the United States before voters there demand protectionist barriers. What, then, are the alternatives?

The gold standard contained an automatic adjustment mechanism that forced trade to balance over time. Unfortunately, there is no possibility of returning to a gold standard—at least not through government decree. The Bretton Woods system was created to replicate the automatic adjustment mechanism inherent in the gold standard and thus ensure that trade balanced. That worked for a quarter of a century, until the United States became unwilling to remain bound by Bretton Woods rules. When the US failed to abide by its commitments under Bretton Woods, the system fell apart.

What are the chances that a new international monetary system could be agreed on and implemented? Realistically, the chances are slim to zero. US policymakers believe (mistakenly) that the current dollar standard, in which US dollars are the principal international reserve currency, is a great advantage for the country since it allows the United States to buy real goods and services in exchange for paper dollars, which the government can create without limit. In reality, however, this arrangement is now doing the United States much more harm than good, since it is expediting the destruction of the country's manufacturing base. Be that as it may, US policymakers are very unlikely to abandon the dollar standard until they are absolutely forced to.

China has recently made highly publicized calls for a new international reserve currency to replace the dollar as the world's principal medium of exchange. This can only be interpreted as a tactic to exert influence on US policy, since a new world reserve currency would have a devastating impact on China's economy. If such a currency came into being, the United States would not have the ability to "print" it in the way it creates dollars. Therefore, the US would have to pay for its imports with the new reserve currency rather than with dollars. Since the United States would have only a limited amount of the reserve currency, it would no longer be able to keep running extraordinarily large trade deficits with China ($268 billion in 2008). China's economy is built to export to the United States. Deprived of its trade surplus with the US, China's economy would collapse. The resulting social repercussions in China would be intolerable. Not only does Beijing not want a new international monetary system that would achieve balanced trade, it will do everything in its power to prevent such a system from becoming a reality. Other trade-surplus countries would be similarly disadvantaged. Therefore, the recreation of an international monetary system aimed at balanced trade is a political impossibility.

A different approach to achieving balanced trade could involve the introduction of a global minimum wage, which the United States could impose unilaterally. A steadily rising global minimum wage is essential if the imbalances created by the gap between high- and low-wage countries are ever to be resolved. The most practical way of achieving that end would be for the United States to impose tariffs on imports from any low-wage country that did not increase the wages of its industrial workers by $1 a day each year. In that way, the prevailing global wage rate could be raised from $5 a day in 2009 to $6 a day in 2010, $7 a day in 2011 and so on. In 10 years, the global minimum wage would have tripled, thereby tripling the purchasing power of industrial workers in those countries. This would lay the foundation for sustainable growth, driven by consumer demand in the developing world. This strategy could make a significant contribution toward gradually bringing international trade back into balance over the medium to long term, with minimal cost or disruption to trade. As the case for a global minimum wage has been made at length elsewhere, it will not be developed further here.[2]

Policymakers and the general public must recognize that the United States no longer manufactures goods the rest of the world wants at an affordable price. The gaping US trade deficit will continue, absent some intervention to resolve it. There is no longer any adjustment mechanism (such as the one inherent in the gold standard) that will force a correction of the deficit. Nor will any new international monetary accord create a framework within which trade will once again balance. A continuation of existing policies and circumstances will in all probability produce a few more years of US industrial erosion and job losses, followed by a vehement protectionist backlash that seriously undermines world trade.

The national industrial-restructuring program outlined in Chapter 11 offers the best chance to avoid that outcome. A multi-trillion-dollar government investment in the technologies of the future would completely change the equation. Rather than producing only goods the rest of the world can buy more cheaply somewhere else, American industry could become the sole source of a large range of indispensable goods that other countries could

---

[2] Richard Duncan, "A Global Minimum Wage". Chap. 12 in *The Dollar Crisis: Causes, Consequences, Cures* (John Wiley & Sons, 2003).

only dream of making at some point in the future. The best way for the United States to bring about balanced global trade is to make a large investment in itself. It must chose between investment and rejuvenation, or deindustrialization and decay.

Monetary reform

Gold has been used as money practically from the dawn of civilization because of its intrinsic value, weight, malleability, and, most importantly, scarcity. It served as a store of value and a medium of exchange by popular convention rather than government decree. As with any other commodity, its value was independently determined by the forces of supply and demand. So long as gold was money, there was a clear distinction between capital and credit; gold and fixed assets were capital, while any agreement to lend or borrow gold was credit. Governments could borrow or confiscate gold from the public, but they could not create it; and consequently, they could not create credit. The value of money was independent of government action and therefore it retained its value regardless of government policy, or even the overthrow of one government by a completely different set of rulers. Gold therefore provided a reliable foundation upon which businesses could be built. Capitalism evolved out of the certainty provided by gold.

When President Johnson asked Congress in 1968 to free the Federal Reserve from its legal obligation to hold gold reserves to back the money in circulation, he said, "The gold reserve requirement against Federal Reserve notes is not needed to tell us what prudent monetary policy should be—that myth was destroyed long ago." He also declared, "The dollar will continue to be kept as good as or better than gold." He was terribly wrong on both counts. Since that year, the dollar has lost 96% of its value relative to gold. Even worse than that, the government has lost control over the amount of dollar-denominated credit that can be created. As a result, the foundations of the nation's prosperity are being rapidly eroded by forces the government cannot control. The need for sound money was no myth. The wild economic swings that have convulsed the country and the world since 1968, culminating in the collapse of 2008, demonstrate the absurdity of the very concept of "prudent monetary policy". The momentum of economic degeneration is now so acute that it is very unlikely to take another 40 years for the dollar to lose a further 96% of its value.

201

Only one generation into this experiment with paper money, it is no longer possible to distinguish between capital and credit. A dollar represents the promise of the United States government to repay the bearer with nothing more than a different dollar. The government can create as many dollars as it pleases. Similarly, a dollar-denominated debt instrument represents the promise of the issuer (whoever that might be) to repay a certain number of dollars in the future. So long as the issuer can issue new debt in the future to repay the debt it issued earlier, that issuer is capable of creating credit. Offshore banks, well beyond any reserve-ratio requirements, are free to create almost as many dollar-denominated loans and, therefore, deposits as they wish. Foreign central banks have facilitated the process of dollar-denominated debt creation by printing the equivalent of trillions of dollars of their own currencies over the past decade, using it to buy dollars in the foreign-exchange markets and then using them to buy newly issued dollar-denominated debt instruments that could not have found buyers had those central banks not waved their magic, money-making wands. Finally, the financial industry has run completely out of control, creating nearly a quadrillion dollars worth of derivatives that are money-like in their ability to manipulate the value of products. Figure 100 depicts dollars held by the public from 1890 to 2009. Does it not demolish any claim that monetary policy has been "prudent" in the years since Washington cut the link between dollars and gold?

Figure 100

UNITED STATES CURRENCY HELD BY THE PUBLIC

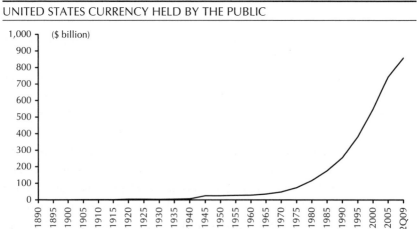

Source: US Department of Commerce, Bureau of the Census, Historical Statistics for the United States: Colonial Times to 1970 (1890-1970); IMF International Financial Statistics (1975-95); Federal Reserve Flow of Funds (2000-09)

The crisis engulfing the global economy is a direct result of the rapid debasement of the US dollar and the loss of control over credit creation that has accompanied it. So is there then any possibility of returning to a sound-money regime, or is it just too late?

Unfortunately, there is no possibility of a government-led initiative to reestablish an international gold standard. There is not enough gold in the world to support global commerce on its current scale. Even if there were (perhaps with gold valued at $100,000 an ounce), it is not distributed evenly enough around the world to make a return to the gold standard possible. Most countries don't have even a fraction of the gold they would need to pay for essential imports. It was the inadequate distribution of gold that prevented a return to the gold standard following World War II. The Bretton Woods system was designed to circumvent the shortage by replacing gold with gold-backed dollars. And, as mentioned above, that arrangement worked only so long as dollars were backed by gold.

The gold standard did not come into existence by government decree in the first place, and there is no chance of it being recreated by government decree. If a gold standard does reemerge, it will be for the same reason that it came about in the past: because individuals refuse to accept unreliable, government-issued money. Extrapolating current trends, there is a real possibility that within a few decades the dollar will have lost all of its value, just as the German mark did during the 1920s. Were that to occur, gold would once again become money. It is unrealistic, however, to anticipate a return to the gold standard through any other set of circumstances.

Therefore, what is the best realistic alternative? The gold standard's greatest virtue is that it prevents the government from creating money and credit. The dollar standard's greatest flaw is not simply that it allows the government to create money (although that is already bad enough), but that it has caused the government to lose its monopoly on money and credit creation. The government can no longer control how much credit is created—and even the distinction between money and credit has become blurred. While there is no hope of reestablishing a gold standard, there is a possibility that the US government could, though forceful reform of the financial sector, regain control over credit creation.

The government lost control of credit because of cross-border capital flows, floating exchange rates and financial-sector deregulation. It could and should regain control over credit creation, and therefore over the economy, by reimposing credit controls, reestablishing fixed exchange rates and reregulating the financial industry. The sooner Washington implements a strategy to achieve those outcomes, the better are the country's chances of avoiding irreparable economic decline. The 40-year experiment with floating exchange rates and unrestricted international credit flows has ended disastrously. The government must now do what it takes to regain control over credit.

That is much easer said than done, however. The United States' balance of payments must balance. So long as the United States has a large trade deficit, therefore, it will not be able to keep out destabilizing capital inflows. Of course, if the US government did take measures that succeeded in radically curtailing capital inflows, the current-account deficit would also correct very sharply in response. However, such a sudden contraction in US imports would create a severe worldwide depression, which would be in no-one's interest. Therefore, a more gradual approach should be devised.

Similarly, there would be no point in fixing exchange rates at their current levels. Doing so would only ensure that global trade imbalances would continue, and very likely intensify over time. Therefore, a strategy must be found for moving gradually to exchange-rate levels that would facilitate the expansion of balanced trade.

Heavy investment in advanced technologies would bring about a surge in US exports and restore equilibrium to the country's balance of payments, from which point it would be far easier to impose strict controls on cross-border capital flows and to peg exchange rates at the appropriate levels. In that way, the needed adjustments could be carried out while international trade continued to expand.

Barring the adoption of a US industrial policy, some other means of bringing the current-account deficit under control will have to be found to prevent the re-eruption and intensification of the present global economic crisis. Either the dollar will have to fall very sharply against the currencies of many of its trading partners (for instance, by 90% or more against the Chinese renminbi) or else the United States will have to resort to gradually raising tariffs until equilibrium on the current account is restored. Those policies would cause international trade to contract, and are therefore much less attractive than an approach that boosts US exports. One way or another, equilibrium in international trade will be restored—that is inevitable. The point is that some routes back to equilibrium are much less painful than others.

"Sound money" generally is sound only when the government cannot create any more of it. As Washington is unlikely ever to restore gold as money or to back dollars with some level of gold reserves, the best alternative would be to block the government from increasing the money supply, or at least to strictly limit the amount of money the government is legally permitted to create. For instance, the money supply could be increased in line with population growth, and attempts by the government to avoid recessions by increasing the money supply would not be allowed. In this way, money would simply serve as a medium of exchange and a store of value, rather than as a means by which the government can generate a short-term economic boom (to win an upcoming election, for instance) at the cost of a medium-term destabilizing bust. A central bank would not be required, as there would be no monetary policy to conduct. The Federal Reserve could be wound down and its highly qualified staff could be incorporated into the FDIC to closely regulate the banking industry. These changes to neutralize money would require legislative action by Congress. That, in turn, would probably require electoral reform, which will be discussed below.

Financial-sector reform

The financial industry has become a menace to society. Its ability to create credit has bought it undue political influence, enabling the industry to deregulate itself and to engage in such excesses that only a massive infusion of taxpayers' money has saved it from extinction. It should be broken into small pieces and very tightly regulated. Credit creation is too dangerous to be left to the discretion of bankers.

The reenactment of Glass-Steagall would be a good place to begin. The banking, insurance, stock broking and investment banking businesses should be completely separated, as they were following the last great banking calamity of the early 1930s. The ability of financial institutions to play off one regulator against another was an institutional failure that allowed the credit bubble to form. A complete regulatory overhaul should be implemented so each business has one and only one regulator.

Next, banks should be turned into utilities—small ones. Their activities should be restricted to taking deposits and extending traditional loans. Uniform ceilings should be imposed on the size of their lending portfolios, as well as on deposit rates, management compensation and, most importantly, the banks' return on assets. Any profits in excess of those regulated returns should be returned to depositors as dividends. Strict capital-adequacy ratios should be enforced, while securitization and off-balance-sheet items should be banned.

These precautions, in combination with very tight regulatory oversight, would eliminate excessive risk-taking and ensure a sound banking system that is too regulated to fail.

The investment banking business should be completely separated from the commercial banking industry and also subjected to size restrictions. The size of each firm should be restricted so that the industry comprises 100 or more medium-sized companies rather than 10 dominant players, as in the recent past. Caps should also be imposed on the size of the "trading books" of investment banks, as well as on the investment portfolios of hedge funds and other investment firms to prevent market manipulation.

The derivatives industry should be radically downsized. All derivatives should be traded through exchanges, and substantial margin requirements should be enforced on every transaction. The Commodity Futures Trading Commission should tightly regulate the business to prevent derivatives from being used to manipulate commodity prices or to facilitate accounting fraud. The use of derivatives for speculation in commodities by non-end users should once again be banned. The insurance industry should be barred from using derivatives and forced to conduct its business prudently, as it did 20 years ago before derivatives came into widespread use. The goal should be to greatly reduce the size of the derivatives industry in order to reduce the extraordinary and unprecedented threat it poses to the real economy. Investment banks that cannot survive without speculating in derivatives should be allowed to fail.

Offshore banking centers and tax havens should be shut down. American banks and investment companies should be given the choice of conducting business in the Cayman Islands (for instance) or the United States, but not both. Similarly, the subsidiaries of US financial institutions in London and elsewhere around the world should be forced to comply with the same laws and be overseen by the same regulators as their parent companies in the US. Should they decide to relocate abroad, those institutions should be banned from conducting any business in the United States. Under those conditions, not many would leave, and for those that did, good riddance. Offshore tax havens that facilitate tax fraud could be put out of business by cutting the travel and telecommunication links between them and the rest of the world. Out-of-control credit creation and unregulated cross-border credit flows, which began wreaking havoc around the world 40 years ago, have now thrown the world into a new depression. They must be brought under control. There are no technological or theoretical impediments to accomplishing this, only political ones.

Finally, financiers must be banned from any positions within the government from which they could influence legislation related to the regulation of the financial industry. Most crucially, bankers should not be allowed to take positions in the US Treasury Department, which at times has taken on the appearance of being a fiefdom of the investment banking industry. The revolving door between Wall Street and Washington must be closed, locked and perhaps even bricked up. Lawmakers and regulators should not be allowed to accept jobs in the financial industry after leaving their government posts. People accepting government jobs in any way related to finance should be made aware that by doing so, they are giving up the possibility of ever working in the financial industry. The risk of a conflict of interest is just too great. Wall Street tycoons must be banned from positions of power in Washington for the same reasons. Regardless of the intentions or motivations of those past or future (or in some cases both past and future) financiers who, while serving in Washington, oversaw the deregulation of the financial industry, this crisis demonstrates that their judgment was disastrously incorrect. Once all of these financial-sector reforms are made, the complexity of the finance industry will be reduced to the point where it will not require a Wall Street wizard to manage it. Economic stability is unlikely to be restored until non-bankers are made responsible for controlling the banks.

Political reform

Paper money and the loss of fiscal discipline have not only led to economic degeneracy, they have also corrupted the political process in the United States. Hard money and balanced budgets force politicians to make hard choices. If they vote to spend money for the benefit of one set of constituents, they must also vote to take money away from a different set, through higher taxes or cost-cutting. Once a country allows its government to create money and amass debt, politicians no longer face hard constraints. They may shower largesse on their financial benefactors and charge the cost to the public tab. Opportunism displaces conscientious management of public affairs. The legislative process eventually comes to resemble an auction, in which the highest bidders write the laws. In politics, it is the creation of money that is the root of all evil.

Wealthy individuals and special interest groups have always bought influence in Washington—and in every other political capital. However, they have never had such a large return on investment as now, when there are no checks on how much the government can spend in their interest. The catastrophic consequences of financial-sector deregulation are a glaring example of the costs to the nation of the undue influence of lobbyists over lawmakers. It would be naïve not to understand, however, that the poisonous influence of this system extends far beyond the financial sector. If every other industry in the country has not bent the legislative process to its will to the same extent that the financial industry has, it was not for lack of trying, but rather because other industries could not create as much credit as banks can.

If a lobbyist-directed government generated effective policies that advanced the interests of the country as a whole, this arrangement would still be shameful and regrettable, but it might be tolerable. However, it doesn't. It is destroying the foundations of American prosperity at a mind-boggling pace. Rather than generating effective national policies, it has simply unleashed a series of wild schemes to allow the few to make a quick buck at the expense of the many. "One man, one vote" is at risk of being superseded by "one million dollars, one vote". Democracy is being undermined and the country is being horribly mismanaged.

Electoral reform is the prerequisite to all the other reforms required to rebuild the foundations of sustainable prosperity. Yet how is electoral reform possible when the institution most in need of reform is the one that writes the laws?

Attempts to regulate campaign finance have a long history and have achieved many successes over the years. The Federal Election Campaign Act of 1971 required the disclosure of the sources of campaign financing and, three years later, an amendment to that act established the Federal Election Commission as the enforcement agency. In 2002 the Bipartisan Campaign Reform Act was passed. It banned unregulated, "soft money" contributions to political parties, but has been challenged on the grounds that it represents a violation of free speech.

Experiments with public financing for elections have been attempted, but they have not achieved the desired results. In their 2002 book *Voting With Dollars: A New Paradigm for Campaign Finance*, Bruce Ackerman and Ian Ayres called for all campaign contributions to be made anonymous so as to limit the influence of financial donors on elected representatives.[3] That proposal has not yet been put to the test.

---

[3] Bruce Ackerman and Ian Ayres, *Voting With Dollars: A new paradigm for campaign finance* (Yale University Press, 2002).

Public disgust at money politics led to a populist movement to impose term limits on Congress, just as the 22nd Amendment imposed a two-term limit on the Presidency in 1951. Newt Gingrich and his fellow Republicans promised to pass term limits in their Contract With America in 1994. They won the election but broke the contract. Separately, voters in 23 states approved congressional term limits by a margin of 2:1 during the early 1990s. However, in May 1995 in US Term Limits, Inc. vs. Thornton, the US Supreme Court ruled as unconstitutional the right of states to impose term limits on the representatives and senators they send to Washington.

Term limits, even if they could be enacted, would not break the grip of special interests over the government in any case. What would work is a one-term limit. If lawmakers could hold office for one term only, lobbyists would have no hold over them. With no possibility of being reelected, there would be no second campaign—and thus no need to support legislation that was detrimental to the national interest in exchange for campaign contributions. Combined with a more appropriate incentive structure and very strict enforcement of conflict-of-interest laws to ensure that lawmakers did not benefit improperly after leaving office, a one-term limit would break the grip of special interests over Washington and improve the chances "that government of the people, by the people, for the people, shall not perish from the earth".[4]

How could this work? In one paragraph, in an ideal world, senators and members of the House of Representatives would be elected to serve one six-year term and given one additional year of training before taking office. They would be strictly barred—at risk of extremely harsh penalties—from accepting any subsequent employment or remuneration from groups they could have benefited while in office. To attract strong leaders and to compensate them for the loss of many opportunities in the private sector after they had served their term, they would receive salaries and retirement benefits that matched or exceeded those of the country's best-paid corporate executives. Within such a framework, the country's elected representatives would have every reason to work for the nation's best interests, with no pecuniary temptations to affect their judgment.

In the real world, of course, such an incorruptible legislative system is more or less inconceivable. The fox is in the henhouse and he is not going to vote himself out. Is there, then, any hope for electoral reform?

The election of President Barack Obama demonstrates that democracy in America is not dead or a lost cause. Using a brilliant internet campaign, the

---

[4] Abraham Lincoln, "The Gettysburg Address" (19 November 1863).

Obama campaign outflanked the lobbyist kingmakers and won by appealing directly to the people. Therefore, if a black man can be elected to the world's most powerful office through a technologically driven grassroots movement, it is not entirely inconceivable that political reform to eliminate the undue influence of vested interests over the government could be achieved in the same way.

Although that kind of political revolution is a long shot, if the public wants good government, the public must fight for reform. In a democracy, the people get the type of government they deserve. Until meaningful electoral reform is passed, the best strategy for the electorate may simply be to campaign against and vote out every incumbent in every election.

The public should also use shame as a tool to bring about political reform. OpenSecrets.org makes available on its website a large, easy-to-use database detailing how much money lobbyists are giving and who they are giving it to.[5] When public servants accept money from lobbyists and then fail to properly regulate the industries those lobbyists represent—banking, for instance—the public should disgrace them into resigning. The Gramm-Leach-Bliley Act of 1999 and the Commodity Futures Modernization Act of 2000 must be counted among the most harmful pieces of legislation ever passed in the United States. Representatives and senators who voted for those bills and who also accepted campaign contributions from lobbyists representing the banking industry should resign. The public should demand it. Regardless of their intentions or motivation, those lawmakers failed to protect the public interest. That, combined with the appearance of conflict of interest—even if they were not influenced by their financial donors—should disqualify them from continuing in office. Accountability need not await the next election. Popular reproach can be a powerful political tool in any society. It must be in a democracy.

Conclusion

The US and global economy are in extreme disequilibrium, which is likely to worsen over time due to the forces of globalization. Eventually, the disequilibrium will be corrected by market forces. This will most probably involve a collapse of globalization and a drastic reduction of the standard of

---

[5] OpenSecrets.org Center for Responsive Politics, http://www.opensecrets.org/index.php.

living of almost everyone alive. Carefully thought-out government policy could avoid this market-induced worst-case outcome and even turn the crisis into an opportunity to advance human wellbeing, through an aggressive government investment program to develop new technologies. However, the chances of that happy scenario actually playing out are far from assured. Misguided conventional wisdom, vested interests, inadequate leadership and inertia are only a few of the impediments. Therefore, while working to achieve a benevolent outcome, it would also be prudent to prepare for a pernicious one. In economic upheavals down through the centuries, gold, land and a broadly diversified investment portfolio have preserved many a fortune.

Conclusion

Over the course of little more than one generation, the global economy has been transformed by three developments: the emergence of the dollar standard, with its inability to prevent or correct trade imbalances; globalization, which caused a 90% drop in the marginal cost of labor and made large trade imbalances between high- and low-wage countries inevitable within the dollar standard framework; and paper-money creation on a previously unimaginable scale, undertaken primarily by the central banks of the low-wage, trade-surplus countries for the purpose of perpetuating their competitive advantage.

These developments are linked. The process of globalization was accelerated by the United States' extraordinary trade deficits. Large-scale paper-money creation would have led to hyperinflation, had globalization not brought about a collapse in wage rates. The United States would have been unable to finance its trade deficits, had its trading partners not created the equivalent of trillions of dollars of paper money and bought US debt instruments. Together, these changes produced the greatest economic boom in history.

Unfortunately, the boom was not built on sustainable foundations. It was built on debt. The expansion of private-sector debt in the United States drove the worldwide economic upsurge but eventually bankrupted the US private sector. Until then the evolution of the "market-based" economic system, most generally thought of as capitalism, had been difficult to notice. In reality, however, capitalism had been corrupted by the creation of paper money and enormous government debt. Capitalism is an economic system based on private ownership of the means of production, within which the role of the government is limited. The economic system that has evolved in the United States over the past 40 years, in which the government creates the money, manipulates interest rates and directs the economy through debt-financed fiscal "stimulus", has little in common with capitalism. It is better described as statism, an economic system in which the government controls the means of production.

The transformation of the US economic system from capitalism to statism was exposed by the government's policy response to the economic breakdown that began in 2008. Had the capitalist forces of creative destruction been allowed to operate, the financial industry would have been annihilated and the global economy would have collapsed. Instead, the state intervened to prop up both through yet more debt and paper-money creation.

There are now three ways forward. First, the government could stop supporting the economy, in which case the economy would spiral into a severe depression. Second, the government could follow the Japanese model, in which it spends just enough to ensure some economic growth, but fails to take the actions required to actually resolve the crisis. This is the current approach. It cannot succeed and will eventually end disastrously when the government is unable to finance more debt.

The third course would be for the government to spend aggressively enough to permanently resolve the crisis. This would require restructuring the US economy to restore its viability and eliminate the imbalances behind the crisis. This is a radical approach, but I believe it is the only one that can succeed. We cannot go back the way we came without enduring economic—and, potentially, social—breakdown. With a clear understanding of what has gone wrong, it may be possible to go forward boldly, making use of the tools available in these changed circumstances. Flaws in the dollar standard are responsible for this crisis. Nonetheless, the dollar standard will enable the United States to finance trillions of dollars in deficit spending over the next decade. Paper money and globalization have produced an unstable new economic paradigm. If Washington makes the most of the possibilities that it creates through an ambitious investment program, not only could this global crisis be resolved, but extraordinary advances in human progress could also be achieved.

The great English historian Arnold Toynbee analyzed the rise and fall of civilizations in terms of their response to challenges. The challenge posed by the collapse of the United States' post-capitalist economic model should not be underestimated. Nor, however, should be that country's prospects for overcoming it.